CHAOS SPACE MARINES

VETERANS OF THE LONG WAR

CONTENTS

PRODUCED BY GAMES WORKSHOP IN NOTTINGHAM

With thanks to the Mournival and the Infinity Circuit for their additional playtesting services

Games Workshop Ltd, Willow Rd, Lenton, Nottingham, NG7 2WS
games-workshop.com

INTRODUCTION

Servants of the Emperor, turn back now, for within these pages you will find acts of treason on an unimaginable scale. Yours to command are the secrets of the Heretic Astartes, a dark brotherhood of traitors hell-bent on the bloody conquest of the Imperium. This book will help you assemble your collection of Chaos Space Marines Citadel Miniatures into a powerful army.

In the legends of the Warhammer 40,000 universe, the Chaos Space Marines are the most reviled of the Imperium's foes. Each of their marauding warbands is a brotherhood of fallen heroes with a shocking history that you will uncover as you delve into the pages of this book. Among their number are counted the Traitor Legions, those Space Marines who renounced the authority of the Emperor during the Horus Heresy ten thousand years ago, and the Renegade Chapters, Adeptus Astartes warriors pushed over the edge by an uncaring Imperium who now exist only to serve their own selfish ends. Marching alongside both factions are hellish Daemon Engines created in the nightmarish soul forges of the Eye of Terror, and Daemon foot soldiers of the Dark Gods themselves, drawn to realspace by the appalling carnage unleashed by their mortal allies.

Whether you decide to base your collection around a force of millennia-old traitors or renegades recently turned to Chaos, this book gives you everything you need to amass a dizzying variety of armies. Simply choose the elements that you like the best, and seek out a battle. Whatever route you take, a force of Chaos Space Marines presents a vision of dark majesty on the battlefield, and has access to powerful daemonically enhanced wargear capable of obliterating anything your opponent throws at you.

Within this book you will find all the information you need to collect a Chaos Space Marine army and field it upon the tabletop.

LET THE GALAXY BURN: This section provides an account of the Heretic Astartes' history, the epic battles of the Long War, and an in-depth analysis of how their armies fight.

SCIONS OF CHAOS: Here you will find a showcase of beautifully painted miniatures showing the full range of Chaos Space Marines and example armies to inspire you.

SLAVES TO DARKNESS: This section includes datasheets, wargear lists and weapon rules for every Chaos Space Marine unit and model for you to use in your games.

THE LOST AND THE DAMNED: This section provides additional rules, including Warlord Traits, Stratagems, Relics and psychic powers, as well as matched play points costs for every entry.

> *To play games with your army, you will need a copy of the Warhammer 40,000 rules. To find out more about Warhammer 40,000 or download the free core rules, visit games-workshop.com.*

Abhor the heretic, for in his heart he fosters only hatred, and in his hands he carries only death. Curse the heretic, for his mind is aflame with unholy passion, and with that fire, he seeks to burn the galaxy to ash. Purge the heretic, for his strength is swollen by the dark power of his gods, and his body hath been wrought anew as a weapon of murder. Abjure the heretic, for he has sworn to sacrifice the faithful upon the altar of darkness. Let the storm of battle rage in denial of his unholy oaths, and cast him out by his heel into the void whence he came!

LET THE GALAXY BURN

The menacing strongholds and hidden fleets of the Chaos Space Marines fester like a canker within the heart of the Imperium. In the roiling depths of the Eye of Terror, amidst the gas clouds of the Maelstrom, upon darkened moons and dead worlds, the bloodthirsty hordes of Chaos plot the downfall of their loyalist brothers. Once proud and majestic warriors armoured with righteousness, these Heretic Astartes are now bitter, selfish champions of dark and hungry gods.

The Chaos Space Marines are a dire threat and rightfully feared by those who have heard their bloodstained legend. They possess not only the superhuman abilities, peerless training and devastating weaponry of their loyalist counterparts, but also supernatural power gleaned from their unholy pacts with the Dark Gods. If that were not enough, they march beside daemonic war engines that function through the application of fell knowledge far beyond that of the Adeptus Mechanicus.

For ten thousand years, Traitor Legions and Renegade Chapters have ransacked the worlds of the Emperor. The scale of their slaughter and conquest is a well-guarded secret of the Inquisition, lest awareness of the heretics' existence tempt others to the service of Chaos. For ten millennia, the Long War has raged unseen and unheard by the vast majority of the Imperium, fought on countless battlefields where loyalists and rebels wage war for the future of Humanity itself.

THE PATH TO DAMNATION

All men of power can choose to devote their lives to great good or great harm, and so it is with a Space Marine. Biologically engineered to be an exemplary warrior, armed and armoured to the highest standard, a Space Marine is the ultimate defender of the Emperor and Mankind. Not only is his body protected against the weapons of the foe, his mind is toughened to endure all pain, despair and temptation. To become a Space Marine is to surrender one's own life to the protection of Mankind and dedicate one's body and soul to that single purpose. Those who prosper behind the shield of the Space Marines can never truly comprehend the sacrifice made on their behalf – the sacrifice of the very humanity the Adeptus Astartes are sworn to defend.

When a Space Marine falls from grace, he falls further than any other man. A lifetime of deprivation and selflessness is thrown aside, and the Space Marine indulges his new-found independence to its fullest extent. Freed from the shackles of tradition and responsibility, this newly fallen heretic can exercise his every whim, whether it is for bloodshed, sensual pleasure, ambition, love or hatred. Given full rein, his incredible physical prowess and mental strength can be turned to the most despicable acts without any sense of mercy or shame. Like a dam holding back a flood, when a Space Marine's will finally breaks, the result is catastrophic.

Having been created purely to fight, most Chaos Space Marines turn to the only thing they know – war. Though their ideals and goals may have been cast aside, their superhuman bodies and military skills remain undiminished. Let loose from the confines of orders, ritual prayers and prescribed missions, a Chaos Space Marine becomes a psychopathic killer without morals or restraint. He pursues his new life to its fullest and most bloody extent, glorying in the unbridled power of his own body and his ability to inflict death and misery upon the weaklings around him. Some never grow beyond this point and will remain bloodthirsty renegades and pirates for the rest of their long lives. Others, having begun to explore the tempting and mysterious galaxy they now inhabit, will reach out in all directions to widen their experience.

Having long been subservient to the lords of the Imperium and the distant Emperor, a Chaos Space Marine relishes the opportunity to be the master rather than the servant, enslaving nations, and even worlds, to his creed. Others may feel free to pursue other avenues, such as the study of illicit texts, or a passion for forbidden knowledge. Some Chaos Space Marines seek to inflict pain and pleasure upon themselves, pushing their bodies and minds to the uttermost limits as they search for a sensual reward they were never intended to enjoy.

To be a Chaos Space Marine is to feel a god-like power over other creatures. Having long since been freed from physical fear, and now released from liability, a heretic does not dread retribution or punishment. For most Chaos Space Marines, all memories of the past are swiftly washed away by blood and sensation, and any thoughts of the future are little more than half-imagined cravings and dreams. By dedicating himself to the gods of Chaos, a heretical Space Marine not only finds a patron who approves of his new life, but who will actively reward him for following it. For one whose existence was denial and obedience, the euphoria of this realisation can be more powerful than the pride he once felt at being accepted as warrior of the Adeptus Astartes.

It is this temptation, this abyss of bloody gratification, that constantly beckons to the Space Marines. They cannot claim ignorance of it, because the teachings of their Chapters and the Chaplains remind them on a daily basis of what lies on the other side of their purpose and stringent duty. A Space Marine's life presents many opportunities to turn away from his duties and follow the path of damnation. To turn to Chaos, he must walk a different road, choosing obscene freedom in place of righteous servitude – whether done with good or selfish intentions, once made, it is a decision that cannot be recanted. From the moment he renounces the Emperor, a Space Marine is truly damned.

THE CREATION OF THE SPACE MARINES

To understand the origins of the Chaos Space Marines, one must delve deep into the prehistory of the Imperium – even as far as the Emperor's first rise to power in the Unification Wars of Terra. During the Age of Strife, swirling warp storms, brutal alien invasions and rampant civil war had isolated many worlds, leaving them vulnerable to attack and leading to their drastic technological decline. When, at the end of this era, the Emperor revealed himself on Terra and began his quest to reunite the race of Mankind, it was

at the head of an army of altered super-warriors – the predecessors to the Space Marines. Following his success in conquering the techno-barbarian tribes of Terra, the saviour of Mankind turned his eyes to the stars.

While his warriors proved more than capable of slaying the rebels and strange beasts of Terra, the Emperor knew that the shadowy threats lurking in the darkness of the galaxy would require something more. He set about improving his biological techniques, perfecting the warrior genes he would need to create an army of post-humans that could reconquer the galaxy. The pinnacle of his success was the Primarch Program, in which the Emperor used his own rich genetic code to create twenty super-beings, each with the strength of a dozen men and intelligence to rival that of the Emperor himself. These gods amongst men were masterpieces of arcane science, destined to reunite the scattered realms of Man.

At the Emperor's moment of triumph, disaster struck. A mysterious force swept up the infant Primarchs and flung them through the immaterium far from Terra, eventually depositing them upon distant human worlds. Perhaps it was during this cosmic voyage that Chaos first touched the Primarchs, whispering in their dreams and sowing the seeds of future tyrannies as they slept. Yet not all was lost for the Emperor's ambitions with the disappearance of the Primarchs. He had gleaned much invaluable knowledge and data from his experiment. Using the genetic structure of the Primarchs, or 'gene-seed' as it would come to be known, the Master of Mankind created the first Space Marines.

THE GREAT CRUSADE

The Emperor formed twenty Legions, each using the gene-seed of one of the Primarchs. Numbering hundreds of thousands of genetically enhanced warriors and boasting fearsome weapons and starships, each Space Marine Legion was powerful enough to conquer whole worlds. With these warriors under his command, the Emperor stepped out into the turbulent galaxy.

World after world was brought into the Imperial fold, some rejoicing at being found by the warriors of Terra, others not so willing to bow before the might of the Emperor. It mattered not, for there was no force capable of resisting the Space Marine Legions for long. As the Great Crusade spread out from Terra, the Space Marines rediscovered the lost Primarchs, one by one. Reunited with the Emperor, they became Mankind's paramount warriors and generals. Each was given a Legion to command – a Legion created from his own genetic material. With joyous vigour and unequalled martial prowess, the Primarchs and their Legions pushed back the boundaries of the wild galaxy, claiming many thousands of worlds in the Emperor's name and reconnecting the distant reaches of space in an ever expanding empire. It was a golden time for the armies and servants of the Emperor of Mankind.

Yet, even at the pinnacle of the Emperor's might, there arose an enemy that would almost destroy his growing Imperium. The insidious forces of Chaos had set into motion the events of their near destruction many decades earlier. The most dire threat to the Imperium was not to come from the xenos filth that infested the galaxy, but from amongst the ranks of the Space Marines themselves.

The leader of this rebellion, after whom the heresy is named, was the most praised and respected of all the Primarchs – Horus.

THE HORUS HERESY

In the dark days of the 31st Millennium, the betrayal of the Emperor by his most favoured son almost tore the emergent Imperium apart. Such was Horus' burning ambition that he turned a full half of the Legiones Astartes against their battle-brothers and personally brought about the downfall of the Emperor himself. Since that cataclysmic act of treachery, the Imperium of Man has been consumed by war within and without; a war so vast it may yet bring the Imperium to its knees.

THE BIRTH OF A NEW ERA

The rise of the Imperium of Man began after the fall of the Eldar. The innate psychic abilities of that ancient race brought about the creation of a new and terrible god – Slaanesh, the Dark Prince of Excess, whose birth almost spelled their extinction.

The psychic apocalypse of Slaanesh's ascendancy had two profound effects. Firstly, its immense catharsis blew away the warp storms created by the build-up to the Chaos God's emergence, thus ending Terra's long isolation and allowing Mankind to ply the stars once more. Secondly, wherever the populations of Eldar were the greatest, the immaterium literally spilled out and mixed with material space. This created many of the scattered zones in the galaxy where the warp and realspace overlap, the largest and most significant of which is known as the Eye of Terror. The Eldar had come face to face with their darkest desires and had been found wanting. For Mankind, the rise of their own empire – and its inexorable slide into damnation – was only just beginning.

THE GREAT CRUSADE

The Emperor of Mankind had long foreseen the birth of Slaanesh and had made preparations for that fateful day. Though his Primarchs had been scattered by the machinations of the Chaos Gods, he strived to track each of them down and enact his vision of a superhuman army. By the time the warp storms around Terra had ended, the Space Marines, bolstered by the Imperial Army and the Mechanicum of Mars, stood ready to begin the reconquest of the galaxy. Many worlds once claimed by Mankind had been taken over by aliens or corrupted by megalomaniacal tyrants. The reclamation of the stars was a long, hard-fought struggle, but the Legiones Astartes were ascendant. With every victory, the Imperium grew as new worlds joined the Great Crusade.

Led by the Emperor and the Primarchs he had gathered to his side, the conquering armies of Mankind swept across the galaxy like a firestorm. Thousands of worlds and untold billions of souls were liberated by the triumphant Space Marine Legions. Foul and sinister holds were shattered, alien dominions were overthrown, and the Imperium of Man was forged in a heroic age of conquest and rediscovery. With the unparalleled vision and skill of the Emperor driving it onwards, Humanity rose to the task of rebuilding its ancient heritage. The minions of darkness retreated to their own realms, and the alien was cast into the void.

PRIDE AND BETRAYAL

Despite the Great Crusade's many victories, the war against the scions of the Ruinous Powers had barely begun. The seeds of corruption had already been sown across the Imperium, tainting the ambition of common men and even taking root amongst its highest echelons. The Chaos Gods whispered to the Primarchs from the warp, disturbing their dreams with promises of limitless power.

In the underground labyrinths of Calth, the vendetta between the Word Bearers and the Ultramarines turned to outright war. Brother fought brother, former allies turned into the most bitter foes by an act of treachery that would resound through the galaxy forever more.

They appealed to their pride, their martial prowess, their perfectionism, and their courage – all the while casting doubt on the Emperor's plans. No single Primarch was wholly resistant. The character of each was sorely tested, and fully half of them eventually failed that test.

When the rebellion against the Emperor came, its leader was to be the Primarch least suspected of any treachery; the great and noble Warmaster, Horus. Horus had always loved and respected the Emperor as a young man looks up to a strong father, and had faithfully remained at the Emperor's side throughout the Great Crusade. After Horus' stunning victories against the Orks during the Ullanor Crusade, the Emperor announced that he was returning to Terra, elevating Horus to the ultimate rank of Warmaster in his stead and giving him free rein to prosecute the Great Crusade as he saw fit. As a mark of honour, the Emperor renamed the Luna Wolves as the Sons of Horus in honour of their mighty Primarch. Yet the announcement bred jealousy and confusion in many of the Primarchs. Did their father really intend to abandon them at this most critical time? Without explanation, the Emperor left for Terra in order to further his mysterious agenda, leaving Horus to deal with the Crusade in his wake.

THE WARMASTER COMETH

Horus strove to carry out the Emperor's will to the best of his ability. Either by fate or sinister design, he came to lead the Sons of Horus to the haunted swamps of Davin's moon, hoping to bring the Emperor's light to that benighted orb. There, beset on all sides, Horus fell to a blow from an eldritch sword. The tainted wound festered, plunging Horus into a fugue state from which he could not be roused.

The Sons of Horus were desolate at the loss of their founding father. Under the advice of Erebus, a respected Chaplain of the Word Bearers, the most senior members of the Legion took their Primarch to one of the Davinite warrior lodges for healing. Unbeknownst to the Space Marines, the Ruinous Powers restored Horus to his full strength, cementing their grip upon the Warmaster's soul in the process. Awed by the 'miracle' worked by the Davinite priests, the Warmaster spread the new-found cult throughout the warrior lodges of the Sons of Horus and beyond, infesting the Legions with heretical notions disguised as beneficence.

THE SLIGHTED SONS

Horus was not the first Primarch to turn to Chaos. Although superhuman in physique, they were all too human in their souls, and therefore fallible. One by one they fell: Lorgar, golden-skinned lord of the Word Bearers; Konrad Curze, the Primarch of the Night Lords, called Night Haunter; Angron, battle-hungry Primarch of the World Eaters. With them were Mortarion, pallid lord of the Death Guard; Magnus the Red, one-eyed Primarch of the Thousand Sons, who unwittingly destroyed the great work the Emperor was striving to create; embittered Perturabo of the Iron Warriors; Fulgrim of the Emperor's Children, formerly thought beyond reproach; and Alpharius of the Alpha Legion, whose part in the heresy remains forever shrouded.

This list of names should have been a roll-call of honour, a roster of mighty heroes that would make the enemies of Mankind tremble. Yet each succumbed to the honeyed promises of Chaos and reneged on their fealty to the Emperor, and each became a figure of infamy that would haunt the Imperium for time immemorial.

Initially, even the mighty Primarchs had little idea that they had fallen to the wiles of the Chaos Gods. When they rebelled, their good intentions and just causes began to fall away as their spirits became saturated with the energies of the warp. Slowly they were remade, body and soul, by the powers that claimed them. The Space Marine Legions that they led inevitably followed the fall of their commanders, blind to the faults of their genetic fathers and ever hungry for more conquest. The corrupting force of Chaos spread into the Imperial Army and the Mechanicum. Soon enough, the rot seeped through to the core of the Emperor's new domain.

HERESY UNBOUND

The final catalyst for the Heresy came from a rebellion in the Isstvan System. The Imperial governor upon Isstvan III had renounced his oaths to the Emperor and declared independence. The Emperor decreed that if the commander of Isstvan went unpunished, other worlds might follow. He ordered Horus to put down the rebellion by whatever means necessary, not knowing of the subtle changes Chaos had wrought upon the Warmaster's soul.

Horus chose to end the Isstvan rebellion swiftly and without mercy, employing virus bombs against Isstvan III from orbit. The voracious life-eater virus consumed every living thing upon the planet in a matter of minutes. Whole continents and cities were burnt to ashes as the mass of gasses released by the rotting organic material ignited in the atmosphere, scouring Isstvan III clean in a devastating firestorm. Twelve billion souls died with a death scream that momentarily pulsed brighter than the Astronomican. It was a signal to the Chaos Gods that Horus was now completely theirs, for it was an act of treachery on a scale never before seen.

Over one hundred companies drawn from the Emperor's Children, Death Guard, World Eaters and Sons of Horus Legions had already taken up arms against the rebellion on Isstvan III's surface at the time of the virus bombing. Horus had ensured their numbers were almost entirely made up of those Space Marines from each Legion who were still loyal to the Emperor, intending to wipe out those who had proved incorruptible in a single deadly stroke. Of these brave warriors, fully two-thirds miraculously survived the bombardment, thanks to warning messages received from the dwindling ranks of loyal comrades left aboard the orbiting fleet of the Warmaster. Angron, headstrong as ever, made planetfall at the head of fifty companies of Traitor Marines to slay these survivors. The ground war began in earnest, signalling the start of the greatest turmoil to ever have engulfed the Imperium.

As the forces of Horus launched their orbital barrage upon the loyal Space Marines on Isstvan III, Captain Garro, of the Death Guard, seized the frigate *Eisenstein* from the traitor fleet. His instinct had led him to warn the loyal warriors on the planet's surface of their imminent betrayal, and he was determined to flee the Isstvan System. Garro was unable to prevent the atrocities that followed, and his vessel was no match against the battleships of Horus' blockading fleet; all he could hope for was that the *Eisenstein* could escape from the Isstvan System and somehow find a way to reach Terra to warn the Emperor of Horus' treachery.

THE IMPERIUM DIVIDED

Throughout the nascent Imperium, armies turned on their commanders and traitorous generals led their troops in attacks on their former comrades. On Mars, the Tech-Priests turned ancient, forbidden weaponry upon each other, further scarring the face of the Red Planet in their bitter struggle for dominance. The Imperium tore itself apart as old feuds were revived and ambitious planetary lords seized the opportunity to declare their secession.

Having been informed of Horus' treason, the Emperor, after overcoming his dismay, ordered no fewer than seven of his Legions to hunt down the Warmaster and destroy the rebels. The Emperor's delay cost him dearly, and the loyal Primarchs had spent precious months mounting their counter-attack, allowing Horus and his rebels to consolidate their grip on the Eastern Fringe and start their advance upon Terra.

THE DROP SITE MASSACRE OF ISSTVAN V

The Warmaster's forces had redeployed to Isstvan V, where the first wave of loyalists made planetfall. According to the Mythos Angelica Mortis, the Raven Guard, Iron Hands and Salamanders Legions made up the vanguard of a massive planetary assault that was caught off-guard by the speed and ferocity of the traitors' counter-attack. As the first wave became pinned at the drop site, they attempted a breakout, only to discover that the four Legions of the second wave – the Iron Warriors, Night Lords, Word Bearers and Alpha Legion – had betrayed them at Horus' behest. The loyalists were attacked from both sides, and very few escaped.

The Imperium was soon entirely engulfed by civil war. All across the galaxy, loyalists and rebels fought tooth and nail to destroy each other, gripped in a bitter conflict that would see all of Mankind fall – or worse, enslaved by the Ruinous Powers. Even with his Space Marines, his daemonic allies and half the Titan Legions behind him, Horus could sense that time was of the essence. He needed to crush the Emperor's followers before they could consolidate, to land a blow that would break the Imperium forever – nothing less than a full-scale assault on the seat of the Emperor's power.

THE INVASION OF TERRA

Horus' numbers grew as his dark creed gained influence, and his hordes pushed on inexorably towards Segmentum Solar. Displaying the tactical brilliance that had once dazzled the enemies of the Imperium, Horus outwitted the Emperor's forces again and again, finally launching a well-orchestrated and audacious attack on Terra and assaulting the Emperor's Palace itself.

The Siege of the Emperor's Palace was the darkest hour in human history. The skies turned black with Chaos Drop Pods and Dreadclaw assault craft. As the traitors sought to conquer the hundreds of square miles of towers, walls and bastions that formed the Palace defences, the dead were piled so thickly that their corridors became blocked by the press of corpses. The forces loyal to the Emperor withstood the initial assault, but they could not prevent Horus' traitor Space Marines from setting up siege lines. Gigantic dropships landed at Lions Gate and many other starports, bringing a second wave of Heretic Astartes to the fight.

The bloodthirsty Berzerkers of the World Eaters Legion were the first to attempt an all-out assault against the Imperial Palace, and were only hurled back by the defenders after days of bloody fighting. With the initial attack stalled, Horus brought his entire arsenal of weapons and warriors to bear. For over a month, the gigantic cannons of the rebel army pounded the walls, foremost amongst them the siege weapons of the Iron Warriors and the Legio Mortis Titan Legion. Eventually, after heavy bombardment, part of the curtain wall came crashing down. The Traitor Legions hurled themselves at the breach to pour into the inner palace. At the heart of the fighting stood the Primarchs. The indomitable Rogal Dorn of the Imperial Fists and noble Sanguinius of the Blood Angels fought a desperate rearguard action to halt the force pouring through the breach. Angron of the World Eaters slew loyalist Space Marines by the dozen, while Mortarion of the Death Guard led his pestilent Plague Marines into the thickest fighting. To the terrified populace of Terra, it was as if their world was drowned in battle.

As the rebel forces slowly closed their grip upon the loyalist troops, the Emperor readied himself for the final conflict. The last hours of Humanity had come, and the few remaining gallant defenders prepared themselves for certain death. The Legions of Horus poured into the Imperial Palace in an unstoppable wave. Shouting praise to the gods of Chaos, the Traitors threw themselves at the final lines of defence. Hundreds of depraved attackers died to salvoes of bolt shells and lascannon blasts, but the Chaos Space Marines were implacable in their advance.

THE FINAL BATTLE

The Emperor had always been guided by his innate prescience, but even he could not be sure which way the tide of this battle would finally turn. The moment of Horus' victory was near, but the Warmaster deemed progress too slow; the defenders still stubbornly resisted. After being notified that loyalist reinforcements were soon to arrive, the Warmaster decided to take a risky gambit and lowered the shields protecting his flagship, hoping to lure the Emperor into a personal confrontation. That very instant, the Master of Mankind saw what he had to do. Gathering his immediate companions, the Emperor teleported directly onto Horus' battle barge with Sanguinius, Rogal Dorn, and a select group of warriors. It was the final chance at victory for both sides, for the future of the human race was at stake.

The Emperor and his entourage were scattered throughout the vessel but immediately saw the full extent of Horus' betrayal. The Warmaster had become an almighty champion of Chaos, and he and his ship writhed with the fell power of the Dark Gods. Nightmarish beyond comprehension, the sight of it drove many of the Space Marines mad. Despite the horror of his surroundings, the Emperor pressed on towards the bridge, seeking the Warmaster.

When the Emperor breached the armoured doors of the bridge, he finally came face to face with his misguided son. Horus, swollen with the power of Chaos, stood over the dead and broken body of the angelic Primarch Sanguinius. Horus faced his creator, and in an instant, the two were locked in deadly battle, likened ever after to a duel between gods. They battled not only with powered blade and claw, but also on the psychic plane, their bodies and spirits locked in a struggle to the death. Though Horus dealt the Emperor several grievous wounds, the Master of Mankind stalwartly withstood the Warmaster's attacks. With a last effort, the Emperor struck home, slaying his beloved son and blasting his psyche to utterly destroy Horus' presence in the warp. In doing so the Emperor paid the ultimate price for his victory, and darkness overcame him as he finally allowed his body to suffer his terrible wounds.

With the death of the Warmaster, the Chaos armies lost the assistance of their daemonic allies – and with it, the resolve to fight. The Battle for Terra was over, but the cost was unthinkable. The Emperor ascended to the arcane life-support systems of the Golden Throne to hold his ultimate death at bay. Terra was in ruins, her cities levelled, her peoples devastated. Even the planet's tectonic plates were shifted by relentless months of orbital bombardments levelled by the traitors. Such was the ferocity of their attacks that nothing short of the complete rebuilding of Terra could even begin to heal the wounds inflicted during the siege.

The loyalists had won, though the Imperium lay in tatters around them. The Traitor Legions retreated to the Eye of Terror, swearing that they would return to set the galaxy aflame once more. Chief amongst them was Abaddon, Captain of the First Company of the Sons of Horus. He took with him the body of the Warmaster, and an unquenchable thirst for vengeance.

Within the giant warp rift, the traitor Primarchs and their Legions found sanctuary amongst the nightmarish Daemon worlds. They warred amongst themselves for dominance and territory, while factions split from the Legions to found other warbands and armies. They have never stopped fighting against the Emperor. This struggle has lasted for ten thousand years and even now besets the Imperium. The Horus Heresy is a distant memory, but the taint of Chaos still threatens to corrupt – the Long War continues.

THE SCOURING

After the traitor Space Marines were hurled back from the walls of the Emperor's Palace, the survivors of the loyalist Legions were united by a desire for vengeance. They sought to purge those brothers that had turned to darkness, following on their heels with the focus of a pride of lions on the hunt. The period that followed was known as the Scouring. The Traitor Legions and their twisted Primarchs continued to fight – no longer for the conquest of the Imperium, but for their own survival. War was so incessant that at times the threat to the Emperor's realm was almost as great as at the peak of the Heresy.

The wars of the Scouring lasted many years and almost exhausted the manifold armies of Terra. The loyalists eventually hounded their turncoat brethren into the Eye of Terror. It became both prison and stronghold to the traitors, the only stable space lane in and out barred by the fortress world of Cadia. Still the traitors launched their raids, wounded animals lashing out with blood-crazed savagery.

As if the traitors were not enough for the badly mauled Imperium to deal with, this time also marked the rise of the alien threat. With so much of its strength committed to its grand civil war, Humanity found itself assailed anew by the very xenos empires it had recently driven back. The Horus Heresy had torn the nascent Imperium from the heights of glory, and plunged it into a nightmare of eternal war.

Upon the colossal death-ship *Vengeful Spirit* did the Emperor's finest face his traitor son, Horus. Though the Angel, Sanguinius, was found wanting, slain by the Warmaster's cruel claw, the Master of Mankind took his vengeance. It was to carry the most terrible cost.

THE TRAITOR LEGIONS

The Traitor Legions have remained the sworn enemies of Mankind since the time of the Heresy. Many strange and hideous changes have been wrought upon them since their retreat, and their bodies have been reforged into forms more pleasing to the Ruinous Powers. Still these killers remain unrepentant, convinced they walk upon the path to everlasting glory.

THE PATH TO GLORY

The Heretic Astartes are united by their hunger for power. At first, this desire is focused towards specific goals, but as time passes, it becomes a bone-deep obsession. Though the Dark Gods are given to rewarding their mortal followers for acts of carnage that further their divine cause, the gifts they bestow upon their favoured are fickle indeed. A particularly extravagant slaughter might be rewarded with a blood-red aura that invigorates the supplicant, but it is just as likely the champion will find his arms being reshaped as axes of bone, or that he has the face of a slavering hound. Eventually, the Chaos Space Marine seeks immortality, to ascend to such lofty heights of favour that he is remade as a Daemon Prince. But for every successful aspirant there are hundreds of failures, mutated beyond recognition into mewling abominations known as Chaos Spawn.

'Those who scale the pinnacles of glory have the furthest to plunge into the abyss.'

- Melothrucius Lux

The ancient events of the Horus Heresy have long since passed into myth within the Imperium; the average Imperial citizen is entirely ignorant of the tumultuous events of the Imperium's founding. Ten thousand years of history have obscured those dark days when Horus almost enslaved Mankind with the shackles of Chaos. Indeed, records of the full horror of the Heresy are only preserved by the Inquisitors of the Ordo Malleus, and perhaps the memories of the Emperor himself.

Within the Eye of Terror, however, time flows differently. Many of the same traitors who howled their praises to the Gods of Chaos before the Imperial Palace still live to this day. Their defeat gnaws at them like a cancer, and their hatred of the Imperium burns undimmed. Those warriors who were once dutiful, honour-bound Space Marines have become cynical and embittered reavers determined to destroy that which they once protected. For these traitors, the Horus Heresy is not some distant, half-forgotten age, but a glorious war still in living memory – a war that is still being fought.

Little remains of the organised Legions that waged war upon ancient Terra. Millennia of jealousies and infighting have broken down the Legions into companies and warbands of varying sizes. Each is led by a captain or champion of Chaos who pursues his own destiny. The most fervent worshippers of the Dark Powers band together to form squads blessed by a patron god and bear their mark upon their bodies and armour. Most have simply sworn themselves to all of the Chaos Gods.

In the ever-changing delirium of the Daemon worlds, many traitor Legionaries have survived the worst of the warping influence of Chaos by keeping their sense of purpose. They are carried forth by ancient warships that have survived from the time of the Heresy, but are now encrusted with millennia of baroque decoration and scarred by old battle wounds. The Traitor Legions also capture drifting space hulks – vast agglomerations of spaceborne detritus and wreckage – and refit them to use as vast battle barges carrying thousands of troops. With these assets, the warbands of Chaos go forth to despoil the worlds of the Emperor, enslave his followers and steal his wealth so that they might carry out further attacks. Thus, the punitive raids of the Traitor Legions are an ever-present threat to the worlds of the Imperium, especially to those systems around the Eye of Terror.

CHAOS RENEGADES

The Traitor Legions are not the only Space Marines to fall to Chaos. With each new millennium, dozens of disillusioned or power-hungry Chapters defect, just as Horus did. Only the High Lords and the Inquisition have any idea of how deep the rot goes. Nonetheless, some renegades have achieved such notoriety that their legends resonate throughout entire sectors.

Over the course of centuries, the forces of Chaos have been further swelled by Space Marines who have turned from the light of the Emperor to pursue their own agendas. Freed from the dogma and traditions of their Chapters, these renegade Space Marines become corsairs and mercenaries, using their unequalled battle skills to gather wealth and power. The most powerful then set themselves up as the tyrannical figureheads of pirate fleets and rulers of bases hidden on desolate planets.

As they explore this new freedom, these Space Marines inevitably turn at some point to the Gods of Chaos to grant them more power to do with as they will. From this point on, they are as doomed to walk the path of the Chaos champion as any Traitor from the Horus Heresy. These renegades are hunted men; they are especially loathed by other Space Marine Chapters, who consider it a duty of honour to crush any renegades lest their perfidious behaviour become a stain upon the honour of all Space Marines.

Though never rivalling the size and power of the Legions, a Space Marine Chapter is a potent military force. When an entire brotherhood turns renegade, it is a grave threat that can destroy armies, conquer worlds and despoil whole sectors of Mankind's realm. Such events always warrant an extreme response from the Imperium, usually involving the intervention of other Space Marine Chapters. It is perhaps the most trying test of faith for a Space Marine to have to pit his skill, training and loyalty against another Space Marine. Though the scions of Chaos do not have the unshakeable faith of their loyalist brethren, the disturbing gifts they receive from the Ruinous Powers in return for their allegiance can more than compensate. Because of this, these internecine conflicts often have a calamitous effect on other Chapters nearby. Inter-Chapter wars tend to escalate quickly, engulfing many worlds in war and bloodshed. On occasion, those forces sent to deal with the treacherous Chapter may actually end up, in whole or in part, joining with those they were sent to destroy.

Just such an occurrence took place during the Obscuran Uprisings of the late 34th Millennium. During the four hundred years of separatist rebellions that were spread across much of Segmentum Obscurus, at least seven Chapters broke their oaths to the Emperor and took part in the pillaging of hundreds of vulnerable or war-ravaged worlds. Of these Chapters, two – the Sons of Vengeance and the Silver Guards – initially fought on the side of the Imperium, but fractured into warbands and turned renegade after their actions against the Free Council of Hannedra II. Insurgencies such as these plague the history of the Adeptus Astartes, and each has been a devastating setback to the Imperium that its masters are eager to suppress.

THE MARK OF THE HERETIC

Whether he be a traitor from the prehistory of the Imperium or a renegade turncoat from a recent war, a Chaos Space Marine will find himself slowly reshaped by the eldritch powers he worships into a form that better echoes the darkness in his soul. The energies of the warp will cause a warrior's flesh and blood to meld with his armour over time until they become one and the same, just as it conjoins his consciousness with the once-pure machine spirits of his wargear. Over the years a Chaos Space Marine obsessed with death may find his helm transforming into a flayed skull that is fused to his own features, whilst one who seeks to glut himself on flesh finds his intestines mingling with the recycler cables of his power armour until he is a living engine of consumption. Often, these perverted anatomies echo the shapes and hues of the Daemon servants of the Ruinous Powers, marking the Chaos Space Marine as the property of his patron, body and soul.

VENGEANCE WRIT LARGE

The Long War has raged for ten thousand years. The bitterness and spite of the Heretic Astartes has spread throughout the galaxy, spilling from the warp before bleeding back once more for time immemorial. Though the Inquisition takes great pains to quell reports of Chaos incursions in order to spare the common populace from unconventional thought, legends of these events persist across the galaxy, handed down through the generations by the foolish and the brave.

M30-M31 AGE OF BETRAYAL
The Great Crusade

The Emperor rises from the anarchy of sundered Terra and creates the Primarchs. The first Space Marines are created in turn. With the warp storms that isolated Terra dissipated, the Emperor goes forth into the galaxy. Over the course of campaigns unnumbered, the Emperor's Legions unite Mankind. The Imperium of Man is born.

The Horus Heresy

The galaxy is torn by rebellion. Horus and his Traitor Primarchs lay waste to the Legiones Astartes and all but overthrow the Emperor of Mankind. The forces of Chaos are eventually hurled back from Terra.

Fall of a Primarch

Fulgrim, the Daemon Primarch of the Emperor's Children, leads his hedonistic armies in a spiteful strike against the Ultramarines upon Thessala. Amongst the swirling pink mists of Slaanesh's favour, Fulgrim hunts down his brother Primarch Roboute Guilliman and fights him in single combat. Though Guilliman is mighty indeed, his opponent is a serpentine giant swollen with daemonic power, each of his four arms wielding a poisoned blade. Guilliman is struck down by a slash across his throat. He is spirited away by his Space Marines and placed in a stasis field before Fulgrim's poisons can kill him outright. For ten long millennia, Guilliman lingers on the very threshold of death.

The Long War Begins

Thirsty for revenge, the Chaos Space Marines strike out against the Imperium from the depths of the Eye of Terror. The Adepts of the Administratum are horrified to find that the number of their invasions increases with every passing decade.

M32-M39 AGE OF RETRIBUTION
Perturabo's Curse

The Daemon Primarch Perturabo perverts the eight rituals of possession, turning them against his enemies. Invoking Nurgle, Perturabo imbues his curse with contagion and releases it into the mechanical systems of Toil, a vassal forge world. Chaos spreads through the machines, and the manufactorums begin to change. On the eighth day, giant cables burst from the earth, daemonic machines hunt the living, and many-legged cathedrals of industry prowl the wastes. The planet is scoured of all native flesh.

The Shattering

Craftworld Lugganath comes under attack from a psychically shielded fleet of Emperor's Children. The Eldar vessels destroy the first wave of fighters, but the sheer number of Chaos Space Marine dropships forces a breach in the craftworld's defences. After a bitterly fought boarding action, a teleport relay is established in the Plaza of Reflection and the Emperor's Children begin to deploy en masse. The Eldar are swift to seal the breach, but they realise their foe's true intent too late. At the heart of the plaza, several hundred Noise Marines combine the output of their sonic weapons into a cacophony that resonates in both realspace and the warp. The damage caused to the craftworld's psycho-reactive architecture is extreme, causing its thin spires to crumble down onto the battle raging below.

The Red Dawn of Iriad IV

Iriad IV, a fortified industrial world, is invaded by a horde of World Eaters. Captain Revellion of the Ebon Knights leads his Chapter against their traitor cousins. The battle tears across the planet until less than a company's worth of warriors remains on either side.

Whilst the World Eaters are unconcerned by their own losses, Revellion is driven to desperation by the deaths of so many of his men. Uttering a dark oath, he leaves his surviving forces to combat the enemy alone. Hours later, the Captain stalks from the shadows covered head to toe in blood. As he strikes down the last of the World Eaters, the surviving Space Marines give voice to victory cries, though their moment of triumph soon turns to ash. In a frenzy, Revellion hacks a swathe through the remaining Ebon Knights. He does not stop there, however – district after district is ravaged as the Captain's pact with Khorne bears slow but terrible fruit. Iriad IV's population is evacuated and the planet declared perditas.

The Great Degeneration

After the unremitting violence of the xenocidal Quietus Campaign, the Annihilators Chapter finally succumbs to blood psychosis. Those of the Chapter still able to act rationally gather at their fortress monastery in the hope of finding absolution. Instead of redeeming their sins, however, their corrupted Chaplains lead them in a ritual that leaves their souls wide open to daemonic influence. Every member of the Chapter is possessed over the course of a single night, shifting forms into armoured half-Daemon monstrosities. Calling themselves the Beasts of Annihilation, the brethren go to war again, though this time it is the Imperium that feels their wrath.

The Abyssal Crusade

Warp Storm Dionys ripples across the galaxy, its empyric energies polluting a swathe of star systems. In addition to billions of Imperial citizens, no fewer than thirty Space Marine Chapters are judged by the charismatic Saint Basillius to be tainted. The Ecclesiarchal lord gives a choice to those so accused – seek redemption in the Eye of Terror or be exterminated.

Without exception, the condemned Chapters – known as the Judged – choose to embark upon a redemptive crusade aimed at purging the Daemon worlds of the Eye of Terror. Within that great warp rift some of the Chapters go missing or are destroyed, whilst others turn renegade in order to survive. The most resolute of the Judged return to the Imperium bloodied but unbowed nearly eight hundred years later, and discover that their accuser, Saint Basillius himself, is a servant of the Ruinous Powers. The corrupted saint's demise is swift.

M40-M41 AGE OF APOTHEOSIS
Double-edged Swords

Agents of the Alpha Legion infiltrate the hive slums of Ghorstangrad, home world of the Emperor's Swords. Through subliminal indoctrination of the dominant sects and gangs, the Alpha Legion seed potential Space Marines with deviant philosophies and subconscious triggers. Though many of these youths are rejected by Librarians and Chaplains, some are recruited into the Chapter nonetheless, a lurking threat unknown even to the recruits themselves.

Almost three centuries later, the Alpha Legion mount an invasion of Ghorstangrad and are met in battle by the Emperor's Swords. The Legion employ psychic attacks that awaken the latent personalities of the unknowing infiltrators amongst the defending Space Marines. Within hours, the Chapter disintegrates into a morass of battling factions, some of which join forces with the invaders. The Emperor's Swords are wiped out, Ghorstangrad is razed and the gene-seed stores of the Chapter are pillaged. The Alpha Legion withdraws to the Eastern Fringe, its numbers bolstered with new renegades.

The 1st Armageddon War

Imperial forces upon the strategically vital world of Armageddon struggle to contain a rebellion across both Armageddon Prime and Armageddon Secundus. At the height of the civil war, a space hulk enters the system and disgorges a horde from the Eye of Terror, led by Angron and his massed warbands of World Eaters. Angron and his armies carve a red path across Armageddon Prime.

The conquest of Armageddon appears inevitable until the Daemon Primarch pauses to draw more chaotic energy to the planet. During the reprieve, the Imperial forces are reinforced not only by Space Wolves from nearby Fenris, but also by the Grey Knights 1st Brotherhood. Though the subsequent battle costs the lives of all but a handful of the Grey Knights, Angron is driven back to the warp.

The Fall of Nova Terra

The sons of Guilliman free Nova Terra from a Tyranid attack. Afterwards, Squad Constantinus hunts down remnants of the hive fleet, uncovering Genestealer Cults within the noble families of the capital. The entire ruling class is executed. To the Ultramarines' horror, the outraged population rises up against their Space Marine liberators. His patience gone, Sergeant Constantinus blames the Imperium for making him a monstrous killer and denounces the Emperor.

Constantinus swears to lead Nova Terra's populace to a better future, and his conviction is infectious. As his oratory takes hold amongst the anarchy, his agenda of martial discipline is beaten into the fabric of the Nova Terran civilisation. The old order is thrown down and statues of Constantinus the Liberator are raised in their place. Other servants of the Ruinous Powers soon arrive, drawn by the anarchy and bloodshed. The rebel sergeant's megalomania escalates until it plunges the whole sector into war. The rebellion ends only when Constantinus is killed by agents of the Officio Assassinorum.

The Badab War

Lugft Huron, Chapter Master of the Astral Claws, declares himself the Tyrant of Badab and secedes from the Imperium. Eleven years of inter-system war follows, embroiling more than a dozen Chapters of the Adeptus Astartes. Huron's reign is eventually brought to an end, but despite suffering grievous wounds, he escapes into the Maelstrom.

The Vaxhallian Genocides

The Chaos renegades known as the Purge vent their hatred of all living things upon the verdant Imperial world of Vaxhallia. The planet's inhabitants are soon riddled with consumptive disease and crippled by famine. Over the course of a single month, the Purge engineer the deaths of no fewer than fourteen billion Imperial citizens.

The Wolf at Bay

Mustering five companies of Space Wolves, the Cadian 301st and the Tallarn 14th, the decorated Inquisitor Pranix attempts to reclaim the nine Hollow Worlds of Lastrati from the Red Corsairs. The Drop Pods of the Space Wolves crash down to the algae-encrusted surfaces of the Hollow Worlds, and war soon rages throughout the tunnels that link them. Huron Blackheart collapses preselected portions of his gate networks with cold precision and timing, isolating and destroying much of the Imperial army sent against him. Heavy casualties are sustained on both sides, and the invading forces withdraw in disarray.

Skulls for the Skull Throne

Having long ago amassed more human skulls than he knew what to do with, Roghrax Bloodhand of the World Eaters, swears to collect a skull from every warrior species in the galaxy. Bloodhand's masterwork takes a dramatic new turn with the coming of the Tyranids. Making haste for the Eastern Fringe, the maniacal trophy collector leads his fleet directly into the path of Hive Fleet Kraken. Delighted at the prospect of collecting such large and varied skulls, he reaps a grisly bounty from the Tyranids.

The Great Awakening

A ripple of psychic activity passes through the Imperium, awakening the dormant powers of latent psykers across the galaxy. The resultant empyric backlash tears open hundreds of warp rifts, and many worlds are lost to daemonic incursion. The Thousand Sons are seen in unprecedented numbers as the psychic apocalypse runs its course.

The Sons of the Maelstrom

A Heretic Astartes fleet emerges from the Maelstrom with over thirty Daemon-infested space hulks. The massed fleet brings the Chogoris, Kaelas and Sessec Systems to their knees, establishing a stranglehold over their space lanes.

The Fall of Vilamus

After a series of raids leaves the fortress monastery of the Marines Errant garrisoned only by a single company, Huron Blackheart sends his Night Lords allies to infiltrate the fastness and bring down its power shields and defence lasers. Teleporting in from low orbit, Chaos Terminators launch a sledgehammer assault upon the fortress' apothecarion as Huron Blackheart moves in to steal the Chapter's relics. Caught in a dilemma, the outnumbered and outmanoeuvred Space Marines fail to repel the invasion. The Red Corsairs withdraw with nearly all of the Chapter's gene-seed, dooming the Marines Errant to a slow demise.

The Great Rift

The principal agents of the Dark Gods are united in a single grand cause, though few of them realise their labours coincide until their efforts yield truly spectacular results. Wars rage, cosmic rituals reach completion, and the barrier between realspace and the warp is weakened across a fault line in the fabric of reality. The heavens themselves split apart, and the Cicatrix Maledictum yawns wide.

THE BLACK CRUSADES

Perhaps once in ten generations, a truly great champion of Chaos will arise in the depths of the Eye of Terror. Through the power of his implacable will and the favour of the Dark Gods, this champion brings about an unsteady alliance between the infernal scions of the warp, drawing together a terrifying army of Chaos Space Marines, Daemons, mutants and renegades.

A Black Crusade is so vast that it darkens the stars. In the years preceding each titanic invasion, the hell-forges of the Daemon worlds echo with the clangour of monstrous machines and nightmare industry, churning out armour and weapons for the wars to come. Daemon Engines are roused from their embittered slumbers and warring factions vie for command of the massed warbands of Heretic Astartes that will form the grand invasion's rank and file.

When a Black Crusade is finally launched, the warp vomits forth the diabolical hordes of Chaos: armies of wretched mutants, hosts of Daemons, twisted monsters the size of buildings, numberless masses of cultists, wild tribes of abhumans and terrifying Chaos Titans. Spearheading these nightmarish hosts are the Chaos Space Marines, united behind their champions in their desire to wreak untold destruction upon the Imperium.

The most destructive Black Crusades have been those led by Abaddon the Despoiler. Thirteen times has the Warmaster rampaged from the Daemon worlds of the Eye of Terror to wreak havoc upon his mortal enemies, his hosts plunging into the Imperium like an envenomed blade. Every attack has sent the Imperium reeling and ravaged worlds close to the Eye, but the Thirteenth Crusade dwarfs all those that have gone before. Many Imperial strategos have theorised that the first twelve campaigns were mere precursors to the current invasion, each seemingly unrelated event paving the way to the same goal – the Fall of Cadia, the coming of the Great Rift and the ultimate invasion of Terra.

THE CRIMSON PATH

Abaddon intends to succeed where his predecessor Horus failed, to break the Imperial Palace wide open and tear the Emperor's corpse from the Golden Throne. Over the millennia, each of his conquests has gradually paved the way from the Eye of Terror towards the Sol System. Less obvious, however, is that, along that path, his actions have gradually unpicked the veil between realspace and the warp.

During the course of his long years on the threshold of the Eye, Abaddon discovered a strange truth about the barrier between the materium and immaterium. Dotted across the galaxy were ancient structures of black stone, stark and monolithic on the outside but extremely complex within. There were many of these upon the fortress world of Cadia. Known as 'pylons' to the planet's militarised populace, they were so old that none gave them more than a passing thought. It was Abaddon's belief that these structures were the very things that maintained the stability of the Cadian Gate – something about them kept the energies of the warp from spilling through the Eye of Terror into realspace.

For thousands of years, the Despoiler sent his agents across the galaxy to locate these monoliths of black stone. He spent many years calling in old alliances, striking daemonic bargains and invoking ancient pacts with the Traitor Legions and their corrupted Primarchs. Thread by tenuous thread, the Despoiler put together a plan to isolate and destroy these structures, using false objectives or even entire Black Crusades to conceal his true motives. Over the course of several world-scouring invasions, Abaddon shattered, toppled or blasted apart these structures wherever he found them – sometimes in person, at other times with his agents, his flagship the *Planet Killer,* or the immense Blackstone Fortresses he co-opted during the Gothic War.

The last of and greatest of these destructive campaigns was levelled at Cadia itself. Abaddon's Thirteenth Black Crusade brought about so much death and destruction that his daemonic allies could breach realspace wherever they wished and be sustained indefinitely by the unbridled mayhem that raged around them. The demolition of the strange black monoliths scattered across Cadia's surface was finally

achieved, the capstone of a grand design that had seen the cataclysmic events of Pandorax, Fenris, the Planet of the Sorcerers and a dozen worlds besides tied together into one galaxy-wrecking whole. Suddenly, all the manifold armies of Chaos were free to pour into realspace like blood from a deep wound. True to his claims, Abaddon had succeeded in ripping open the gates of hell.

As the galaxy has split along its length, with warp storms raging in a hundred locations and more, those Traitor Legions and Renegade Chapters who have sworn allegiance to the Warmaster have formed the vanguard of the invasion. They are a broad-headed spear that has plunged deep into the heart of the Cadian System and emerged from the other side. Abaddon cares little how many casualties are amassed as his great agenda comes to fruition. His only concern is that enough blood be spilled to saturate the battlefields of the Imperium's defenders, and in doing so summon more daemonic armies to his cause. This is a strategy Abaddon intends to see replicated on world after world as he extends the Crimson Path, each planetary invasion taking the Chaos Space Marines closer to Terra, with the armies of the Daemon lords following in their wake.

With Cadia reduced to ruin, the Cicatrix Maledictum is being effectively weaponised by Abaddon's invasion. It spills out behind the Thirteenth Black Crusade, roiling and growing more violent in Abaddon's wake, agitated by the scale of the Black Legion's many slaughters. Simultaneously, dozens of Renegade Chapters from the warp anomaly once known as the Maelstrom are pouring out into Segmentum Solar, forcing the Space Marines and their Primaris reinforcements to spread themselves thin as they fight on hundreds of fronts. Abaddon has driven a talon of unreality into Segmentum Solar, its onset heralding the doom of the Imperium. The High Lords of Terra live in constant fear of realspace collapsing entirely, and are sending every military force they can muster to halt Abaddon's rampage. As the drama plays out to its desperate conclusion, one thing remains certain – unending war.

BLACK LEGION

The Black Legion are the only Traitor Legion to have changed their name in ten thousand years of exile. Originally created as the Luna Wolves, the Emperor renamed them the Sons of Horus in honour of their actions during the Ullanor Crusade. After the Horus Heresy, Abaddon renamed the Legion once more, rejecting the name of their Primarch, whom he regarded with contempt after the rebellion's failure.

During the Heresy, the Sons of Horus served as the Warmaster's praetorians throughout his campaigns. They were the first to remove the icons of the Emperor from their armour, replacing them with the Eye of Horus, an image that would become a symbol of dread throughout the Imperium. They fought with pride and unthinkable ferocity, knowing that they were the chosen amongst the Warmaster's new order. When the Emperor defeated Horus, the Legion's morale was extinguished; their patron, their father, had been taken from them, and they launched a costly but successful raid to recover Horus' body from the loyalists.

Factions in the other Traitor Legions later blamed the Sons of Horus for initiating the rout from Terra by retreating into warp space with the body of the Warmaster, leaving the horde below leaderless. But the battle for Terra was lost the moment Horus fell, and no power in the universe could have brought victory to the forces of Chaos after that. In the Eye of Terror, the Sons of Horus fought ferocious battles with the other Legions for possession of key worlds and resources, fighting to re-establish themselves as the pre-eminent Legion.

The Sons of Horus worshipped one Chaos God after another, and each time more and more of their number gave themselves up to possession by Daemons. Over the centuries they were bled white in a succession of conflicts with the other Traitor Legions. This internecine warfare eventually culminated in the destruction of the Sons' fortress by a combined force of their rivals. To add to the ignominy of defeat, the body of the Warmaster was stolen and attempts were made to clone him, much to the horror and revulsion of his remaining Legionaries. Denied their genetic and spiritual father, the Sons of Horus swore allegiance to Ezekyle Abaddon, Captain of the 1st Company, and hailed him as the new Warmaster.

One of Abaddon's first edicts was to reject the name of Horus and the Legion's title. He ordered the remaining Chaos Space Marines to paint their armour black to mark their shame, and then led them in a lightning raid to destroy Horus' body and the misshapen clones created from it. The Legion's gigantic command ship, the *Vengeful Spirit*, and its attendant fleet disappeared into the obscuring nebulae at the very edge of the Eye of Terror, which were to serve as a hidden base for Abaddon and his warriors, who were now known as the Black Legion. The Legion has launched attacks across the breadth of the Imperium ever since, often vanishing as swiftly as they arrive.

Abaddon and his warriors fought hard to regain their honour and rebuild their reputation, throwing themselves into the most dangerous conflicts they could find. At first, Abaddon won the grudging respect of the surviving Traitor Legions, but as his deeds became ever bolder and his list of extraordinary achievements grew, respect turned into active support. His impassioned words have since fanned the smouldering resentment of the Traitor Legions into the raging fires of hatred. Champions of many Legions and gods now vie to fight for Abaddon in the colours of his Black Legion.

The Black Legion is made up of many warbands whose appearance and motivations vary wildly, but all are guided by the implacable will of Abaddon the Despoiler and so broadly employ the same tactics in battle. The Legion has a preference for close assault over ranged combat, and the swift application of extreme force to disrupt or neutralise key targets. The frequency of these attacks increases exponentially, applying a constant and escalating pressure on the enemy and gradually crushing their ability to muster a coordinated defence. Eventually, the Black Legion commanders and their Chosen launch a devastating strike at the crucial moment – usually a teleport strike by warriors in Terminator armour – which breaks the back of the enemy forces.

BLACK LEGION WARBANDS

The Black Legion is the largest of the Traitor Legions inhabiting the Eye of Terror, vastly outnumbering even their closest rivals. As long as a warrior is willing to bow before Abaddon the Despoiler and take the oath of obedience, he may join the Black Legion. During the centuries of warfare and acts of vengeance since the Horus Heresy, Space Marines from dozens of Chapters and other Legions have joined the Despoiler. Now, the Black Legion boasts warlords and warbands from almost every permutation of Chaos worship, depraved doctrine and ruinous faith.

Usually, these warbands work in isolation, raiding planets and pillaging the Imperium in the name of their master, but largely pursuing their own agendas. Their preferred style of warfare is to engage the foe swiftly in close-quarters combat and to cut off any chance of retreat. They advance relentlessly towards the lines of their enemies, laying down hails of fire and bellowing dark oaths as they press forwards. Wherever their foe presents weakness, the Black Legion are swift to exploit it, sending their elite warriors to eradicate a collapsing flank or to slaughter enemy champions who have left themselves exposed.

Warbands vary greatly in size, from a few score Heretic Astartes to as many as several hundred. Each such force boasts its own transports, Battle Barges, heavy landing craft, war machines and Daemon Engines, as well as throngs of fanatical cultists who charge screaming into the fray. A lone warband can reduce an Imperial or xenos outpost to ruin, bombarding the enemy's defences from on high as warriors on the ground close in for the kill. This gives the tyrannical Chaos Lords who lead these warbands free rein to maraud as they please, sating their thirst for carnage and power without the need to form lasting alliances with their brethren.

However, when Abaddon calls, the warbands gather. Their oaths to the Warmaster force them to put aside their hatreds and feuds to fight alongside the Legion united. Even so, there is no denying that the Black Legion remains an alliance of traitors; the warlords therein are constantly scheming against their rivals, vying for prominence and glory, and undermining their contenders' achievements, even when they are not openly battling amongst themselves. Only their collective fear of the Despoiler forces them to suffer cooperation – fear and the chilling memory of the fates of those who have crossed him.

The Black Legion bear the Eye of Horus upon their shoulder pads.

Brother Narghast has wielded his boltgun Hateslaker for millennia, and has put it to gruesome use on countless planets throughout the galaxy.

LEGION OF A THOUSAND HOSTS

The Black Legion has recruited countless warbands of every stripe to their cause – though some of these still claim autonomy, they have all bent the knee to Abaddon the Despoiler, and all wear some variant of gold and black in honour of their adopted faction. Many warbands worship one of the Chaos Gods above the others, adorning their black battle plate with icons, trophies and the favoured colours of their patron in the hope of attracting more divine favour – and perhaps ascending beyond the Black Legion to claim mastery of their own fate. Many traitor legionnaires are counted amongst these hosts, for Abaddon's strength as a leader is impossible to deny.

HOUNDS OF ABADDON

Within the ranks of the Black Legion there are thousands of devotees of Khorne. The Hounds of Abaddon revel in close combat, where they can spill the greatest volume of blood for their god, using chainaxes, lightning claws or even their own fangs. The Hounds are currently led by Threxos Hellbreed, Admiral of the Black Fleet. He has won great favour with Khorne due to his skill at launching ship-to-ship ambushes, and has a reputation for initiating spectacular boarding actions.

Kharmak Heartripper, the Butcher-Knight of Azmoreal's Reach

SONS OF THE CYCLOPS

Consisting of the followers of Tzeentch, Sorcerers and their Rubricae, the Sons of the Cyclops hold a disproportionate amount of power within the Black Legion. This is largely through the ceaseless efforts of the warlords that have led them; invaluable psykers such as Zaraphiston and Ygethmor the Deceiver. Gifted seers and diviners, they make up the core of Abaddon's advisers, peering into the future for him and guiding his Black Crusades.

Athoth the Voiceless, Privy to the Nine Unholy Secrets

BRINGERS OF DECAY

The Plague God has a strong following within the Black Legion. Under the dominance of Skyrak Slaughterborn, the Nurglites have converted many to their cause. In battle, the Bringers of Decay are Abaddon's plague carriers and heralds of contagion, appearing before other warbands to sow infection and sickness. This could also be why many other warbands will have little to do with the Bringers, repelled by the blessings of the Plague God they bear.

Gholbax Ghlaur, host to the dreaded Byleworm Gutpox

CHILDREN OF TORMENT

Under the guidance of such warlords as Devram Korda and Zagthean the Broken, the followers of Slaanesh that have joined the Black Legion are collectively called the Children of Torment. These traitors have sided with the Despoiler so they might wallow in the anguish he spreads and bathe in the gushing blood of his victims. The Children of Torment are despised by the Emperor's Children, who see them as traitors to Fulgrim and puppets of Abaddon.

Devolus the Obscenitor, Twistflesh Desecrator of the Tomb of Saint Solus

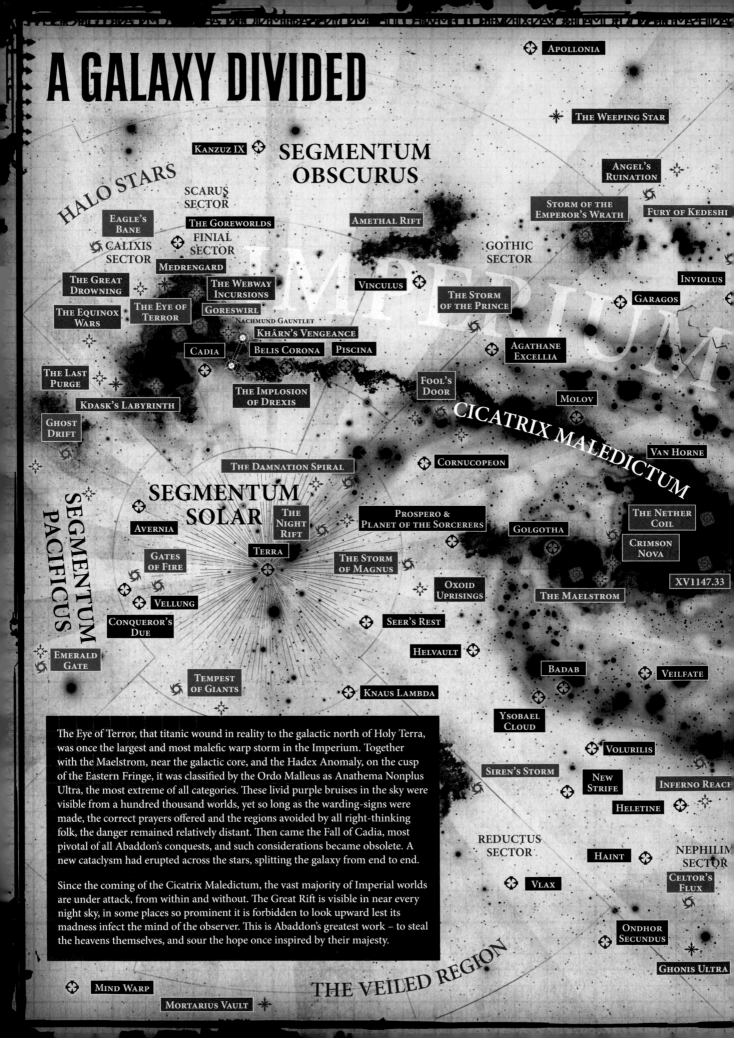

A GALAXY DIVIDED

APOLLONIA

THE WEEPING STAR

KANZUZ IX

SEGMENTUM OBSCURUS

ANGEL'S RUINATION

HALO STARS

SCARUS SECTOR

STORM OF THE EMPEROR'S WRATH

FURY OF KEDESHI

EAGLE'S BANE

THE GOREWORLDS

AMETHAL RIFT

FINIAL SECTOR

CALIXIS SECTOR

GOTHIC SECTOR

MEDRENGARD

IMPERIUM

INVIOLUS

THE GREAT DROWNING

THE WEBWAY INCURSIONS

VINCULUS

THE STORM OF THE PRINCE

GARAGOS

THE EQUINOX WARS

THE EYE OF TERROR

GORESWIRL

Nachmund Gauntlet

KHÂRN'S VENGEANCE

AGATHANE EXCELLIA

CADIA

BELIS CORONA

PISCINA

THE LAST PURGE

THE IMPLOSION OF DREXIS

FOOL'S DOOR

MOLOV

KDASK'S LABYRINTH

CICATRIX MALEDICTUM

GHOST DRIFT

VAN HORNE

THE DAMNATION SPIRAL

CORNUCOPEON

SEGMENTUM SOLAR

THE NETHER COIL

AVERNIA

THE NIGHT RIFT

PROSPERO & PLANET OF THE SORCERERS

GOLGOTHA

CRIMSON NOVA

SEGMENTUM PACIFICUS

TERRA

GATES OF FIRE

THE STORM OF MAGNUS

XV1147.33

VELLUNG

OXOID UPRISINGS

THE MAELSTROM

CONQUEROR'S DUE

SEER'S REST

EMERALD GATE

HELVAULT

BADAB

VEILFATE

TEMPEST OF GIANTS

KNAUS LAMBDA

YSOBAEL CLOUD

VOLURILIS

SIREN'S STORM

NEW STRIFE

INFERNO REACH

HELETINE

The Eye of Terror, that titanic wound in reality to the galactic north of Holy Terra, was once the largest and most malefic warp storm in the Imperium. Together with the Maelstrom, near the galactic core, and the Hadex Anomaly, on the cusp of the Eastern Fringe, it was classified by the Ordo Malleus as Anathema Nonplus Ultra, the most extreme of all categories. These livid purple bruises in the sky were visible from a hundred thousand worlds, yet so long as the warding-signs were made, the correct prayers offered and the regions avoided by all right-thinking folk, the danger remained relatively distant. Then came the Fall of Cadia, most pivotal of all Abaddon's conquests, and such considerations became obsolete. A new cataclysm had erupted across the stars, splitting the galaxy from end to end.

Since the coming of the Cicatrix Maledictum, the vast majority of Imperial worlds are under attack, from within and without. The Great Rift is visible in near every night sky, in some places so prominent it is forbidden to look upward lest its madness infect the mind of the observer. This is Abaddon's greatest work – to steal the heavens themselves, and sour the hope once inspired by their majesty.

REDUCTUS SECTOR

HAINT

NEPHILIM SECTOR

CELTOR'S FLUX

VLAX

ONDHOR SECUNDUS

MIND WARP

GHONIS ULTRA

THE VEILED REGION

MORTARIUS VAULT

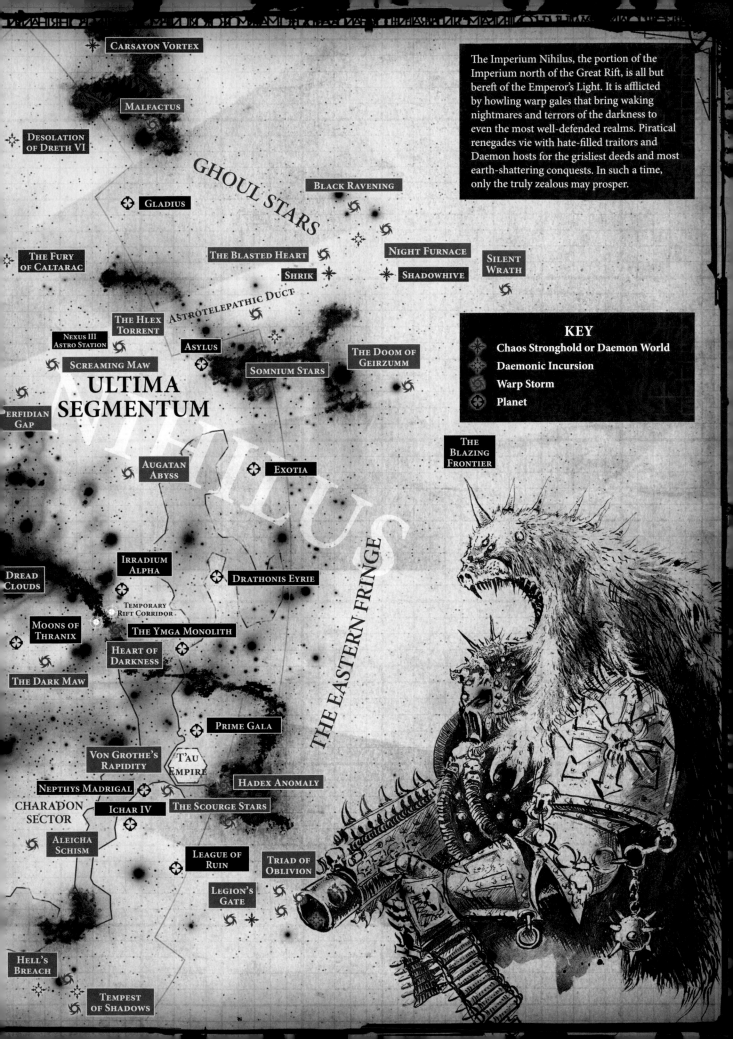

CARSAYON VORTEX

MALFACTUS

DESOLATION OF DRETH VI

GHOUL STARS

BLACK RAVENING

GLADIUS

THE FURY OF CALTARAC

THE BLASTED HEART

SHRIK

NIGHT FURNACE

SHADOWHIVE

SILENT WRATH

ASTROTELEPATHIC DUCT

THE HLEX TORRENT

NEXUS III ASTRO STATION

ASYLUS

SCREAMING MAW

ULTIMA SEGMENTUM

SOMNIUM STARS

THE DOOM OF GEIRZUMM

PERFIDIAN GAP

NIHILUS

THE BLAZING FRONTIER

AUGATAN ABYSS

EXOTIA

The Imperium Nihilus, the portion of the Imperium north of the Great Rift, is all but bereft of the Emperor's Light. It is afflicted by howling warp gales that bring waking nightmares and terrors of the darkness to even the most well-defended realms. Piratical renegades vie with hate-filled traitors and Daemon hosts for the grisliest deeds and most earth-shattering conquests. In such a time, only the truly zealous may prosper.

KEY

◈ Chaos Stronghold or Daemon World

⊕ Daemonic Incursion

꩜ Warp Storm

⊕ Planet

DREAD CLOUDS

IRRADIUM ALPHA

DRATHONIS EYRIE

TEMPORARY RIFT CORRIDOR

MOONS OF THRANIX

THE YMGA MONOLITH

HEART OF DARKNESS

THE DARK MAW

THE EASTERN FRINGE

PRIME GALA

VON GROTHE'S RAPIDITY

T'AU EMPIRE

NEPTHYS MADRIGAL

HADEX ANOMALY

CHARADON SECTOR

ICHAR IV

THE SCOURGE STARS

ALEICHA SCHISM

LEAGUE OF RUIN

TRIAD OF OBLIVION

LEGION'S GATE

HELL'S BREACH

TEMPEST OF SHADOWS

A LEGACY OF HATE

Thirteen times has Abaddon led the Black Legion in a grand assault against the Imperium. Every time, the Despoiler and his hordes have achieved a great victory, slain millions of loyalists or completed some obscure objective before vanishing back into the Eye of Terror. At the close of the 41st Millennium, Abaddon has led his Thirteenth Black Crusade in the final conquest of Cadia, emerging stronger than ever before at the head of a vast army of traitors, heretics and Daemons.

M30-M31 AGE OF BETRAYAL
Heresy and Aftermath

The spiritual rot spread by Warmaster Horus takes root in a full half of the Legiones Astartes, and ten thousand years of war is put in motion.

The Great Crusade

The Emperor unites the warring tribes of Terra and sets out to restore Mankind's place among the stars. At his side, Horus and the Luna Wolves fight with great fervour, laying waste to countless foes in his name and helping to create the Imperium of Man. In the aftermath of the Ullanor Campaign, the Luna Wolves are renamed the Sons of Horus in honour of their Primarch.

The Horus Heresy

Tainted by the touch of the Dark Gods, the Warmaster Horus turns against the Emperor. Fully half of the Legiones Astartes join with him as he attempts to bring the Imperium to its knees and destroy the loyalist Space Marine Legions. In the final battle for Terra, Horus is struck down by the Emperor in mortal combat aboard the *Vengeful Spirit*. Abaddon seizes the Warmaster's body and flees with the Sons of Horus into the Eye of Terror.

The Legion War

The traitor Astartes fight among themselves within the Eye of Terror in a war for resources and slaves that further fractures the already broken Legions. In the culmination of the war, the Emperor's Children attack the Daemon world of Maeleum and raze the Sons of Horus' fortress, stealing the body of their Primarch and vanishing into the warp.

The Black Legion Rises

Ascending to dominion of the Sons of Horus, Abaddon embarks on a quest to slay the clones Fabius Bile has crafted from Horus' remains. Destroying the Primogenitor's hidden laboratories and the abominations he created, Abaddon leaves behind no trace of his gene-father. With the final and utter destruction of Horus, Abaddon renames his Legion the Black Legion.

M32-M39 AGE OF RETRIBUTION
The Long War

Swearing to succeed where his forefather failed, Abaddon takes up the mantle of Warmaster and begins the Long War anew.

Abaddon the Despoiler's First Black Crusade

Mustering a vast army of traitors and Daemons, Abaddon leads the Black Legion out of the Eye of Terror to lay waste to the Imperium. In a great battle around the worlds of Cadia, the traitors are turned back by newly raised Space Marine Chapters and the Legio Titanicus. During the fighting, Abaddon secretly travels to the world of Uralan and claims the ancient Daemon sword Drach'nyen.

The Tormented Mine

Faenroc the Forgotten of the Black Legion discovers a world formed from warp-infused iron ore. He constructs a vast mine to harvest its wealth for the Warmaster. Slaves prove too fragile to work the mine as the ore mutates them uncontrollably, while some mine shafts secrete fluids that dissolve the workers within. Faenroc remedies this problem by binding daemonic entities to his mining machines in a ritual that involves the mass sacrifice of the entire mortal workforce.

Abaddon the Despoiler's Second Black Crusade

Abaddon places a death-curse upon the worlds of the Belis Corona Sector, infusing them with the touch of the warp. His fleet attacks the sector's shipyards, destroying dozens of Imperial cruisers under construction or repair. The Imperium, focusing on the war in space, musters a naval force to fight back. Entrusting his flagship to his Sorcerers, the Despoiler then teleports to the Inquisitorial stronghold of Nemesis Tessera. He topples its hexagrammic 'Eldritch Needles', ravaging the black stone with sustained melta fire before withdrawing. The Inquisition later find that a critical vault cell has been opened and its daemonic prisoner – the legendary nemesis for which the planet is named – is missing.

The Traitorous Eye

Drecarth the Sightless forms the Sons of the Eye out of those Sons of Horus who refused to join Abaddon after the Heresy. In the Battle of the Keening Deep, the Sons defeat Voslok and his World Eaters, claiming their fortress and hurling their skulls into the soulfires that rage beneath the planet's crust. Drecarth personally wrests Voslok's daemonic axe from his grip during the battle, turning the weapon upon its former owner.

Abaddon the Despoiler's Third Black Crusade

The Despoiler sends the Daemon Prince Tallomin against the Cadian Gate in a reckless frontal assault. The daemonic horde that follows in Tallomin's wake accounts for millions of lives and draws in Imperial Guard regiments and Space Marine Chapters from across Segmentum Obscurus. Eventually, the Space Wolves manage to banish Tallomin back to the warp. Under the cover provided by the attack, Abaddon leads a strike force to desecrate the shrine world of Gerstahl, breaking the ancient seals on the eponymous saint's tomb and destroying his remains while the Imperium's attention is directed elsewhere. This act of supreme violation banishes the saint's spirit, thwarting the prophecy that he would one day rise again whilst weakening the planet's psychic defences.

Zaraphiston's Penance

The Thousand Sons Sorcerer Zaraphiston travels deep into the heart of the Eye of Terror at the behest of Tzeentch, where he is granted the power of prophecy. Gifted with a profound understanding of the millennia to come, Zaraphiston pledges his loyalty to Abaddon the Despoiler.

Abaddon the Despoiler's Fourth Black Crusade

During the El'Phanor War, the Black Legion besiege the Citadel of the Kromarch. Abaddon leads the charge against the gates of the fortress, but so great is the firepower of the citadel that only a handful of his Chaos Space Marines make it past the kill zones of the Imperial defenders to the fortification's walls. With a single blow from Drach'nyen, the Warmaster sunders the towering doors of the fortress. In the process he shatters not just a portal of immense strength, but an ancient empyric barrier, for the citadel's gates incorporated ancient monoliths that had kept a potent warp node sealed. The Black Legion and their daemonic allies fall upon the Kromarch and his kin, conquering the citadel and extinguishing their ancient line.

The Nightmare Well

Zagthean the Broken pillages Helosian in the Agripinaa Sector. Taking the Convent of Alabaster Maidens prisoner, he exposes them to the energies of the warp, triggering their latent psychic gifts. Zagthean then uses warp-tech to fuse the maidens into a single entity, before using the resultant abomination as a living warp portal to unleash a daemonic invasion.

The Ragged King

Imperial cruisers orbiting the feral world of Skyrro destroy the traitor vessel *Talon of Rage*. A single Black Legionnaire escapes the ship's destruction and makes his way down to the surface of the world. Skyrro's indigenous populace come to worship the Chaos Space Marine as a god whom they hail as the Ragged King, and are gradually turned to the service of the Ruinous Powers. It takes the Imperial Guard more than a decade to destroy the legionnaire's cultist armies and reclaim the world.

Abaddon the Despoiler's Fifth Black Crusade

Abaddon scours the Elysia Sector, ordering the destruction of specific cities, shrines and temples across dozens its worlds. Each act of violation shatters the warp-seals that had held psychic mutation stable in that region of space. On Tarinth, the Despoiler lures the Warhawks and Venerators Chapters into the ruins of Kasyr Lutien where he traps them between the daemonic hordes of Khorne and the Black Legion. In a bitter last stand, both loyalist Chapters are completely destroyed, their skulls taken by the Daemon Prince Doombreed to be mounted upon Khorne's throne.

Abaddon the Despoiler's Sixth Black Crusade

The Warmaster visits his wrath upon Drecarth the Sightless. Abaddon aids the Sons of the Eye in an assault on the forge world of Arkreath, fighting with them side by side until the planet's Adeptus Mechanicus defenders are

finally crushed and its complex durasteel ziggurats battered to shapeless lumps of metal that no longer fulfil their function as sophisticated flux-cages. As the two leaders address their respective forces in the war's aftermath, Abaddon strikes Drecarth down, forcing him to watch the arrayed Sons of the Eye kneel before slaying him in a ritual display of violence.

The Tournament of Blood

Displeased with his Chosen, Abaddon pits them against each other. For eight days, the Chosen fight in the gore-spattered holds of the *Vengeful Spirit* until only one of them remains. Impaling the victor on the Talon of Horus, Abaddon seals a pact with Khorne, gaining a powerful daemonic ally in the form of the Bloodthirster Hakk'an'graah.

Abaddon the Despoiler's Seventh Black Crusade

During the Ghost War, a strike force of Blood Angels joins battle against Abaddon's forces upon the world of Mackan. The Despoiler singles out the sons of Sanguinius, personally leading a band of Khorne Berzerkers in a charge against their lines. The traitors that survive the loyalists' gunfire reap a bloody toll. So frenzied is the assault that the surviving Blood Angels are unable to recover the bodies of their fallen.

The Prison of Madness

Abaddon conducts experiments on captured loyalist Space Marines, torturing them with repeated visions of a future in which the Imperium falls to Chaos. Despite the psycho-indoctrinated mental resilience of the Adeptus Astartes, such is the ring of truth in these prophecies that those who do not take their own lives are left as soul-blasted husks that eventually swear allegiance to the Despoiler.

Abaddon the Despoiler's Eighth Black Crusade

On worlds throughout Segmentum Obscurus, Abaddon's forces cull precise numbers of Imperial citizens in the name of Tzeentch. The living-metal monoliths beneath the crater-cities of Teekus glow

brighter with each ritual slaughter until, at the culmination of the ninth, the structures begin to melt. By the time agents of the Inquisition identify a pattern in the Black Legion's actions, Abaddon has already achieved his aims.

The Ark of Damnation

Flesh Tearers Terminators board the space hulk *Soul of Damnation* as it drifts dangerously close to the core worlds of the Scelus Sub-sector. In the depths of the hulk, they uncover a stasis chamber containing a single casket. Inside is an ancient warrior of the Luna Wolves. When told of his Legion's fate, the ancient Space Marine is filled with rage and takes one of the Flesh Tearers' craft before disappearing into the void.

The Feast of Daemons

The Black Legion ravages the desert world of Sanisor, staining its dune oceans red with blood. In the Warpwind Canyons, the Chaos Space Marines erect a towering steel-framed device with a sail-like membrane of flayed skin. The creatures of the immaterium are drawn to the world to feed on the soul-stuff caught in the nightmarish construction. When the Cadian 232nd Expeditionary Force land on Sanisor, they find it crawling with Daemons like flies on a corpse.

Abaddon the Despoiler's Ninth Black Crusade

As part of a wider strategy to disable the naval fortress Cancephalus, Abaddon leads his Ninth Black Crusade against the heaving population of nearby Antecanis. The seat of the world's Imperial commander, Monarchive, is besieged by Abaddon's vanguard. Black Legionnaires butcher their way through the lower levels of the hive, whilst the Despoiler himself storms its inner sanctums. By the time Imperial Guard from Cancephalus arrive to reinforce the surviving defenders, Abaddon and his forces have already left the planet's surface.

As a gesture of contempt, the Black Legion drop a dozen cyclonic warheads onto the ruins of Monarchive. The seventeen-year war that ensues eventually robs both Antecanis and Cancephalus of their most precious resource – manpower. Without the fleets of the naval fortress to stop him, Abaddon is able to ravage the sector at will, and his Sorcerers are free to conduct the rituals required to weaken the walls of reality in that region of space with impunity.

The Forgotten Company

Almost eight millennia after it was sent, an astropathic distress signal reaches the Black Legion's Sorcerers from a lost company of Luna Wolves. Abaddon travels to the planet located at the coordinates in the message to find his ancient brothers have become a twisted parody of his original Legion, perverting their own gene-seed with primitive rituals and dwelling with the native inhabitants. Expecting no mercy from Abaddon's forces, the debased Luna Wolves are surprised when he welcomes them into the Black Legion.

Abaddon the Despoiler's Tenth Black Crusade

Abaddon's armies and Perturabo's Iron Warriors invade the Helica Sector. While the Black Legion assault the capital world, Thracian Primaris, the Iron Warriors focus their attack against the Iron Hands Chapter, seeking to settle an old blood debt. The Iron Warriors lay waste to the worlds of the Medusa System and push the Iron Hands to the brink of extinction. Only when the loyalist Chapter receives heavy reinforcement do Abaddon and the Iron Warriors disengage, taking with them valuable intelligence concerning Medusa's defences.

The Daemonic Shipyard

Deep within the Eye of Terror, Abaddon discovers an ancient shipyard drifting through the warp. Amongst its rusting gantries and crumbling manufactorum towers, the Warmaster finds a half-constructed vessel, vast in scale and terrible in its design. His Warpsmiths examine the ship, marvelling at its dark majesty, and promise that, when complete, it will be the doom of worlds.

Abaddon the Despoiler's Eleventh Black Crusade

The Despoiler's fleet becomes lost in the warp, finally returning to realspace in the path of Waaagh! Murgor. In the ruins of Relorria, the Black Legion bring the greenskins to battle. After months of fighting, Abaddon orders the Black Legion to leave Relorria to its fate and return to the Eye of Terror – but not before the Warmaster fills the holds of his fleet with captured Ork Weirdboyz. In conjunction with a coven of his most powerful Sorcerers, he uses the volatile psychic energies of the greenskin abductees in a daemonic hybridisation ritual that weakens the fabric of reality across the Relorrian System.

Fall of the Savage Swords

The Chapter Master of the Savage Swords mistakenly believes the Imperial governor of the planet Hyboras has stolen an ancient relic blade belonging to his Chapter. Caught up in their wrath and righteous retribution, his Space Marines commit a series of atrocities on the world. Only when their Chapter Master sits on the governor's gore-stained throne does he realise the extent of his folly, but by then it is too late. When the Black Legion arrive to push the world over the brink of disaster, the Savage Swords have already fallen to the worship of Khorne. It does not take much for Abaddon to persuade them to join him.

M40-M41 AGE OF APOTHEOSIS
The Hungering Prince

Glutgora, a Daemon Prince of Nurgle, invades the agri world of Pilentos with a massive force of Black Legionnaires. While the Chaos Space Marines crush every vestige of Imperial resistance, Glutgora gorges itself on the weave-worms of the planet's sprawling silk farms. Insatiable in its hunger, the Daemon Prince consumes everything and everyone in its path, swelling to immense proportions with the meat of worm and man. Eventually, Glutgora bursts in a tide of festering organs and rancid effluvia, and a million Nurglings crawl out from its corpse. The planet is declared perditas and quarantined indefinitely.

The Penumbra Prophecy

Abaddon is guided by the visions of Zaraphiston to an Eldar crone world. In the ruins of an ancient wraithbone city littered with skeletons, the Sorcerer leads the Warmaster to a room where a tapestry of flayed skin covers the walls from floor to ceiling. Upon its surface Abaddon reads a prophecy that reveals the secrets of six weapons of immense power.

Abaddon the Despoiler's Twelfth Black Crusade

Abaddon leads his fleet into the Gothic Sector, capturing three of the prehistoric star-forts known as the Blackstone Fortresses. Under Abaddon's control, the might of the Blackstone Fortresses is used to destroy the star Tarantis, consuming several of the system's closest worlds in the process and ravaging the Imperial fleets sent against the Black Legion. Eventually, the Despoiler's fleet is driven back, though at the end of this period – known in the Imperium as the Gothic War – Abaddon escapes into the Eye of Terror with two of the Blackstone Fortresses. The vast engines of destruction are to emerge once more in realspace during Abaddon's Thirteenth Black Crusade.

The Iron Labyrinth

A Chaos fleet spearheaded by the Black Legion cuts a path into the worlds of the Cadian System. With the aid of the Imperial Fists, the Astra Militarum manage break the Chaos forces at the battle of the Iron Labyrinth, driving them back to the Eye of Terror. However, what their enemy's seemingly reckless thrust so far in-system achieved remains a mystery to the Imperial commanders.

The Skull of Ker'ngar

Abaddon travels to the maiden world of Ildanira, seeking the Skull of Ker'ngar. Though initially confounded on the planet's surface by Eldar snipers from Craftworld Alaitoc, he orders all cover around his position to be levelled by orbital bombardment. Eldar reinforcements react swiftly to drive the Despoiler back, but not before he secures his prize.

The Pilgrimage of Dark Lament

Struck by a vision of Abaddon, millions of pilgrims abandon their worship of the God-Emperor and turn their ships towards the Eye of Terror. After a long and perilous journey in which thousands perish, the pilgrims finally reach worlds held by the Black Legion, where they are immediately enslaved. Even as they fall beneath the lash of their new masters, the pilgrims give thanks to the Warmaster.

The Damnation Cache

The Despoiler invades the Pandorax System with an alliance of Traitor Legions. Sweeping aside Imperial resistance, Abaddon breaks into the vaults below the world and opens the Damnation Cache, an ancient portal to the warp. A combined force of Dark Angels and Grey Knights come to Pandorax's aid in an attempt to stop a daemonic incursion from engulfing the sector, and eventually succeed in closing the portal. Unbeknownst to the Imperium, however, the Despoiler has already left Pandorax, taking with him a rogue psyker of prodigious strength.

The Promethean War

The Salamanders fight an urban war against the Black Legion on Heletine. The Order of the Ebon Chalice arrives to reinforce the Space Marines, and together they push forward, but their advance is halted by the Daemon Prince Gralastyx. Saint Celestine appears suddenly, storming through the Chaos hordes and slaying Gralastyx, before vanishing once more.

The Cage is Cracked

Lord Xorphas of the Black Legion invades the planet Amethal alongside the World Eaters of Khârn the Betrayer and the Crimson Slaughter. An alliance of Blood Angels and Adeptus Mechanicus repels the invaders, but as the planet is consumed in a rising tide of carnage, the ancient 'Daemon cage' that forms the planet's interior has its structural integrity breached. The Chaos invaders are driven off, but the damage has been done. Within the year, a nearby warp storm breaks the Daemon cage entirely, plunging the system into warp-haunted mayhem and adding to the empyric tempest raging across the galaxy.

The Wrath of Magnus

With the aid of the Tzeentchian trickster known as the Changeling, the Daemon Primarch of the Thousand Sons, Magnus the Red, gathers his Sorcerers and, at the head of several war sects of Rubricae, visits his revenge upon the beleaguered world of Fenris.

Abaddon the Despoiler's Thirteenth Black Crusade

The armies of Chaos invade Cadia and its many surrounding worlds. The forces of the Dark Gods read like a roll call from epic battles of the ages. Always in the vanguard are the Black Legion, followed by the Death Guard, World Eaters, Alpha Legion, Thousand Sons, Night Lords and other Legions from the annals of the blackest days. Renegade Chapters long thought extinct renew their assaults on the Imperium of Man. Before them run scabrous cultists, deranged mutants and traitorous scum in numbers too great to count. Behind them march Daemons of all the Ruinous Powers, the nightmares of mortals made real, led by their infernal overlords.

After a gruelling campaign with a death toll that spirals into the trillions, Abaddon the Despoiler succeeds in tearing down the strange pylons that for thousands of years had held the Cadian Gate as a stable region of space. Cadia falls soon thereafter, and a wave of warp storms roars into being across the length of the galaxy. Astropaths everywhere fear to open their minds to receive or broadcast messages, for the immaterium rings with mind-splitting peals, possibly the sound of the myriad tears ripping open in the barrier between the material universe and the warp, or perhaps the laughter of the Dark Gods…

The Great Rift Opens

A chain reaction of warp cataclysms rips across the Imperium, plunging its worlds into disaster and awakening the dormant powers of latent psykers across the galaxy. The Imperium is torn in two along its length, giving rise to the phenomenon known as the Cicatrix Maledictum. Countless civilisations are lost to daemonic incursions as the galaxy burns.

Crippling Terror

Thousands of Imperial planets lying along the edge of the Great Rift are evacuated as the tapestry of warp storms threatens to consume them. On the forge world Raeddon, the Adeptus Mechanicus Tech-Priests gather their most sacred manufacturing relics in preparation of shipping them off-world. But before the frigates are loaded and launched, an armada of Black Legion warships emerges from the warp, forming an impenetrable blockade around the planet.

Before long, hordes of Chaos Space Marine shock troops descend upon the forge world. The bulk of its Skitarii defenders are deployed to guard the basilica logisticum where the Mechanicus have stored their invaluable archeotech. However, the Chaos forces do not even attempt to lay siege to this complex. Instead, they conduct a series of devastating orbital bombardments on the planet's spaceports, obliterating their static lascannon arrays before sending in waves of ground troops to mop up the remaining Skitarii. With Raeddon stripped of its transport capabilities, the Black Legion armada recedes, leaving the Tech-Priests and their precious relics untouched as the warp storms envelop them.

Blacker Pastures

The rampant advance of the Hounds of Abaddon through the Bellicose Stars comes to a grinding halt when they are met by the Imperial Fists on Gandor's Providence. The sons of Dorn deploy numerous squads of Intercessors, creating a series of heavily defended redoubts across the surface of the agri world. Rather than allowing themselves to become bogged down in a prolonged siege, the Hounds of Abaddon withdraw to wreak destruction elsewhere.

Gods from the Warp

After a months-long battle in the Aralest System, the Imperial Navy are all but wiped out by a massive war fleet comprising several Black Legion warbands. The few remaining Imperial forces retreat to Everwatch Stanchion, the heavily fortified orbital docking platform above Aralest VII, to consolidate their strength. Meanwhile, on the planet's surface, Governor Melachron Indis marshals his planetary defence forces and prepares for invasion.

As the Black Legion ships approach, dozens of Chaos cults emerge from amongst the indentured populace of Aralest VII. These deluded fanatics do not see the Chaos Space Marines as invaders, but rather as saviours who have emerged from the Great Rift that burns across the sky day and night. Indis is forced to expend his troops in bloody fights deep inside the hive cities to prevent the planet from falling to the savage cultists before the Black Legion even arrive. These battles do not go in the governor's favour, for with each passing hour, more and more members of the citizenry join in the anarchic uprising.

Indis and the remaining fragments of his armies barricade themselves inside the spire of Aralest VII's capital hive and pray to the Emperor that the naval garrison on Everwatch will soon be able to send them aid. Their prayers are not answered. The Black Legion, having captured Everwatch Stanchion days earlier, dislodge the platform from its orbit and send it plummeting down to the planet's surface, directly towards the capital. The explosion created by the colossal impact leaves only a crater where the hive city once stood, and the ensuing quake is felt across the planet. This display of raw power is the final proof the Chaos cults need. No one on Aralest VII now doubts that the warriors of the Black Legion are gods.

ALPHA LEGION

The Alpha Legion was the twentieth and last Legion created during the First Founding. Under the critical eye of their twin Primarchs, Alpharius and Omegon, the Legion became renowned for its discipline and strict organisation during the Great Crusade. Though the youngest Legion, the Alpha Legion sought to outshine their brethren in all things, as if to prove their worthiness amidst the older Legions.

The Alpha Legion are devious beyond measure. Where other Legions seek to dominate through raw strength, divine favour or inspirational charisma, the Alpha Legion impose their will through intelligence and skill. The tools of war they value most highly are misdirection, confusion, treachery and duplicity, but when the time comes for them to spring their traps, they are such a focused and well-coordinated force that they can set a world ablaze in a single hour of blitzing assault.

When Horus made his pact with Chaos, the martial pride of the Alpha Legion was their downfall. The Warmaster was a mighty warrior himself – he commanded armies and fleets, and fought at the forefront of the Emperor's wars. By comparison, he made the distant Emperor on Terra seem a weak and cowardly individual. The Warmaster was a leader worthy of the Alpha Legion's respect, while the Emperor sought only to exploit Horus' conquests and crush the liberated humans of the galaxy beneath his stifling regime.

So the lies of Horus and his agents were insinuated into the hearts and minds of the Alpha Legion, and if any lie is repeated often enough it begins to be accepted, and once accepted, it ultimately becomes truth.

With relish did the Alpha Legion fight loyalist Space Marines on Isstvan V, and in many campaigns thereafter. At last they had found an opponent as tough, as trained and as ferocious as themselves. The brethren of the hydra inflicted

stinging defeats on the loyalists at Tallarn, Yarant and dozens of smaller outposts before moving onwards into the Ultima Segmentum. The Alpha Legion became entirely separated from the forces of Horus, but continued to wage war on all they came across. By the end of the Heresy, they were inventing objectives and missions of their own to fulfil their war-lust without reference to their allies. The last of the Legions to be founded, they were considered by others to be latecomers bereft of any true experience, and hence were keen to prove themselves as capable as any other. With the Ultramarines being held up as the exemplars of what a Legion could be, it was not long before the Alpha Legion sought to match themselves against the standards of Macragge – and in the end, match themselves in battle against those who had dismissed them or looked upon them as pale by comparison.

Even after the Heresy ground to a halt, the Alpha Legion continued to fight a covert war against the Imperium. Raiding parties still sally out from secret bases to

catch the defenders of Humanity unaware – sabotaging bases, attacking shipping, terrorising settlements and destroying small outposts with merciless efficiency. Their spy networks and double agents are without number; the Alpha Legions' connections with humans on the settled worlds of the Imperium are unparalleled.

The Alpha Legion coordinates and directs the activities of Chaos cultists across entire sectors and they instigate massive insurrections against Imperial rule. These revolts are often used as a cover for a series of shattering Heretic Astartes raids or as a precursor to a full-scale invasion from the Eye of Terror. The Inquisition holds a special loathing for the Alpha Legion for their role in spreading Daemon-worshipping cults and fanning the embers of discontent into the fires of outright rebellion, but for every cult they put down, two more spring up elsewhere.

Tactically, the Alpha Legion believes in striking from several directions at once. This requires meticulous planning and skilful infiltration. Extensive use is made of spies and corruption to weaken the enemy's resolve before any decisive move is made. Amongst the Traitor Legions, the Alpha Legion makes the most use of cultist troops. As they tend to operate as raiders deep within the Imperium, they require local support to bolster their numbers. Considerable effort is expended to spread propaganda inciting revolt and acts of sabotage. Once the Alpha Legion is committed to action, events move very quickly. The Legion attaches great importance to its field commanders, who use their initiative to outwit the enemy, magnifying the advantages that Traitor Marines have over more conventional troops. The Legion is prideful of its abilities and welcomes opportunities to demonstrate their skills against loyalist Space Marines. They have even been known to hold back some of their forces to test themselves more thoroughly in such circumstances.

The Alpha Legion's warriors have adopted the symbol of the hydra as their Legion's icon. This many-headed, dragon-like creature from ancient myth serves to remind the Alpha Legion of their unity in body and spirit. On the battlefield, the terrifying coordination of the Alpha Legion is their hallmark, as their multi-pronged attacks apply relentless pressure while they search for weak points in their enemy's defences.

HYDRA DOMINATUS

The Primarch Alpharius was the last to be found by the Emperor, their relationship distant and formal even before Horus revealed his true colours. Those outside the Legion believed this was because the Emperor had already completed his galactic odyssey to reclaim the Primarchs by the time the two met in person, and that his focus had shifted elsewhere. Some legionnaires realised that their relationship was likely more complex, and others whispered that Alpharius was one of two twins who were all but identical. Many of the Alpha Legion were uncannily similar in appearance and temperament, and their Primarch used this fact to his advantage – the claims that Alpharius was so efficient he could appear in two places at once had their basis in reality. Unusually for a Primarch, Alpharius was not a giant by comparison to the battle-brothers that followed him. He was able to assume the identities of his minions – and vice versa – whenever it would serve him to wrong-foot his enemies. Many was the warrior who claimed to be Alpharius to throw his foes off the scent; indeed, in some ways, every member of the Legion is an echo of his primogenitor in some manner. This grand misdirection is reflected across the Legion to this day. Alpha Legion warlords are rarely where they appear to be; inside the armour of a famed leader may be a new recruit, whereas a bolter-wielding trooper may in truth be the mastermind behind a sector-wide conquest. In this way do the Alpha Legion echo their totem and embody their war cry 'Hydra Dominatus', for their foes find it impossible to land a decapitating blow.

THE LEGION'S LONG WAR

The military actions of the Alpha Legion are so artfully swathed in misdirection, so efficiently planned and prosecuted, that barely one in a hundred has been correctly attributed to them. Nonetheless, as Chaos Space Marines they strike with terrifying force, and the worlds that they attack are scarred by the violence they unleash for the rest of their days.

I Am Alpharius

Word reaches the High Lords of Terra of a Chaos Lord claiming to be Alpharius ravaging the adamantine-laced moons of the Danevra Sub-sector. Debate rages about whether this could potentially be the case, for the Primarch's death has been recorded more than once across the span of Imperial history. The Grand Master of the Officio Assassinorum despatches a force of six Vindicare marksmen. Over a number of years they identify and slay a dozen Alpha Legion champions bearing the name of Alpharius upon the scrolls of their battle plate, but the reports of raids upon the sub-sector's mining operations only intensify. Five years later, the decapitated heads of all six Vindicare Assassins are found frozen in the food storage halls of the High Lords.

'War is simply the galaxy's hygiene.'
- attributed to the Primarch Alpharius

War of Hidden Lairs

The brotherhood of Chosen known as the Shrouded Hand infiltrates the way station world of Zharastia Jensen, a principal link in the supply chain of the Golgotha System. In their delvings amongst the lower strata of society to recruit more agents to their cause, the Shrouded Hand uncover a hive of Genestealer Cultists. In doing so they trigger an uprising that sees the industrialised populace rise up to seize rulership of the planet. The sleeper cells placed by the Alpha Legion are awakened by the coded messages of the Shrouded Hand, and the streets run with blood as the hidden cults of Chaos fight a savage guerrilla war against those who bear the mark of the Great Devourer. Content that Zharastia Jensen is now a broken cog in the Golgotha war machine, the Shrouded Hand disappear without trace.

The Hunt for Voldorius

Kernax Voldorius of the Alpha Legion is elevated to daemonhood by the Dark Gods. Kor'sarro Khan of the White Scars is tasked to hunt down the Daemon Prince and to return with the monster's head, or not at all. After driving Voldorius from his foremost stronghold, Kor'sarro Khan tracks him to the planet of Quintus. There, the White Scars find no mere warband but a whole planet of traitors and renegades. Upon making planetfall, Kor'sarro Khan finds unexpected allies in the form of Kayvaan Shrike and the Raven Guard 3rd Company. Such is the grievous threat posed by Voldorius that the two rival loyalist Chapters put aside their differences and join forces, eventually slaying the Daemon Prince in the streets of the planetary capital Mankarra.

Dreams of the Serpent

A plague of nightmares engulfs the psyker-rich world of Seer's Rest. Each of the planet's oracles, hedge wizards and soothsayers reports having the same recurring dream – that of a rain of serpents that covers the land. Such is the intensity of these dreams that the subconscious gestalt of the planet's psykers manifests them in reality, and the planet's populace is halved in a day. Millions die to venomous snake bites before the psykers fall into a fugue state and the rain stops. The Adeptus Arbites investigation finds,

too late, that the atmosphere processors of the world's terraforming engines have been spiked with psychotropic gas. When the Alpha Legion descend to destroy what remains of the planet's guardian provosts and Astra Militarum regiments, the storm of psychic energy intensifies to such a degree that Seer's Rest is reclassified as a Daemon world. The Alpha Legion abduct thousands of comatose psykers.

The Planetary Heist of Avernia

A coven of Alpha Legion Sorcerers, using a combination of psychic hypnosis and double agents seeded within the Administratum, convinces the Imperial authorities that their maps have the system of Avernia in the wrong place. When the Alpha Legion invade the industrial worlds of Avernia III and Primavernia, psychic distress calls are sent out into the void. The Adeptus Terra, spurred into action by reports of a Heretic Astartes attack, divert a formidable battle group from the war for the jewel world of Negligence towards Avernia's coordinates in Segmentum Pacificus. They make their warp translation in good time, but in entirely the wrong segmentum. Both Avernia and Negligence fall within the year.

The Nest of Serpents

The long-seeded plans of the Alpha Legion come to fruition when the Great Rift ripples into being across the heavens. Billions of mortal eyes look to the night sky, and in a thousand locations and more, networks of sleepers and hypno-indoctrinated agents blink in confusion as the mental imperatives of the Alpha Legion are triggered. A wave of anarchy blossoms across every seeded world as newly revealed demagogues decry the Imperium that has failed to protect them, stirring up swathes of Imperial citizenry that have been forbidden from looking at the night sky by heavy-handed and reactionary new laws. Dozens of worlds fall when the Alpha Legion arrive to turn rioting into outright war.

THE FACES OF THE HYDRA

The Alpha Legion wear many skins and don many guises in the prosecution of their covert agendas, but when the time to land the killing blow is nigh, they go to war in the colours of their Primarch Alpharius. It is not unusual for the Legion's warriors to incorporate designs based on the scales of serpents into their battle plate, or even to have similar icons tattooed under their skin, visible only when the wearer wishes them to be. Ostentation is rare, giving more of a sense of unity to their armies.

The pre-Heresy colours of the Alpha Legion are not markedly different from their latter-day incarnations, an outward testament to the fact the Alpha Legion has – in spirit if not in body – remained much the same since its creation.

Brother Talas, Knifemaster of the Third Harrow

The twentieth and final Legion created by the First Founding, the Alpha Legion was commanded by the twin Primarchs Alpharius and Omegon. The Sons of the Hydra have always favoured subterfuge and misdirection over the blunt ferocity employed by many of their fellow Legions. Their foes, distracted and thrown off balance by feints, betrayals and vicious coordinated strikes, rarely understand the inevitably of their doom until it is far too late.

Brother Lepsys, Keeper of the Eight Stolen Truths

The most experienced of the Alpha Legion are specialists in the arts of the infil-traitor and the thoughtsmith. The chosen agents of their warband's leader, these master operatives are able to bind their victims in spiralling webs of suspicion, confusion and doubt before springing their lethal traps.

Brother Hathmor, Liemaster of the Whispering Forge

Anonymity is a potent weapon in its own right. The vast majority of Alpha Legionnaires go into battle helmed, conversing in code across baffled vox-channels and with the ancient data-signifiers of their armour and weapons occluded. Enemies are left with no idea as to the rank, role or physical appearance of the legionnaires they face. They cannot predict the heretics' developing battle plans, cannot identify command personnel to target for elimination, and are soon thoroughly outmanoeuvred and utterly bewildered.

Legionnaire identified by six different names and titles in Imperial records to date.

IRON WARRIORS

The Iron Warriors once formed the Emperor's most formidable siege troops. They fought alongside the Imperial Fists on a hundred worlds in the Great Crusade, laying waste to alien citadels and the palaces of rulers who denied the Emperor's authority. Their Primarch, Perturabo, excelled in the planning and execution of siege and trench warfare. However, his stoicism and patience saw his Legion relegated to the shadows of the Great Crusade. Those shadows were to darken, and corrupt the Legion beyond recovery.

The Iron Warriors see themselves as titans of old who are loose in the universe, acting as they please in the knowledge that no natural or man-made law can stop them. They honour the Chaos Gods as a pantheon, but are not truly devout themselves. Their greatest loyalty is to their Primarch, Perturabo, whom they believe saved them from being sacrificed by the False Emperor.

The Iron Warriors are the most heavily armed of the Traitor Legions; as siege specialists, they rely less on close combat and more on withering salvoes of fire. Even when fighting outside their strongholds their approach remains the same, with great importance being placed on detailed fire plans. They are adept at quickly erecting formidable battlefield fortifications, establishing strongpoints that will tie down the enemy and thereby allow the Iron Warriors reserves to achieve

superiority elsewhere. As with their Primarch these traitors are methodical and thorough, always seeking to grind down their opponents by attrition until the moment comes when they can be swept away in a concerted attack.

When they were loyal to the Emperor, the Iron Warriors had a reputation for being fearsomely efficient and capable. Not for them the grandiose heroism of their brother Legions, nor the quest for glory that would resonate down the ages. Instead the Iron Warriors were pragmatic and cold in the execution of their duty, seeing the pursuance of excellence and the craftsmanship of war as reward in itself. This was an echo of the philosophy held by Perturabo, a Primarch with the mind of a genius but the temperament of a recluse. A master artisan, Perturabo crafted wars with the same methodical approach and attention to detail with which he crafted

the intricate inventions that decorated his sanctums. Content to rule alone, he often spurned the company of his brothers – even in battle he had been known to fight not with his fellow warriors, but with the towering robots known collectively as the Iron Circle.

The pursuance of crafting the perfect war was put aside in the name of duty time and again, for in Perturabo, the Emperor had a commander who would enact any duty without complaint, no matter how gruelling or unsavoury. In quickly and effectively completing every task assigned to them, the Iron Warriors became the recipients of those missions no other Legion wished to undertake. Where the likes of Sanguinius and Fulgrim won glory under the golden rays of alien paradise worlds, Perturabo and his Legion slogged through muddy hinterlands of perpetual gloom. Where Rogal Dorn and the

THE TYRANTS OF MEDRENGARD

Freed from the shackles of physical laws, the battlements and turrets of the Iron Warriors' fortress world of Medrengard rise spiralling upwards for miles. Spiked oubliettes and labyrinthine dungeons pierce the world to its core, and bastions cover it like fungi. Medrengard is a dizzying tangle of insane structure, a mad architect's vision of iron and stone where twisted stairs run at right angles to one another and pinnacles plunge eternally downwards. This planet-sized stronghold is the domain of the Primarch Perturabo – reincarnated as a mighty Daemon Prince by the Ruinous Powers that guide him, he has become a being of inconceivable destructive power whose warp-infused hammer, Forgebreaker, can shatter the rockcrete walls of a fortress with a single blow.

Countless warbands of the Iron Warriors have used Medrengard as their base of operations for centuries, plotting as to how to crush and imprison their enemies, the Imperial Fists foremost amongst them. Now is the time for those plans to come to fruition. As Abaddon flings open the gates of the Eye and leads the hosts of Chaos past Cadia's burning husk, Perturabo and his Legion of embittered traitors march to war once more, their sole intent to wreak such devastation upon the Imperium that no stone stands upon another.

Great Khan refused to split their Legions, Perturabo obediently garrisoned those fortresses his Legion had built as they brought ever more worlds into compliance. He gradually expended his Legion's strength in the process, and did so stoically – until the seeds of doubt were planted by Horus. Was the Emperor taking Perturabo for a fool?

The idea was pervasive, and after a disastrous return to Perturabo's home planet of Olympia, the Legion fully embraced their dark side. The Iron Warriors' treachery was revealed in the wake of the massacre at Isstvan V, where the Iron Warriors joined with the Night Lords, Word Bearers and Alpha Legion to destroy the three Legions in Horus' task force who remained loyal. In accordance with Perturabo's doctrines, the Iron Warriors had rapidly established strongholds and trench systems around their drop zones. The loyalist Space Marines, who had suffered tremendous casualties during their initial deployment, found themselves driven back against the Iron Warriors' fortifications by the ravening Traitor Legions. Instead of offering the hard-pressed loyalists respite, the bunkers and bastions proved to be their graveyards, as the Iron Warriors mercilessly gunned down anything that moved within range. With the booming rattle of heavy bolters and the slicing beams of lascannons, the Iron Warriors declared for Horus.

After Isstvan, the Iron Warriors were let loose. On many worlds, their Warsmiths replaced governors and tithes were paid to the new masters under the shadow of fortified battlements. The Iron Warriors split up to fight on a dozen other worlds in the Heresy. They fought on Vanaheim, reducing its armoured hive cities to twisted ruins one after the other. They battled across Thranx and Avellorn, worlds where every scrap of ground is covered by plasteel and rockcrete. They struck at loyalist fortresses, temples, keeps and palaces across the galaxy and ground them beneath the tracks of their siege tanks. A strong contingent of the Legion accompanied Perturabo to Terra where he supervised the siege of the Emperor's Palace. There the Iron Warriors found a sublime pleasure in tearing down the edifices of the Imperium.

Wherever the Iron Warriors fought, they raised great citadels in their wake. Jagged towers mounting heinous weapons of destruction dominated the surrounding terrain, each a monument to Perturabo's cunning. Fields of trenches and forests of razor wire surrounded the strongholds of the Iron Warriors, such that the loyalists began to dread the bloody assaults needed to destroy them. Even after Horus' defeat, the Iron Warriors were only driven out of the Imperium's worlds at a terrible price. The rest of the Legion defended the small empire they had built centred around their home world of Olympia, but there was no refuge from the retribution of the loyalist Legions. The Imperial Fists supported the Ultramarines in a decade-long campaign to liberate the subjugated worlds. They discovered the Iron Warriors to be a barbed hook that, once embedded into a victim, could only be removed with great risk of further injury. The Olympia garrison held out for two years, eventually triggering their missile stockpiles when defeat was unavoidable. They left a blasted wasteland that, like the other Traitor Legion home worlds, was declared perditas. The surviving Iron Warriors were driven into the Eye of Terror, where they took a world for their own: the impossible fortress of Medrengard.

THE ENDLESS SIEGE

The galaxy has felt the remorseless wrath of the Iron Warriors on numerous occasions. The death toll taken by Legions such as the World Eaters or the Black Legion is likely higher, for the Iron Warriors believe in attacks long-planned and painstakingly executed, but when they strike, they do so with such calculated and unremitting savagery that nothing can survive.

A Rebellion Crushed

A mountainous edifice encrusted with gargoyle-mouthed cannons, Cornucopeon's capital hive of Steelstone Keep supplies tithes of war materiel to the Iron Warriors. When the industrialist Korothrodd Vessh doubles his tithes after a costly campaign, Steelstone Keep's defenders rise up against the iron-collared cultists that keep them beneath the lash. The cult leader that oversees the hive's infernal industry is battered to death by smithy hammers, but not before he swears a mighty oath of vengeance with his last breath. Perturabo hears its echo in the warp. Within a week, Cornucopeon is infested by locomotive-sized Daemon Engines that burrow through the planet like maggots gnawing through an apple. They rise up under Steelstone Keep itself, erupting in geysers of magma to disgorge Iron Warriors from their fleshmetal bellies. The rebellious defenders fight level by level as Perturabo's kill teams gut the hive from the inside out. Beneath them a rising tide of magma burns away all evidence of Steelstone's rebellion. When the Iron Warriors leave from the hive spires, the only evidence of the uprising is a metallic mountain filled with cooling igneous rock.

The Humbling

Endt Thrinn, the genius planetary governor of Inviolus, completes his dynasty's planet-girdling fortress network. In his cups, he is much given to boast that his home planet is unassailable. Agents of the Alpha Legion relay this claim to their Iron Warriors brothers, and before long Lord Mandrakk has made warp translation in-system at the head of a large fleet. Instead of attacking Inviolus directly, he invades the nearby agri world of Dalathro's Rest.

The bread basket of the Inviolus System, Dalathro's Rest is well defended by the Astra Militarum. Mandrakk bombards it from orbit whilst launching boarding actions against every craft bound for Inviolus. Within the year the people of Inviolus are crippled by starvation. Though reinforcement arrives in the form of a company of Mentor Legion Space Marines, Mandrakk has ensured that Inviolus' half-starved defence forces are easy prey for his teleporting annihilation squads. The planet is seized and repurposed as a Chaos base.

The Technovirus Rages

The transmogrifying plague known as the Technovirus spreads from Medrengard's deepest dungeons across the worlds of the Eye of Terror. It infects metal construct and mortal body alike, turning one to the other and blending warriors with their weapons and wargear until only sentient-metal machine-things remain. After the resultant conflicts, known as the Wars of Flesh, the nihilistic Cult of Destruction proliferates massively. Obliterators and Mutilators join the ranks of the Iron Warriors in ever greater numbers.

The Machine Eyrie

The Iron Warriors flagship *Merciless Spite* is forced to crash land in the salt-rich Glowing Ocean of the feudal planet Prime Gala. Colonised by House Terryn several years earlier, the planet's Imperial Knight defenders stride out into the shallow waters to attack the crashed spaceship. The first wave, led by King Dontros, scales one flank of the *Spite*, only to find its upper reaches infested by Heldrakes. The Knights fight bravely, but the Daemon Engines attack in such numbers they are toppled into the sea or ripped apart.

The second wave, attacking some weeks later, is confronted by the corrupted remnants of their former comrades – the *Merciless Spite*'s master, Lord Admiral Vaen, has replaced each Throne Mechanicum's incumbent with one of his own Chosen lieutenants. Over the next three months, the terrifying combination of Renegade Knights and Heldrakes allows the Iron Warriors to enslave the feudal world's population from one pole to the other.

Temporia Emerges

In a feat of engineering only the truly insane could devise, the Dark Mechanicum stronghold world of Temporia is dragged out of the Eye of Terror by an armada of gravitic tugs and possessed haulers. The mutant machines churned out by the planet's sprawling Daemon-foundries assail the Cadian System by the thousand.

The Grand Siege Begins

Having studied the Imperial defences of Segmentum Obscurus in detail via a combination of remote scrying, methodically applied torture of captive loyalists and a network of techno-cultist informants, Perturabo learns much of their capabilities and limitations. When Cadia finally falls and the Cicatrix Maledictum splits the galaxy from end to end, the Daemon Primarch mobilises a thousand armies and coordinates them in a grand strategy that targets the most heavily defended Imperial worlds in the segmentum.

So begins a brutal blockade of the Imperium itself. As Perturabo's embittered armies march forth, menageries of Daemon Engines and batteries of artillery machines at their side, a dozen fortified worlds previously thought inviolable are brought to the edge of total disaster by the Iron Warriors' merciless siege tactics.

THE CHILL OF IRON

The Iron Warriors wear largely plain power armour of a deep metallic hue marked with yellow and black industrial symbols. They care little for trophies and embellishments, instead preferring to prove their strength and prowess through acts of large-scale destruction. Though each warband wears markings of allegiance to their champion, these are scoured off and repainted whenever circumstance dictates that a change of loyalty would be advantageous.

Mk IV Maximus armour is worn by many amongst the ranks of Perturabo's traitors, as are the weapon patterns and configurations dating back to the final days of Perturabo's contribution to the Great Crusade. This armour sacrifices a modicum of manoeuvrability in order to incorporate larger inflexible casings, making it perfectly suited to the Iron Warriors' attritional style of war.

Darnoch Polaid, Veteran of the gruelling Siege of the Loathenhold

The Iron Warriors were once the Imperium's foremost siege troops, capable of breaching the defences of even the most formidable of fortresses. Since the Legion followed their Primarch Perturabo into heresy, they have turned this skill towards the destruction of Imperial worlds. With cold-blooded relentlessness and the thunder of heavy artillery, they level the greatest strongholds of Mankind and reduce to ashes those who seek to oppose them.

Corprax the Wall-breaker

Beneath their armour, many Iron Warriors have cybernetic limbs and organs, and are often wired directly into their battle gear so as to more closely commune with its twisted machine spirits. Some join body and soul with their wargear, either because the twisting power of the empyrean shapes them into reflections of their obsessions, or because they have contracted the dreaded Technovirus of the Cults of Destruction.

Gornoth the Unbending, Thrice-Forged in the Baleful Furnace

The Iron Warriors value the psychological impact that their grotesque wargear and monstrous size has upon their enemies. Many go out of their way to festoon their armour with spiked chains, gory fetishes and jutting horns, the better to present a truly terrifying aspect when forcing their way through the breach into some luckless enemy's fortress. Many are the foes whose nerve has broken at the sight of such a daemonic gathering of armoured monstrosities massing around their beleaguered stronghold and baying to get in.

Bathalorr Steelhelm, Cannonmaster of the Blazing Battlements

NIGHT LORDS

The Night Lords were the eighth Legion formed during the First Founding. Their Primarch, Konrad Curze – later known as Night Haunter – grew up on the mining planet of Nostramo, a world shielded from its sun by a huge moon, which consequently rested in almost perpetual darkness.

The days on Nostramo were only slightly lighter than the pitch-black nights, giving the inhabitants of the planet a deathly grey pallor. Suicide and depression were facts of life on the world, and were it not for the huge deposits of adamantine ore beneath the planet's surface, it is doubtful it would have settled by Humanity at all. Violent crime was also endemic on Nostramo – that is, until the young Primarch Curze took it upon himself to single-handedly wage a vigilante war against the crime lords of the planet, taking on the name 'Night Haunter' as one that would strike terror into the hearts of his enemies. His methods were simple, vicious and direct: if you broke his law, you died. There was no appeal – Night Haunter was judge, jury and executioner.

The Great Crusade finally reached even this dark world, and the Master of Mankind was reunited with Curze. Night Haunter was placed in command of the Night Lords, who quickly gained a reputation for ruthless efficiency and an almost cynical disregard for human life. Their Primarch's methods became the way of the Night Lords themselves, and as long as the Legion achieved their objectives, the means just did not matter. Soon, stories began to circulate of large-scale massacres and brutal atrocities being committed by the Night Lords, some under the supervision of the Primarch himself, until finally the Emperor was forced to recall Night Haunter to answer the charges that had been made against him and those under his command.

But the Horus Heresy erupted before Night Haunter could return, and it quickly became apparent that all of the charges against him and the Night Lords were true. Night Haunter had no hesitation in joining Horus against the man he started to see as a weak-willed hypocrite. Operating from a planet deep in the wilderness area of space known as the Eastern Fringe, he led the Night Lords on a campaign of terror and genocide that has rarely, if ever, been equalled. Even after Horus was defeated, the Night Lords continued to attack, although increasingly without any discernible motivations for their steadily more murderous actions. Finally, the Imperial Assassin M'Shen was able to infiltrate Night Haunter's base and slay the Primarch, and with this act, the Night Lords quickly ceased to be an organised threat to the Imperium.

The Night Lords fought their way to the Eye of Terror, from where they continue to take part in raids on the worlds of the Imperium. They do not appear to worship any one of the Chaos Gods, but rather fight solely for pleasure and material gain. They look down on their more dedicated brethren, be they fanatical Chaos Space Marines such as Khorne Berzerkers or zealous loyalists like the Dark Angels. In place of faith and devotion, they respect only strength – that, and the use of terror as a weapon. No Legion is as careful as them in severing enemy communications and making visible examples of those who dare to oppose them.

The merciless and sickeningly inventive atrocities the Night Lords perpetrate are their way of sapping their enemy's will to resist. Many planetary governors have capitulated rather than face the wrath of the Night Lords, though none have been spared as a consequence. Darkness is their ally, and they ruthlessly use their innate abilities to give themselves an advantage over their enemies. Aggressive patrolling and surprise raids are their stock in trade, and they will patiently win a hundred small victories in order to achieve their objectives rather than pin everything on one large-scale conflict.

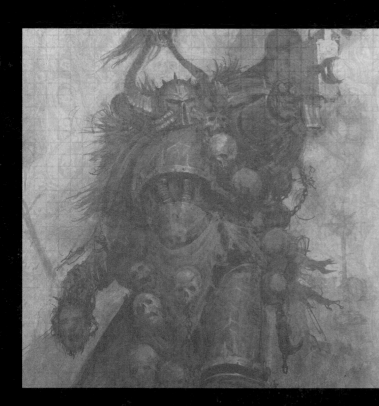

FEAR INCARNATE

The Night Lords thrive in sowing terror and confusion amongst the enemy. It is common practice for the Legion to shut down the communications of a target planet and broadcast hideous messages and screams across the airwaves as they begin slaughtering the populace at their leisure. Repeated instances have shown that they will give no quarter, and are entirely bereft of mercy. Any poor soul offering to surrender will have their pleas answered with mutilation and death.

Night Haunter's Legion have no holy crusade, no belief that causes them to spread murder and misery to the worlds they prey upon. Similarly, they have no martial creed, all concept of honour eroded by their age-old habit of recruiting vicious criminals into their ranks.

The Night Lords are masters of stealth and infiltration. This skill appears to be innate to the Legion, and comes to the fore during the sick games they play to drive their prey into paroxysms of fear. They are extremely versatile in their use of the forces of Chaos, employing the powers of each of the Dark Gods with equal favour in order to further their horrific agendas.

THE VISIONS OF KONRAD CURZE

The last words of Night Haunter stand as one of the great enigmas of Imperial history. It is thought that the Assassin M'Shen was consciously allowed to infiltrate Night Haunter's grotesque palace on the world of Tsagualsa, an edifice constructed entirely from still-living bodies. Expecting to have to deal with numerous guards and loyal retainers, she was surprised to find the halls of flesh and bone completely deserted. The vid-log built into M'Shen's baroque vambraces, kept in stasis at the heart of the most venerated Callidus shrine, shows the final confrontation between the twisted Primarch and the avenging angel.

Sitting in a pool of shadow upon a throne made from the fused bones of his victims, a carpet of screaming faces leading up to bare, gnarled feet, sits Night Haunter himself. His madness and hate radiate from him, palpable even through such a remote medium as a vid-log. M'Shen stops in her tracks when the fallen Primarch raises his head, her face reflected in his impassive, jet-black eyes. Long moments pass. Then, in a voice thick with contempt and pain, Night Haunter speaks.

'Your presence does not surprise me, Assassin. I have known of you ever since your craft entered the Eastern Fringes. Why did I not have you killed? Because your mission and the act you are about to commit proves the truth of all I have ever said or done. I merely punished those who had wronged, just as your false Emperor now seeks to punish me. Death is nothing compared to vindication.'

Then the vid-log blurs for a fraction of a second as M'Shen leaps forwards. The last image in the recording is of dark, staring eyes brimming with madness above a lipless smile, before the recording inexplicably shorts out.

FEAR ETERNAL

Across the aeons, the Night Lords have done more to traumatise the psyche of the Imperium than any other Traitor Legion. As the Time of Ending intensifies, the terror raids and cruel hunts of the Night Lords increase in frequency. Long scattered, they are uniting, warband by warband, in the name of some dire cause. It can spell only doom for the worlds of Mankind.

False Saviours

Together with the Alpha Legion, the Night Lords save the algae-mining Garagos Entrenchment from being completely overrun by Waaagh! Krushbakk. The members of this seemingly benevolent strike force are largely clad in the colours and insignia of loyalist Space Marines, giving the populace of Garagos a few blissful days of hope. Only when the Orks are driven off-world do they realise they have merely exchanged one set of persecutors for another – and that the second doom to befall them is far more malevolent.

The Sons of Grendel

In M34, the Imperial frigate *Hand of Mercy* answered a residual distress call from Grendel's World, only to find every single inhabitant had been hunted down and killed, the symbols cut into their corpses identified as those of the Night Lords.

Though Grendel's World is resettled a century later and the massacre of its people rendered into a folk tale, that exact same scene occurs seven millennia later in M41. This second incidence triggers a full-scale crusade from the Mortifactors, who take the fastest ships in their fleet and set off in search of the perpetrators.

Twisted Justice

After millennia of slaughter, the Night Lords warmonger Anvrex Rarth becomes disenchanted with indiscriminate violence. He vows to embody his Primarch's early days, punishing only those whom he believes deserve it – but doing so with such grievous acts of retribution that none who hear of them dare stray from the path of righteousness. For a time, he finds a kind of peace, but his notions of morality are broken beyond repair. Within the year he is wreaking the most terrible of atrocities as a response to everything from the breaching of shipping contracts to the incorrect pronunciation of High Gothic.

The Claws Descend

The warband of Ghilus Venst mounts a series of crippling hit-and-run attacks, focusing on the orbital waystations and macrofibre lifts that surround the infamously criminalised cargo world Chokehold. They escape with not only copious amounts of ammunition and fully charged power units, but also dozens of new recruits.

Empire of Fiends

The Great Rift spreads panic and madness across the Imperium. The Night Lords are in their element, with many establishing small empires amongst those systems cut off from the Emperor's Light.

An Ill-Fated Crossing

The Navigator Guilds identify a temporary channel of realspace near the Corinthe System that leads through the Cicatrix Maledictum. With the need to travel between segmentums so desperate, it is not long before several Imperial fleets are inbound, intending to make the crossing with all haste. They plunge deep into the Great Rift. Only then do the Night Lords, whose daemonic pacts engineered the 'safe' region of space, launch their attack. In a series of boarding actions, they capture dozens of Imperial vessels.

The Long Night

With the light of the Astronomican cut off, thousands of star systems are plunged into blindness across the Imperium. The warbands of the Night Lords, seeing a gory harvest to be reaped, raid and pillage more than ever before.

IN MIDNIGHT CLAD

Even before they turned to Chaos, the Night Lords adorned their armour with the imagery of death. They know fear can be used as a weapon just as effectively as a chainsword or bolter, and revel in the twisted anatomies that the powers of Chaos sometimes lavish upon them. It is common to see the Night Lords adorned with malefic symbols – fanged skulls, bat-like wings and glowing red eyes all feature heavily upon the battle plate of these murderous traitors.

Brother Arkalon claims to have once fought at Night Haunter's side

Even before the Night Lords rebelled against the Emperor, their midnight blue, lightning-streaked power armour lent them a sinister appearance at odds with the bold livery of Legions such as the Imperial Fists and Emperor's Children. There are still those amongst their ranks that wear the Mk IV armour that was so common amongst the Legion during the Horus Heresy.

Deimar the Eyetaker, Butcher of the Amnission Fields

The Night Lords Traitor Legion revel in terrorising and tormenting their foes. Their lightning raids and sadistic acts of atrocity have haunted the Imperium for thousands of years. Masters of stealth and infiltration, these murderous traitors never opt for the clean kill when they can instead spread fear and panic amongst the ranks of their prey. They adorn their battle plate with nightmarish symbols – bat-winged skulls, blazing red eyes and other malefic images.

Thraktar Hexx, whose malevolence is so great that it darkens the air around him

Many Night Lords incorporate human bones into their wargear. Skull faceplates are laid over – or even sorcerously melded into – helms, femurs are inlaid along greaves, splayed ribcages adorn breastplates, and even compacted ground bonemeal is used to trim shoulder guards. The bones themselves come from the most terrified of the Night Lords' victims, the Chaos Space Marines believing that their last moments radiate from them as an aura of pure fear.

Relchim Charredsoul hunted down the Heroes of Bastvale and murdered them all

Some of the original Traitor Legions have retained a degree of their old fraternal loyalty, in however twisted a fashion it may manifest. The Night Lords had little enough to begin with, however, and have only become more self-centred and cruel as the millennia have slipped past. Each warrior amongst them vies with his comrades to claim the most glorious kills, to spread the most terror and adorn his wargear with the most baroque warrior trophies.

WORD BEARERS

The Word Bearers are the most devout of all the Dark Gods' servants, taking pride in their favoured status as servants of Chaos. They raise their damned standards high and march beneath cursed icons, bellowing catechisms of hate at the foe as cultist war drums beat out a heart-pounding thunder. The advance of the Word Bearers is a terrifying sight even before they invoke the daemonic pacts that conjure their fiendish allies from the warp.

The Word Bearers are a Legion of warrior fanatics whose history is steeped in blood. They are religious zealots whose conviction is so powerful it can drive them to the heights of personal valour or the depths of villainy. Chanting devotional hymns in deep, sonorous voices, their mighty Legion storms into war, grinding all before it in the name of belief itself. And yet there was a crux point in their history where beatific devotion curdled to the most unholy hatred.

As the Great Crusade spread further and further across the stars, the Emperor became a divinity in the eyes of his people. The Master of Mankind forbade such irrational thoughts; his goal was for logic and reason to rule the galaxy, not blind faith. Even so, when the Emperor was reunited with Lorgar upon Colchis, vast displays of devotion and rapture were laid before him. The warriors that became the Word Bearers felt such devotion for their spiritual father their admiration crossed the line into worship. The scale of their sacraments was so great that the Emperor became impatient, demanding war, not veneration. Lorgar soon led the Legion he had been bequeathed into the stars, but still his progress lacked urgency – each conquest would be followed by a period of reconsecration and monument-building to the glory of Humanity's saviour. The Emperor took exception to these indulgent displays and the slow progress they represented, chastising Lorgar and ordering the Ultramarines to cast down his works, including Monarchia – known to the Word Bearers as the Perfect City.

Slowly, like a seeping poison, Lorgar's bitterness at his censure spread throughout the Word Bearers Legion. Some amongst them – notably the Chaplain Erebus – turned their sorrow into hatred, their dark faith infecting those under their sway. Erebus and his accomplice, Kor Phaeron, used their position of trust to draw Lorgar ever further from the Emperor's secular philosophy. There were other powers in the universe that would gladly accept the worship of mortals, and that had the power to reward them copiously for acts of devotion and sacrifice. What started as a noble quest to understand the spiritual worlds beyond mortality crossed into the studies of the occult, and then into the worship of more sinister entities. Though the Word Bearers' new creed was at first covert, when Horus declared his plans of secession, Lorgar was swift to offer his allegiance.

By necessity, the Word Bearers had to keep their activities hidden at first. Secret covens were set up on the planets that the Word Bearers controlled or conquered, and these worked covertly to create followings for the Chaos Gods. As the first Legion to embrace the worship of Chaos, once the Horus Heresy began the Word Bearers revealed their true nature, and on a thousand worlds the Chaos cults they had founded erupted into open rebellion. Freed from the need to keep their devotion to Chaos a secret, the Word Bearers dedicated themselves fully to the gods of Chaos. As the atrocities carried out in the name of devotion rose to new heights, Lorgar was rewarded by his patrons with the gift of daemonhood. Finally, he truly was the equal of a god, and the birth scream of this newest Daemon Primarch was said by Astropaths to have echoed through the warp with triumphant vindication.

From the Daemon world of Sicarus, Lorgar watches over his Legion as it launches twisted wars of faith against the Imperium, directing its myriad wars and engagements whilst orchestrating the vast corruption from within that the Imperium suffers at the hands of his innumerable cults. Unlike their peers, the Word Bearers have remained a unified, if loosely organised, Legion.

Many of Lorgar's champions have become amalgamations of brutal war leaders and divinely inspired preachers of Chaos known as Dark Apostles. Each is gifted an army roughly equivalent to a Space Marine Chapter, known as a Host. On the worlds these forces attack, the Word Bearers build huge monuments dedicated to the Dark Gods, and vast cathedrals are erected in which the chants and prayers of the faithful intermingle with the screams of those being sacrificed in the name of Lorgar. Their war against the Imperium of Man is total, and it will not end until every icon of the Emperor who betrayed them lies shattered at their feet.

The Dark Apostles of the Word Bearers enforce a strict regime of religious observance upon their brothers. All Word Bearers are expected to spend a considerable portion of each day in acts of ritual sacrifice, occult study or acts of worship. In battle the Word Bearers are zealous in the extreme, marching forwards under huge banners dedicated to Chaos in its myriad forms, reciting catechisms as they fight, and slaying the enemy for their failure to follow the one path to righteousness. Forced conversion is a common fate for those conquered by their armies, often as a precursor to a short, brutal life as a slave labourer building an immense temple to the Chaos Gods.

The Word Bearers follow the words of their Dark Apostles with utter loyalty in battle, and they in turn interpret the will of Lorgar by a myriad esoteric means. The strategy to win a battle may be contained within the entrails of a particular captive, an alignment of the stars or the pattern of cast bones. The Dark Apostles decree how the battle is to be fought and the warriors of the Host obey unquestioningly. The night before each battle, the enemy can hear dark mutterings emanating from all around, echoed in pounding drums and fever dreams, straining the nerves and instilling every man with fear. When dawn comes, a bloody enlightenment is unleashed, for the Word Bearers believe that they alone can save the galaxy through embracing Chaos. This unshakeable creed sees them marching towards certain death as often as glorious victory, yet regardless of the carnage around them, they remain unwilling to take a single step back.

THE ANNALS OF DARKNESS

The Word Bearers have woven a rich tapestry of disaster across the millennia. Only those truly steeped in arcane lore can discern the patterns within. No idle raids are these, but the sacrificial acts of a grand ritual designed to tear open reality and empower the Chaos Gods. Each betrayal, each act of hideous devotion, has been for the furtherance of this bitter crusade.

The War of Statues

The Iconoclastic Brotherhood invades the world of Conqueror's Due. The planet was once host to a great Imperial triumph, and is covered with statues hundreds of feet high depicting the Primarchs and the Emperor. The Word Bearers and their cultists disfigure many of the statues and tear down many more with ropes and melta charges, toppling them even as the fires of a full-scale planetary war rage all around. The Cyclopeans, a Titan Legion from nearby Vellung, counter-invade from enormous bulk landers and take a grievous toll on the Word Bearers – though the god-machines are toppled after the Chaos Space Marines perform a grand ritual in the name of Tzeentch that imbues the disfigured statues with a semblance of life.

The Counter-Crusade

During the Thorados Crusade, the Black Templars burn a white-hot scar of retribution across the rebellious Invernus Sector. The Word Bearers that instigated the insurrection mount a fleet-based crusade of their own, clashing with the Black Templars on a hundred battlefields. The war escalates massively as other Traitor Legions and Daemon hosts join the fight. By the time the two crusades grind to a halt, the once-populous Invernus Sector has been decimated, with six of its worlds consumed by radioactive flame.

'Cast down the idols! Destroy the temples! Slay the priests! Show these fools that they worship nothing more than a rotting corpse!'

– Dark Apostle Harzhan

The Saint's Beacon

The shrine world of Nepthys Madrigal is the last bastion of resistance against the empyric incursion led by Lord Vileblight, a Greater Daemon of Nurgle. So holy is the ground and so valorous its Adepta Sororitas defenders that every outbreak of Vileblight's initial gambit, the Deathly Pox, is contained and sanctified within minutes of it occurring. In frustration, the Great Unclean One calls in an old debt with the Dark Apostle Kor Daradan. Within the month, the Word Bearers attack Nepthys Madrigal. As mortals, they are not repelled by the banishment sigils of the world, and cross the barriers that kept the Daemons out. They take the fight to the Sisters of Battle there with such vigour they force a full-scale evacuation of the populace. The conflict becomes a war of attrition in which the Chaos Space Marines prioritise casting down the temples and altars of the Imperial Creed, disrupting their wards. The planet falls to a wave of contagion and the subsequent Plaguebearer assault.

The Blood Tithe

T'au diplomats establish an uneasy peace upon the planet of Ur-Clemait, a world that has long been ravaged by civil war. Though most of the population seems content with the T'au's enforced ceasefire, the elders and priests of the old faith are distraught, insisting that the 'blood tithe' must continue to be met. The puzzled T'au continue their assimilation, but before the year is out, the Word Bearers arrive to enforce the tithe. They attack Ur-Clemait in force, chanting prayers of appeasement to the Dark Gods as they cut down human and xenos alike. The T'au Fire caste meet the invasion head-on, and the world is plunged into an ongoing war far worse than the ritual struggles of old.

The Cursed Moons of Thranix

The Word Bearers harness industrial cults to scorch titanic eight-pointed stars into the moons of Thranix. The capital world they orbit is blighted by a wave of daemonic possession soon after.

Daemon Tide

The frontier world of Gruelbowl is the site of a painstakingly planned mass sacrifice – not only of humans, but also captured Ork Freebooterz, Eldar Outcasts and T'au ambassadors. Despite the intervention of Craftworld Alaitoc, the Word Bearers complete their ritual. The Great Rift tears open across the space lanes around Gruelbowl, stranding it and leaving it at the mercy of the Dark Apostles who engineered its demise.

The Blackstone Pylons of Irradium Alpha

Sent by Abaddon to blast apart the null-field megaliths of what seems to be a deserted world, the Word Bearers become embroiled in a grinding land battle when a self-repairing Canoptek swarm leads a Necron assault from under the planet's surface. Only by summoning Daemons of Khorne with offerings of their own blood do the Word Bearers break free of the counter-attack and complete their mission.

The War of False Prophets

The Cult of Impurity takes root after Word Bearers are sighted on the Macharius pilgrimage route. Its members thrive in secrecy, the only outward sign of their allegiance a blasphemous mockery of an Adeptus Astartes purity seal melted onto the flesh above their hearts. Led from afar by portents sent by the Dark Apostles, the cult spreads across Segmentum Pacificus before uniting in a massive civil war that sees six Space Marine Chapters matched against billions of the lost and the damned.

Exile's End

After the Horus Heresy's earth-shattering climax at Terra, Lorgar retreated ever further from the matters of the material realm, and went into seclusion indefinitely, cloistered in a locked sanctum on the planet Sicarius to atone for his deeds. As the 41st Millennium comes to a close and the Great Rift boils across the sky, rumours persist that Lorgar has finally ended this self-imposed confinement, and has been seen walking the mortal realms in terrible splendour, preaching the word of Chaos at the head of a Word Bearers force of shocking strength and conviction.

THE WORD OF LORGAR

Since their worship turned from the Emperor to the Chaos Gods, the Word Bearers have adorned the deep crimson of their armour with runic script in the Dark Tongue. Devotional parchments made from human skin are inscribed with excerpts from the Book of Lorgar, blasphemous texts that detail the philosophies of the Primarch, and scraps of ritual that attract the eyes of Daemons. The Word Bearers have become a literal manifestation of their name – though their creed is no longer a celebration of the Emperor's Glory, but of the Ruinous Powers that cast their shadow across reality.

At the behest of the first Dark Apostles, the armour of the Word Bearers was changed from steely grey to the scarlet of dried blood. The script that once adorned their armour changed too; where their ceramite once bore Imperial truths in High Gothic, after their great censure the Legion replaced the text with runic sigils and arcane symbols redolent with hidden meaning.

Brother Gharshor of the Chapter of the Tainted Solstice

As a Word Bearer garners ever more favour from the Chaos Gods, his appearance changes to reflect his station. One who excels in a battle – or in an especially violent ritual sacrifice – may have Colchisian runes inscribed on his battle plate by a Dark Apostle or Sorcerer, lending an extra measure of esoteric protection that hardens his soul against horrors both metaphysical and corporeal.

Brother Kar'Gorax, the Arch-Tormentor of Hadravar VII

Veteran Word Bearers often wear hermetic icons, stylised after the geometric symbols devised by Lorgar to summon and bind entities from the empyrean. The most extreme of these symbols invite daemonic entities to possess the wearer entirely – only the most devoted go to such lengths to become one with the darkness of the universe, for though they gain tremendous power, they forfeit their soul.

Dar'thassak of the Unshackled Truth, whose soul teeters upon the brink

Before the Horus Heresy came to light, the book icon of the Word Bearers represented the pursuit of gnostic truths. Now it is seen as emblematic of arcane tomes and daemonic summonation. The Chosen of the Legion are walking encyclopaedias of arcane lore, the blasphemous syllables spilling from their lips weakening the veil between realspace and the empyrean so that Daemons might force their way through.

Shaddoth Gnur, Lorespeaker of the Iron Veil and bearer of the Litany Malifactum

WORLD EATERS

The World Eaters were the twelfth Legion created in the First Founding, and still regard themselves as holding true to their original beliefs. To them, it is the later foundings under the False Emperor that have become decadent and depraved. Even before the Horus Heresy, the World Eaters were noted for their bloody-handed approach to warfare and the savagery of their training, rituals and combat doctrine.

The World Eaters were censured by the Emperor for their use of psycho-surgery on new recruits. This process was forbidden for good reason, for in times of stress it essentially turned the recipient into a madman obsessed with bloodshed. Nonetheless, the World Eaters were invaluable terror troops in the Great Crusade. It was a simple matter for Horus to pervert the World Eaters' bloody Legion rituals to the worship of Chaos. Under his corrupting influence, Angron, the Primarch of the World Eaters, soon became devoted to Khorne. It was not long before his prowess in battle and immense martial pride saw him take the first steps on the path towards daemonhood.

Though once synonymous with loyalty to the Emperor, the name of the World Eaters became a byword for carnage and terror during the Heresy. They fought in the vanguard of every assault, and their Legion records show it was they, and not the Sons of Horus, who first breached the walls of the Imperial Palace.

The World Eaters retreated from Terra only grudgingly before fighting their way to the Eye of Terror, carving a bloody swathe through anything that stood in their way. There they strengthened their blood-rites, tying themselves ever closer to Khorne and his Daemons. All pretence of forming balanced, tactical strike forces fell away as chainaxes and chainswords became the favoured tools of battle. Competition to be the first into the fray and the first to kill for the Blood God was fierce.

As more and more of the Legion's officers became fully fledged champions of Khorne, all discipline broke down. Finally, at the end of the savage Skalathrax campaign, Khârn the Betrayer, an exalted Berzerker-champion of Khorne, set upon his brethren with such bloodlust that the whole Legion tore itself apart in a great battle. By the time the smoke cleared, the Legion had been shattered into dozens of warbands of crazed butchers. Even now, some of these warbands are hundreds strong, while others are no more than a lone champion leading his Berzerkers on a quest for carnage. Dressed in armour of red, black and brass, Khorne's chosen are the first into any battle and the last to leave the field. Their delight in bloodshed and death is so strong that they have been known to fall on their own chainswords as sacrifices to their god. Such warbands will join with any Chaos Lord who is gathering his forces for conquest, asking nothing more than to spill blood and take skulls for Khorne. However, even these Chaos Lords must be wary in case their own heads are added to the tally.

Though Khorne despises sorcery and sees it as beneath a true warrior, he does not rely on swords and axes alone to gather skulls. Technology, and even arcane relics, are all tools to increase the tally of the fallen. Greatest of Khorne's weapons are the part-magical, part-technological Daemon Engines. Covered with heavy armour of black steel and marked with brass skull-runes of Khorne, these nightmarish war machines resemble hulking beasts and twisted colossi. Their advance is all but unstoppable as they clank forwards on rattling tracks, segmented legs or spiked wheels.

The Daemon Primarch Angron is still an active force in the galaxy. In the mid-38th Millennium, the Red Angel rampaged from the Eye of Terror at the head of an army of fifty thousand Khorne Berzerkers, who slaughtered their way across three dozen star systems. In the wake of the carnage, the flames of war and rebellion burned across seventy sectors for a further two and a half centuries. Many Imperial commanders threw off the yoke of the Emperor's rule, and petty warlords rose up to seize control of the sundered territories. Eventually, four Chapters of the Adeptus Astartes, two Titan Legions and over thirty Imperial Guard regiments crusaded to cleanse the fallen worlds. After a total of seven centuries, ninety per cent of the afflicted sectors were once more under Imperial law, and the period known as Angron's Dominion of Fire was brought to an end.

OCEANS OF BLOOD

The World Eaters have kept true to Khorne's battle-hungry creed ever since their Primarch allowed himself to be completely consumed by his rage during the Horus Heresy. Across the millennia, this shattered Legion has spilled enough blood to drown worlds, stacking high the skulls of their foes until their mountainous offerings to Khorne reach the clouds above.

The Feast of a Hundred Duels

The centennial Feast of Blades, where the descendants of the Imperial Fists compete against one another in ritual duels, is the target of a massive World Eaters invasion. The sons of Dorn quickly unite against the Khornate maniacs smashing their way through the world's defences. The finest Space Marine bladesmen of the age match their power swords against the chainaxes and flails of the World Eaters. Though the Chaos Space Marines finally fall to superior numbers, the skies rumble with Khorne's approval, for the feast halls are awash with the hot blood of champions.

Gladius Anathema

Upon the quarantined world of Gladius, the Drukhari Wych Cult of the Seventh Woe fight their way into the great fang-lined fighting pits of the World Eaters in search of a challenge. The violent duels that result are amongst the fastest and most vicious that Gladius' Daemon Prince masters have ever seen. Though dozens of Wyches and World Eaters die upon one another's blades, Khorne is pleased by the intensity of the carnage, and blesses the occasion with a rain of blood that brings the dead back to life. A bond of wary respect is forged between the two factions, ultimately leading to the invasion known as the Great Blood Wager of Anathema Quartus.

Red Tide

The peaceful commune world of Exotia falls into the worship of a charismatic but sinister figure known as the Red Messiah. After a planet-wide chanson held on the solstice of a blood moon, the planet is harried by midnight attacks from roving bands of Bloodletters. The Red Messiah reveals himself as a devotee of Khorne, and forces his astropathic choir to call out to the raiders of the Maelstrom. Soon after, a force of Red Corsairs bolstered by no fewer than three hundred Khorne Berzerkers descends to push the planet over the edge of madness.

The Skull Hunt of Octarius

The Skullhunt of Vodha Bloodprice invades the Octarius System. After hearing about the Tyranids and Orks that clash there in an ever-escalating spiral of violence, they reason that the fighting there will be intense indeed, and that Khorne's eye will be drawn to the furore. The World Eaters are not disappointed – within the space of a single year, over eight thousand skulls are offered to the Blood God, the smallest of which is the size of a boulder. Vodha ascends to daemonhood after slaying a Hierophant bio-titan with the greataxe of the fallen Ork warlord Magza da Kollossus.

The Fall of Ebon Vale

The watch fortress of Ebon Vale is assailed by the gore-slicked World Eaters of Lord Invocatus. Together with Daemon Engine allies from the Brazen Beasts, Invocatus raids the arsenals of the Deathwatch to claim state-of-the-art wargear and powerful artefacts of battle from Ebon Vale's reliquaries. When the attack is quarantined and whittled down by the Deathwatch air cover, the World Eaters make their departure, leaving empty weapons vaults and hundreds of black-armoured corpses in their wake. With the Deathwatch greatly reduced in strength in the region, a Hrud infestation spreads throughout the Ebon Vale soon after, reducing several civilised worlds to useless mulch.

Blood Runs Hot

The famously ferocious T'au Fire Warriors of Vior'la face an incursion of World Eaters. The Chaos Space Marines are so thoroughly lost to the worship of Khorne that their ranks contain as many Spawn as they do Berzerkers. The T'au's impeccable fire discipline sees the World Eaters warbands kept at arm's length – that is, until the infectious rage of the Khorne devotees begins to catch in the souls of Vior'la's foremost cadres. The T'au, voices raised in primitive Fio'taun war cries that have not been heard for centuries, begin to engage the Chaos Spawn at close range and even charge in to engage them in close combat. It does not end well for the T'au. Millions die before a council of six Ethereals are scrambled to the site to lend their calming influence to the Fire caste cadres, restoring order and allowing the T'au to withdraw into low orbit before the World Eaters can complete the slaughter.

The Maelstrom of Gore

Khârn the Betrayer and his Berzerkers are sent by Abaddon to wreak havoc upon the forge world of Amethal, a planet that houses a relic from the Dark Age of Technology that keeps innumerable Daemons caged beneath its crust. Alongside the renegades of the Crimson Slaughter, Khârn and his warriors kill so many Cult Mechanicus servitors and cyborg Skitarii that blood rains from the skies as a sign of Khorne's favour. When the Blood Angels descend to bolster the Adeptus Mechanicus' troops, the World Eaters find themselves matched against a worthy foe, but Khârn still proves unstoppable. Once the Warmaster's objective – the cracking of the Daemon cage – is achieved, his forces withdraw. Shortly afterwards, Khârn and his Berzerkers disappear in a tempest of gore.

Hounds at the Gate

A sudden invasion of Khornate Daemons assails Holy Terra; led by eight Bloodthirsters, it causes utter havoc before being hurled back by the defending echelons of the Emperor's Palace. Word travels far of their defeat. Inspired by the prospect of victory erasing the defeat of ten millennia hence, the World Eaters gather in great strength to make their own attack upon Terra.

++ Commander. They beg for mercy–

++ Mercy! Oh Lord Khorne, truly have you led us to a land overflowing with blood and skulls!

Give them the mercy of death.

++ Affirm. Blood! Blood! Blood for my Lord!

++ Chosen of Khorne, lead us in the final assault.

++ Blood for the Blood God! Suppressing fire. Forward and centre. Heavy bolters range two hundred and fifty.

Move, scum…

(Communications intercept ends. The Portrein defenders are assumed to have detonated their armoury.)

- Ordo Malleus Secret Report: Portrein Raid 8106960.M41

ANOINTED WITH THE BLOOD OF WORLDS

The World Eaters care for one thing above all else – the thrill of slaughter. Even if they cleaned and sanctified their wargear after each engagement in the manner of loyalist Space Marines, it would be caked in the sticky, clotted lifeblood of their victims within minutes. Wherever they go, whatever enemy they face, the deep crimson battle plate of the World Eaters is covered in another layer of arterial red, and then another. Each new jet of gore or splash of vital fluids is a sacrament offered unto Khorne himself.

Before Angron's Legion turned upon their brothers at the Isstvan V Massacre, his warriors were clad in stark white and deep blue – in theory, at least. Such was the violence with which these warriors brought worlds into compliance during the Great Crusade that more often than not they were spattered with copious amounts of blood – a fact that did not go unnoticed amongst their brother Legions.

Brother Olvarr, who fought in Angron's wake in the Choral City

The warrior elite of the World Eaters have long histories of slaughter. Many have fought at the side of Angron himself, the waves of unnatural energy that radiate from the Daemon Primarch leaving their mark on body and soul. It is considered a blessing second only to that of Khorne to kill within Angron's sight – those who truly earn his favour are granted a nod of respect or a growl of recognition in the midst of battle.

Ghrodd the Slaughterlord, herald of the Bloody Dawn

The Berzerkers of the World Eaters use a variety of weapons optimised for close-range slaughter, but the most favoured amongst them is the chainaxe. This massive weapon has rows of grinding teeth that whir around the axe's edge with speed enough to gnaw through armour and hack through rockcrete – should they make it through to the flesh beneath, the destruction they cause is catastrophic.

Akkatar the Cleanser, whose genocidal rampage is never-ending

The World Eaters give only the barest thought to the condition or appearance of their wargear, for time spent on maintenance is time that could be better used committing murder. Their blood-red battle plate is chipped and battered, its battle scars worn proudly or given no thought whatsoever. Their blades are forever crusted in dried blood, gore and gristle spattering from them as the Berzerkers swing them savagely into their foes' faces.

Vastyx Khade, the infamous Gore-hound of Yhellos Alpha

EMPEROR'S CHILDREN

All the First Founding Legions were created to take part in the Great Crusade. After their inception, several decades slid past before the Emperor's Children saw action. An accident during gene-seeding almost destroyed the Legion as it was born. Once the Emperor's Children had been re-established with rescued gene-seed, they proved to be loyal and efficient, distinguishing themselves in several campaigns.

The Emperor's Children were one of the first of the Legiones Astartes to defect to the Warmaster. The Legion's Primarch, Fulgrim, and his highest ranking officers, were corrupted by the decadent pastimes that Horus and his Chaos-worshippers offered. Drugged, pleasured beyond endurance, and finally broken, they agreed to aid Horus. The rot quickly spread to the whole Legion, and the Emperor's Children willingly embraced the gratifying worship of Slaanesh.

Once a Legion dedicated to perfection in all its pursuits, the Emperor's Children succumbed to the call of forbidden knowledge, and their drive for perfection was perverted to an obsession with excess. As one of the Traitor Legions, the Emperor's Children invaded Terra but took little part in the fighting around the Imperial Palace. Instead they descended upon the civilian population of the Administratum, the complex infrastructure of clerks, bureaucrats, curators and menials who coordinated the efforts of the far-flung Imperium. Whole families of staid scribes and haughty prefects fleeing the battle zone were hunted down and incarcerated in dreadful conditions. Simple pleasures had given way to complex debaucheries. While their allies fought and died the Emperor's Children slaughtered more than a million people and rendered them down to create endless varieties of drugs and stimulants. Countless thousands more died to give the Emperor's Children more direct, if cruder, enjoyment.

When the assault failed the Emperor's Children fled with the rest of the Traitor Legions. Those Imperial vessels that pursued Fulgrim's fleet from Terra followed a trail of devastated worlds, where corpses were piled high, survivors pleaded to be allowed to die to escape their nightmares and, ominously, thousands more were simply missing, never seen again. Eventually, after countless atrocities, the Emperor's Children reached the Eye of Terror. They were the first to begin raiding Imperial worlds for captives and plunder. Their excesses soon knew no bounds, and simple raiding could not supply enough raw human material for their orgies of worship.

The Emperor's Children quickly exhausted their supplies of slaves and playthings, and began to prey upon the only victims available: the slaves and servants of the other Traitor Legions, an action that began a series of wars within the Eye of Terror. The struggles of the Emperor's Children continued until the destruction of the clones of Horus by the Black Legion. The resulting wars were terrible and bloody, but there could be only one eventual result, and finally the Legion of the Emperor's Children was shattered.

The Emperor's Children have retained some of their former organisation as Space Marines, but have altered it to suit their new loyalties. Psykers are particularly highly regarded by the Emperor's Children, both as enemies and within their own ranks. The broadcast terror of an enemy psyker can be enjoyed in its own right as new, exotic sensations, while an Emperor's Children Sorcerer can kill his enemies with excesses of pleasure or pure sensation – the greatest act of worship for a servant of Slaanesh. Close combat, where the enemy can be touched and directly destroyed, is also much favoured by the Emperor's Children. Few of them enter battle without some form of close combat weapon.

While corrupt beyond human comprehension, the Emperor's Children are a savage fighting force. The danger of combat is a rediscovered thrill and aphrodisiac, allowing them to reach new extremes of debauchery. Many of these crazed followers of the Lord of Pleasure have become Noise Marines – depraved and totally decadent warriors who seek and find a perverse enjoyment in battle and pain. The louder and more discordant the noise, the more extreme the emotional reaction provoked, until only the din of war and the terrified screams of the enemy can stir them. To further enhance their enjoyment, Noise Marines carry outlandish weapons that produce deafeningly loud and pyrotechnically explosive attacks.

Because the senses of the Emperor's Children have become so distorted, only the most extravagant patterns and colours register in their minds. Each suit of armour, every bolter or chainsword, is worked into fantastic patterns and coloured in praise of Slaanesh. Each Emperor's Children Traitor Marine alters and changes his armour slightly, adding to its quality and 'beautifying' it. For the most favoured, the weaponsmiths of the Legion sometimes carve scenes of debauchery into pauldrons and breastplates. Only the most extreme sensations can provoke a reaction from these jaded veterans, causing them to decorate their armour in dazzling, clashing colours, and adorn it with shimmering silks and golden chains. Despite their insanity, they remain vicious, savage warriors, delighting in the destruction they cause and injuries they sustain in battle, willing to serve any master in return for fresh slaves upon which to practise their devotion to Slaanesh.

Of the fate of the Primarch Fulgrim, none are sure. The enemies of Slaanesh claim he was killed during the battles against his fellow Legions, but robot-crewed Mechanicus trawlers recovered neither his body nor the remains of his Battle Barge. Among the remains of the Emperor's Children, it is rumoured that he was rewarded for his devotion to pleasure and elevated by Slaanesh to become a Daemon Primarch, lord of a Daemon world. Over the millennia, many of the Emperor's Children, along with other Slaanesh-worshipping Space Marines, sought Fulgrim's world, hoping to discover limitless pleasure, but none have returned. Even after ten thousand years, the Inquisition still maintains a strike force devoted to pursuing rumours, however slight, of the traitor Primarch's existence.

PINNACLES AND NADIRS

For the Emperor's Children, the quest for excess never stops. Such is their need for endless depravity they have plumbed the depths of experience, from the most sublime thrills to the most intense acts of barbarism ever committed by the human race. To catalogue them all would be to give one's mind to insanity; as a consequence, only a few are matters of Imperial record.

Flesh Meets Steel

The Sensorians, a newly formed warband of Slaanesh-worshipping Chaos Space Marines, treat with the Dark Mechanicum in an attempt to pioneer Daemon Engines equipped with suites of sonic weaponry. In doing so they learn of the sombre Skitarii of the forge world Agripinaa, ancestral enemies of the Eye of Terror's machine-hereteks.

Appalled by the notion that the Skitarii voluntarily exchange their flesh for cybernetic replacements, the Emperor's Children stage a grand raid upon the planet under the cover of a Dark Mechanicum invasion. They capture several maniples of Skitarii, overloading their circuits with barrages of intense noise and deafening scrapcode, before bearing them back to the Eye of Terror. There they cut out the Skitarii's bionics and replace them with fleshy equivalents taken from mutants, from corpses, even from fallen Chaos Spawn, until barely an ounce of metal is left. The Fleshlings of Sensoria, though driven mad by the process, prove a potent asset in the Long War.

'Thrill in the noise that breaks the skin and ravages the mind! Savour the shuddering, shaking screams that shiver the spine and shatter the skull! Let sensation wash over you, through you, claim you and cast you aside!'

- Bellerophid, Scarlet Marquis of the Emperor's Children

The Eternal Duellist

Lucius the Eternal leads a motley warband across the galaxy on the trail of the deadliest opponents his network of admiring torture-cultists can locate for him. He intends to hunt down the best melee fighters in the galaxy and beat them in one-on-one combat or die in the attempt. Over the course of several centuries he defeats the Dark Eldar Archon Vraesque in cursed Shaa-dom, the Emperor's Champion of the Black Templars at Veilfate, and the Ork Warboss Two-klaws at Octarius Sigma.

Eventually, on a nameless moon near Damnos, Lucius is cut down by the shape-shifting Necron duellist known only as the Phasing Sword. Not even the Necron's body of living metal can prevent the Slaaneshi champion's strange possession-curse from taking hold, however, for it takes a cold pride in its victory, and that is the seed of its undoing. Lucius is reborn inside his killer within days, the xenos warrior's body drizzling away to reveal the twisted swordsman, as arrogant and maniacal as ever.

The Cacophonicum of Knaus Lambda

The warband of Revellian Thrice-Burned captures the Basilica Morbidus, centrepiece of the shrine world Knaus Lambda's majestic Faithful City. Six Dreadclaws slam through the cathedrum's stained-glass ceiling and disgorge their battle-hungry passengers. The sonic weaponry of the hedonistic killers shatters priceless glass sculptures and a king's ransom in jewels. The barefoot supplicants and pilgrims that were making their devotions are shredded body and soul by the deafening cacophony, which is enhanced by the basilica's perfect acoustics. In response, the nearby Schola Progenium complex scrambles its Tempestus Scions to the site, and a gun battle takes place that sees the city filled with terrified screams. The cacophony grows so intense that reality itself shimmers and convulses, and a carnival of Slaaneshi Daemonettes joins the feast.

The Faithful City is eventually reconsecrated as the Cacophonicum, becoming a base of operations that sees Revellian Thrice-Burned and his Emperor's Children reduce every one of Knaus Lambda's fortified settlements to rubble.

Revenge of the Silver Prince

After a long and difficult journey through the warp, the Khorne Daemonkin warband known as the Skullsworn overtake their Emperor's Children rivals on the approach to the civilised planet of Hunter's Haven. The Skullsworn launch a bloody strike three days before their fellow Chaos Space Marines arrive. When the Emperor's Children make planetfall, there is little left of the capital city's populace but dismembered corpses and decapitated heads stacked in pyramidal piles.

Enraged by the Skullsworn's actions, the Daemon overlord known as the Silver Prince leads his bodyguard of Chaos Terminators in a sorcerous strike directly at the Khornate warband's commanders. The sudden conflict escalates into a grinding war of attrition that sees both warbands sustain grievous losses; however, both sides revel in the carnage to such an extent neither will back down. The remaining citizens of Hunter's Haven make use of the reprieve to evacuate, leaving the Chaos Space Marines to fight amongst themselves.

The Primogenitor Primaris

The deranged fleshmaster Fabius Bile is upon the world of Agrathane Excellia when he witnesses a strike force of Primaris Space Marines in action. Attacking from above, a strike force from the newly founded Nemesors Chapter takes a fortified Black Legion bastion complex in the space of an hour. Impressed despite himself, Bile develops an obsession with the capture and dissection of these statuesque warriors. His intent is to blend them body and soul with the dark energies of Chaos in order to breed his own twisted versions of Primaris Space Marines.

THE BROTHERHOODS OF EXCESS

The Emperor's Children have always taken great pride in their appearance. Once, they considered magnificence of form to be epitomised by statuesque armour and finely wrought blades, but since they turned wholly to Slaanesh they have become ever more extreme and bizarre, bearing garish and clashing colours that offend the eye to mutant anatomies that only a madman could consider a gift from the gods. Provided the end result allows them to sample ever more excessive sensations, the Emperor's Children are more than happy to adopt Slaanesh's perverse tastes as their own.

The pre-Heresy heraldry of the Emperor's Children was rich purple with gold trim and embellishment. As reward for their excellence in battle, they alone amongst the Legiones Astartes were permitted to wear the Imperial Eagle upon their chests. This bolstered their already considerable pride to the point where Horus' flattery and Fulgrim's obsessions took root all the more easily, eventually leading to their downfall.

Brother Lythaen, whose marksmanship record remained unsullied for six centuries

The Emperor's Children are hedonists of the most extreme kind, and revel in the pleasures of the flesh. Yet none would survive the flames of war for long outside their battle plate. Slaanesh gifts his favoured warriors with the ability to feel pleasure and pain through the layered ceramite of their armour as if it were their own skin, making every bullet or blade that rebounds from its contours a thrill of sublime pain.

Mandrakh Blyss, Devourer of the Severed Souls

Many Emperor's Children relish the cut and thrust of close combat above all, revelling in the slash of the blade and the sharp sting of the riposte. Each drop of blood shed is exquisite nectar to these specialists; some even learn to taste with their blades. Fuelled by sensation, they find pain as invigorating as any intoxicant; to land a blow upon these demented warriors is to give them a vitalising ecstasy that no mortal could comprehend.

Marquis Sularashian the Sadistic, Bringer of the Bladed Caress

Those Emperor's Children who give themselves over completely to the sensations of battle become Noise Marines. Their armour slowly grows laud-hailer screamers, noise vents and organ batteries that allow them to produce ear-splitting dins, the perfect complement to the sonic weaponry that has made their kind infamous throughout the Traitor Legions. Even other Space Marines are deafened by the proximity of these maniac thrill-seekers.

Threshling Vainglariadh of the Kakophatine Temple of the Unsated Shriek

RENEGADES AND TYRANTS

None truly know how many Space Marine Chapters have turned renegade throughout the Imperium's history. The galaxy is so vast that reliable data is extremely hard to come by, and the first sign of a Chapter's rebellion is often when their new incarnation preys upon the Imperium's worlds – usually bearing a different identity and markings. Only the most dedicated scholars of the Ordo Malleus have succeeded in tracing the disastrous events, decisions or tragedies that have led to once-loyal Chapters going rogue. At the close of the 41st Millennium, these investigators are busier than ever before…

THE SCOURGED

Chapter Master Herodicus of the Seekers of Truth was an honourable man, and every innocent he was ordered to kill during his service to the Imperium of Mankind tore at his soul. He prayed for a way to know when a person was lying. Unfortunately for Herodicus, Tzeentch granted his wish. From that moment on, he and his brothers could hear every lie spoken by Mankind. The Chapter turned renegade within days, naming themselves The Scourged.

Brother Thanatossus the Aether-sighted

FLAWLESS HOST

The Flawless Host believe they are the embodiment of justice and purity. The rigid training of their former incarnation, the Shining Blades, gave the Chapter an unshakeable faith in its own abilities. They convinced themselves they could not fail, and their overweening pride and wilful delusion caused them to attack, in a frenzy of indignation, any who questioned their magnificence. Renaming themselves the Flawless Host, they have scarred the Imperium ever since.

Persidius of the Coiled Tongue

BLOOD DISCIPLES

In 888.M37, a Chaos cult rose on the Goreworlds. The Emperor's Wolves were sent to destabilise the threat. After weeks of searching, their 8th Company located the cult's Red Prophet as he preached from a pillar of blood. Soaring on their jump packs, the 8th cut him down, but all those touched by the blood fell instantly to the worship of Khorne. The Blood Disciples, as the 8th Company is now called, have led raids on the Segmentum Obscurus ever since.

Balthor the Neverquenched, whose flesh is molten gore

COMPANY OF MISERY

Since the degradation of their gene-seed in M32, the Desolate Brotherhood found themselves assigned to impossibly dangerous duties. Each time they won a reprieve, they were sent on an even more hazardous mission, plunging them into a spiral of dissolution and despair. After a catastrophe in the acid swamps of the world Misery, the Chapter took a new name and left their duties behind, forever becoming sworn enemies of the Imperium and the illusion of hope.

Abomnis Mourne, the Red Knight of Tragedy

The Khorne Daemonkin are a breed of renegade like no other. United by their fanatical worship of the Blood God, they flood onto the battlefield in a chanting, gore-drenched horde. Their hymns are the screams of the dying, and the tools of their faith are the edges of their blades. The ultimate desire of the Daemonkin is – through acts of bloodthirsty devotion – to summon the Daemons of Khorne and fight in battle alongside them. Their rituals of massacre do not go unnoticed by their patron. The zealotry of the Daemonkin acts as a beacon for the footsoldiers of Khorne; the veil is sundered as blood-red Daemons spill into realspace, and the remaining renegades continue their massacre in enraptured vindication. Ultimately, such warbands are destined for daemonhood, or for death.

CRIMSON SLAUGHTER

The Crimson Sabres were once regarded as unimpeachable. In 928. M41, however, their genocidal purge of Umidia's jungle cults left a terrible shadow on their honour. The entire Chapter was literally haunted by the butchery of the Balethu Cults, and a pall of paranoia spread through the Chapter like a disease. The voices of the spectres could only be drowned out by indiscriminate killing. Soon the Chapter was reborn, becoming the Crimson Slaughter.

Makhtos Narr-Desh, He Whose Soul Lurks in the Beyond

BRAZEN BEASTS

Roaring, clanking packs of Daemon Engines lead the charge of the Brazen Beasts. They tear through the enemy like the gouging claws of some almighty monster, leaving behind nothing but mangled corpses and blazing devastation. Following these metal monsters come the Daemonkin, howling praise to Khorne as they carve the Blood God's rune into the bodies of their victims and consecrate the carnage in his name.

Dakmar Vrax, the Flenser of the Eighty-eight Saints

THE CLEAVED

The Cleaved first appeared during the insurrection of Magma Cordelian. Amongst the fury of an Astra Militarum counterstrike, the rebels conjured reinforcements – not Daemons of the immaterium, but Chaos Space Marines with oil-like blood oozing from the joins in their armour. Though the new arrivals were massively outnumbered, they fought on through mortal wounds to eventually secure the planet for the insurrectionists.

The Faceless Dirge, conjured from the strands of unreality to punish the just

THE PURGE

The Purge loathe life in all its forms. They have waged their pitiless war against Mankind and alien alike since late M36, consumed by their self-imposed quest to exterminate all living creatures. Having seen first-hand the dread threat of Chaos, they believe that the galaxy is hopelessly corrupt and that the only salvation lies in the sterility of death. The Purge pray to Nurgle, the God of Plagues, for a pandemic that will destroy every living being.

Ghrouvas Marinnon, Sower of the Great Spoil

RED CORSAIRS

The Astral Claws had been stationed near the Maelstrom for over three centuries when a fleet was despatched to investigate their lapsed gene-tithes. Chapter Master Lugft Huron had every Imperial ship destroyed. The backlash saw several Chapters diverted onto a punitive mission to slay the Tyrant of Badab. However, so inspirational was Huron's rhetoric that several Chapters defected to his empire. His Red Corsairs raid from the Maelstrom to this day.

Brother Skarvjelsson, formerly an over-proud Space Wolf of the Blackmanes

SONS OF VENGEANCE

After the brutal suppression of the Obscuran Uprisings, the Sons of Vengeance ran wild, slaughtering and looting ostensibly in the name of the Emperor. Soon they dropped even the pretence of punitive action, taking their campaign of violence to Laskaria. By the time the Adeptus Terra intervened, the Sons of Vengeance and Silver Guards had spilt the blood of fourteen star systems in a savage war for dominance.

Garvus the Damned, the Beast in Genewrought Flesh

INVOCATORS

Known for the daemonic hosts they summon before each battle, the Invocators are a rag-tag assortment of minor warbands that now seek power through bringing as many daemonic rituals to fruition as they can. Once known as the Clerics of Steel, they have fallen so far from the light of truth that their only recourse is to court the favour of all four of the Ruinous Powers – and some rumour other empyric gods besides.

Maeloc Threnn, Caster of the Tainted Auguries

THE HEDONISTARII

Slaanesh-worshipping renegades that raid the extremities of the Eastern Fringe, the Hedonistarii are fleet-based pirates that revel in war for its own sake. So ready are they to tear down law and order wherever they find it that they have a long-standing pact with the anarchist Lord Drathoni, whose Heldrake eyries are famed amongst the renegade Warpsmiths of Ultima Segmentum.

Languith the Perfumed, whose musk drives mortals to deranged slaughter

The 37th Millennium saw thirty thousand Space Marines embark on a redemptive crusade into the Eye of Terror. Barely half returned, and many of those left behind were horribly altered, caught in thrall to the very forces they had sought to purge. The catalyst for this event, known as the Abyssal Crusade, was Warp Storm Dionys. Many of the Chapters with home worlds in the path of the storm found that the secret imperfections in their gene-seed were writ large upon their new recruits, giving rise to a wave of disturbing mutations. This was but a precursor to the mayhem that would unfold at the opening of the Great Rift – the number of Chapters forced to turn renegade by the corruption of their own forms is at an all-time high.

CORPUS BRETHREN

The Sentinels Chapter took war to the fleshy crust of Oliensis, a Daemon world in the shape of a morbidly obese man. The battle-brothers of the Sentinels hunted down the goat-headed hedonists that frolicked there. Then, from the planet's yawning pores, came Noise Marines. The Sentinels fought hard until the planet itself stirred, awoken by the din. Oliensis devoured the combatants, later regurgitating them as the cannibalistic Corpus Brethren renegades.

The Gnawing Brute, whose chewing teeth are never still

MAGMA HOUNDS

The Knights Excelsior never returned from their invasion of the machine planet Temporia, for the Warpsmith Valadrak set upon them a ravenous electroplague. With the controls of their warships rebelling and their wargear pulsing with static, the Space Marines were seized up in the piston-driven claws of Temporia's Daemon Engines and thrust into the red-hot soul-forges of Valadrak's fortress. They emerged reborn as the renegade Magma Hounds.

Mastrec Tahn, weldblade of Athmar Rivetheart's warband

DEATHMONGERS

Upon the crone world of Belial IV, the Brothers of the Anvil scoured the spires of the original Eldar empire, only to be brought to battle by Drukhari Kabalites searching the ancient planet for ancient treasures. After a year of nightmarish ordeals in the Commorrite arenas, the broken remains of the Brothers of the Anvil slaughtered their way back into realspace, where they killed every living thing they found. They are now known as the Deathmongers.

Brother Harnal, bladefingered lord of the murderous arts

THE GREY DEATH

After the Death Guard crippled their fleet, the Iron Drakes Chapter became marooned on the plague world of Anathrax in the Eye of Terror. For over a century, Plague Marines harried the stranded loyalists, always aiming to debilitate their targets and damage their wargear rather than slay them. The last time the Iron Drakes were sighted in the Imperium, they fought under the name of the Grey Death, and their new loyalties were plain to all.

Brother Brohxial, whose very exhalation rots iron and flesh

A planet attacked by the hordes of Chaos is cursed twice over. The invasion strikes home with the violence of a spear thrust into the heart, for the heretics know their prey well. They send forth veteran warriors, engines of war and daemonic machines until all that is good and pure has been torn down. Even should these conquerors be driven away, the world will be irrevocably tainted by their presence. All too often a second damnation is brought by the planet's saviours, forced to burn the lands clean in order to prevent the spread of madness and corruption.

DAEMON PRINCES

Daemon Princes are infernal monsters that tower over the mortals they lead to battle. These paragons of evil take many forms, though all exude a palpable aura of terror and power. In battle, a Daemon Prince strides through the pitiful bullets of the enemy without pause, his unnatural laughter driving men to the edge of fear. Warp energy sizzles from his eyes, and black flames curl from his mouth as he speaks dread phrases that kill as sure as any blade. These are creatures of nightmare – a living expression of Chaos given form.

The ultimate ambition of most champions of Chaos is to achieve immortality. For the devotees of the Ruinous Powers, this is far from an impossible goal. Those few who climb the path of the champion to its apex are granted the prize of eternal life. Though thousands of lesser aspirants will fall by the wayside, a supremely talented devotee will clamber over mountains of the slain until he reaches the pinnacle of his bloody craft. Over the course of centuries, such champions offer up sacrifices on a planetary scale, risking death and mutation in the hope of attracting the gaze of the gods. And yet murder alone is not enough. Only those who further the causes of their masters are given the precious gift of daemonhood. They are raised up to become demigods, roaring their triumph into the night as their new bodies swell and bulge with the energies of the warp.

Yet a Daemon Prince is just as much a tool of the Dark Gods as his mortal followers. If anything, he becomes even more of an extension of his master's will. Daemons cannot truly be killed, only banished back to the warp for a time – one who ascends to daemonhood can look forward to an eternity of servitude at his patron's behest. Even death is no respite.

CHAOS LORDS

A Chaos Lord is a tyrannical warrior king who lives to bathe in the blood of worlds. He strives to bring whole star systems to their knees in the name of his patron deities. Typified by merciless ambition and fierce pride, many of these champions of disorder were once noble Chapter Masters and Captains of the Adeptus Astartes, but long years of unremitting war have twisted their souls beyond recovery.

All Chaos Lords are imposing in stature, their enhanced physiques made even more impressive by the protean caress of the warp. Their wargear is often as outlandish as their physical appearance; a Chaos Lord may hack his foes apart with a massive chainaxe, blast them with an ancient combi-weapon, or slice open their vehicles with a screaming Daemon sword. Regardless of affiliation, these conquerors of worlds invariably prefer to lead from the front. There, the visceral thrill of war is strong enough to eclipse any glimmering sense of betrayal they may feel as they rend their loyalist brothers limb from limb.

Possessed of a wrath so intense it often clouds their vision, the lords of Khorne lead by example. Each lord is a looming brute in gore-stained armour. Many such lords retain their intellect and conqueror's instincts, but their blood-greed is so strong that, upon the battlefield, they could easily be mistaken for mindless savages.

Tzeentch grants his lordly devotees access to an almost limitless supply of sorcerous power. Such beings have a supernatural ability to outguess their foes. They often manifest arcane mutations such as haloes of dark flame or third eyes, whilst mystical auras protect them from harm, transmuting attacks into harmless energy.

The lords of Nurgle are lumbering, filth-encrusted hulks that devote their lives to spreading disease across the stars. Their guts are bloated sacs of gas and rancid fat, and their sagging skin has the waxy pallor of a corpse, but their resistance to injury is legendary.

Lords of Slaanesh are gifted with strange sensory organs and mood amplifiers that allow them to better savour the shocking stimuli of open warfare. The life of such a lord is a whirlwind of excess that inspires his followers anew with every new battle.

EXALTED CHAMPIONS

For every Chaos Lord making his grisly mark upon the galaxy, there are dozens, if not hundreds, of champions vying for the favour of the Ruinous Powers. Each is an exceptional warrior; whether he is known for his martial prowess or sheer animalistic brutality, the Exalted Champion inevitably leaves a trail of corpses in his wake. In seeking out and slaying the most vaunted of enemies, Exalted Champions hope to draw the eye of the Dark Gods. Unlike so many other deities given obeisance across the galaxy, who remain distant and unknowable, if they exist at all, the gods of Chaos are very real, and willing to reward or punish their supplicants on the whim of the moment.

An Exalted Champion that proves a capable pawn in the Great Game will find himself rewarded with abilities far beyond those of even the most accomplished mortal. Warp-given rewards usually appear first as blemishes or stigmata that become ever more pronounced over time. A bloodthirsty butcher may become possessed of insane strength, whereas a leader of men might find his commands obeyed without question. Other gifts might be hideously disfiguring, or even physically crippling, for what the Ruinous Powers consider a blessing might be seen by mortals as the vilest curse. But even those champions who sprout extra limbs, razor-sharp horns or extra eyes soon find ways to turn their new gifts to slaughter.

SORCERERS

Sorcerers of Chaos shape destiny itself with arcane rituals and unspeakable pacts with the malefic entities of the empyrean. They channel the soul-blasting energies of the warp into potent hexes and blasts of wyrdflame, and they mould the fabric of the material universe with little more than a hate-filled curse. Because of their constant exposure to the power of Chaos, Sorcerers are inevitably haunted by the prospect of eventually succumbing to crippling mutation or insanity. Though they believe they are above mortal concerns, the truth is that they, too, are pawns, raised up and then expended by the Dark Gods for their own amusement.

The line between psychic power and sorcery is fine indeed. The Chapters of the Adeptus Astartes may seek to deny it, but every time a Space Marine Librarian calls upon his mental might he risks tainting his soul. In the heat of battle, even the most capable psyker may overreach his abilities, and instead of recoiling in horror from the resultant carnage, he may feel a forbidden thrill. Such emotions are the first step on a path to limitless evil. From that moment on, the psyker may endure honeyed whispers in his dreams and visions of immortality. Those who succumb to such temptations become Sorcerers, able to channel the malefic power of the warp.

Sorcerers are forever driven to expand their influence and knowledge. They see themselves as having ascended; no longer hindered by blind loyalty to the corpse-lord of the Imperium, they become even more callous and inhuman than those who follow them. Some are cold-hearted strategists who vent their hatred upon as much of the universe as possible; Ygethmor the Deceiver once orchestrated a doomsday cult that resulted in the depopulation of every inhabited world in the Corriallis System. Others act as advisors for the lords of Chaos, subtly redirecting them to their own ends under the illusion of servitude. A rare few roam the hidden paths of the universe, unlocking the secrets of the ancients to better plunge the galaxy into the embrace of Chaos.

Regardless of their goals, all Sorcerers revel in the anarchy of the Long War. It takes only a flicker of resistance to spur them into unleashing the destructive energies of the immaterium. Their bitterness manifests upon the battlefield as a palpable force; red-hot skulls hammer down from the skies, disease chokes the souls of those nearby, and men are turned into monsters in their wake. The martial prowess common to all Chaos Space Marines is magnified greatly when combined with the weapons of the Sorcerer, baleful artefacts saturated with the energies of Chaos that can rip the soul from the body of their victim.

THOUSAND SONS

The Thousand Sons gave rise to the first Space Marine Sorcerers. Even before the Heresy, the Legion of Magnus the Red had a thirst for knowledge that proved impossible to slake, and ultimately proved their undoing. Most of their number were reduced to unliving automatons by the Rubric of Ahriman, though the most powerful among them were able to resist the unforeseen consequences of that grand ritual. Many of these ancient Sorcerers have forged pacts with Abaddon the Despoiler, joining the Warmaster in his quest to overthrow the Imperium of Man and adding the strength of their Rubricae bodyguards to that of the Black Legion.

MASTERS OF POSSESSION

Masters of Possession lead warbands of devoted warriors in pursuit of untold power. These sorcerous figures have mastered the darkest and most blasphemous lore: the art of using hosts of living flesh to house daemonic spirits. It is they who perform the profane ceremonies of binding that imbue the Daemonkin with their warp-born power. Gouging a breach in the fabric of realspace, the Master of Possession draws a willing entity from the immaterium, channelling its terrible energies into the body of a supplicant or the chassis of a war machine. So thoroughly are these dread figures steeped in blasphemous sorcery that where they walk, reality itself recoils. In battle they bolster their Daemon-possessed followers, stitching together rents in fleshmetal carcasses, or imbuing their creations with a demented, predatory fury. Enemies are despatched with bolts of searing warpflame, or with precise shots from a bolt pistol sidearm. With a touch from their corrupted staves, Masters of Possession can even blast asunder the souls of their foes, spilling daemonic energy into the now hollow shell. This hideous act can cause mortal frames to erupt with hellish energies, transforming the unfortunate victim into a slavering Chaos Spawn, or a willing Chaos champion into a towering Greater Possessed.

All amongst the Daemonkin believe that by trafficking with the creatures of the warp they can gain true power. Their insistence that the daemonic possession of mortal flesh is the most effective method of achieving this enlightenment is a cause of contention amongst their Chaos allies. This divide is most clearly observed in the long-held rivalry between the Masters of Possession who act as the spiritual leaders of the Daemonkin, and the Warpsmiths who scorn doctrine in favour of cold, merciless logic. Masters of Possession are inclined towards traditionalism, believing that the bonding of mortal flesh with a daemonic spirit is the most potent and sacred form of ascension. For them, Daemon Engines are valuable assets, but little more than crude creations of necessity. It is raging emotion that grants power, not the iron resolve of the machine. Masters of Possession often demonstrate how effectively hatred fuels a Daemon Engine by ripping apart the soul of a nearby combatant and using the wrathful shreds to reinvigorate the monstrous construct – such sacrifices are particularly fruitful when the raging soul is taken from a rival Warpsmith.

Masters of Possession are viewed by their fellow Heretic Astartes with a combination of awe and bitter suspicion. They are prophet-like figures, often speaking of when and where great warp breaches will appear to spill daemonic beings into realspace. Yet they speak in riddles, twisting their own words to have multiple and contradictory meanings. They may foretell of a world upon which a great sacrifice will bring forth the denizens of the warp in plenitude, and a Chaos Lord, learning of this and seeking to bolster his warband with daemonic forces, might travel to this world and eradicate the populace of a bustling hive city in a profane mass sacrifice. But the truth of the Master of Possession's prophecy may be that the Chaos Lord themselves is destined to become the sacrifice, their tainted soul consumed to create a rupture in the fabric of reality. In their arrogance, most heretical champions are sure they will not succumb to such a fate, and risk treating with a Master of Possession in the hopes of adding daemonic warriors to their ranks. Should this lead to the demise of the Chaos Lord, the Master of Possession will swiftly take their place and begin their own tyrannical reign.

Crusev's skull bulged outwards, pressing against the inside of his ancient helm. In his long and loathsome existence he had never experienced such agony, such horrific sensations in every cell of his body, yet still he laughed with insane joy. Through his distending eyes he could see the Master of Possession standing before him, calling out to the warp, compelling the Daemons into their awaiting hosts – and Crusev could feel one of the hateful entities entering his flesh. They were reshaping him body and soul, carving out and discarding what weakness remained in him. He felt a jet of fire running through his right arm, shattering the bones and swelling the muscles to massive proportions. The surrounding armour burst open to reveal an enormous clawed limb, though it was not his to control – it belonged to the Daemon within. His consciousness receded, his body overtaken completely by its new owner, and he heard the Master of Possession speak.

'You are complete.'

WARPSMITHS

Warpsmiths are the masters of the machine. Most can trace their origins back to the priesthood of Mars, whether through the schisms of the Magi or the rigid doctrine of the Techmarines. However, where the Adeptus Mechanicus regard technology as sacrosanct, the Warpsmiths seek to subjugate and control it.

Warpsmiths tend to be obsessive characters who believe that Mankind's ambition is limited by his mortal nature. Daemons are ultimately insubstantial of form, and machines, though physically indomitable, are all but inert. Because of this, all Warpsmiths are engaged in an eternal quest to combine the strengths of all three elements whilst eradicating their weaknesses. They would conquer the galaxy and remould it into one giant, tainted flesh-engine if they could. The Warpsmiths themselves seek to embody this unholy fusion of man, machine and Daemon; in their search for the perfect form, they often become more metal than

flesh. Some are little more than a brain and a spinal cord wired into a metallic approximation of a Chaos Space Marine – pincer limbs, mechatendrils and fusion claws sprout from the Warpsmith's altered form next to melta crucibles and searing welder blades.

Though each Warpsmith is an expert in battlefield repair and siege craft, his true calling lies in the soul forges of the warp, especially those in the Eye of Terror. There, the spirits of captured Imperial machines are driven to madness as their physical forms are rebuilt into bestial and terrifying new shapes. Daemons are thrust into the cogs of giant, mechanoid birth-factories that crank out red-hot engines of destruction from their cabled wombs. Acolytes of the Dark Mechanicum combine flesh, bone and steel with daemonic essence in ever more inventive and sickening ways. Presiding over this infernal industry are the Warpsmiths themselves – pioneers of mechamorphosis, grim and silent as the

grave save for the occasional barked order or spell of binding. When the time for conquest is finally at hand, entire armies of these growling battle engines stomp and soar into realspace – the Warpsmiths' bitter ambition writ large and set loose upon the Imperium of Man.

DARK APOSTLES

Dark Apostles make up the priesthood of the Dark Gods. Just as the Chaplains of the loyalist Space Marines uphold the creeds of their Chapters, the Dark Apostles devote their lives to the propagation of the unholy word, actively spreading the worship of Chaos across the galaxy. Their efforts do not go unrewarded – Dark Apostles are surrounded by daemonic auras of protection that shimmer and writhe as they chant their blasphemous prayers.

The Dark Apostles preach that, compared to the blood and thunder of their own faith, the falsehoods of the Ecclesiarchy are but cobweb-thin tissues of superstition. These are more than idle words – most Dark Apostles can act as direct conduits through which the Ruinous Powers can speak to mortal men. It is not unknown for a Dark Apostle to suddenly straighten, his eyes glazing over as his mouth spits guttural and blood-flecked gibberish. Those who can understand this glottal tongue claim that it is the language of the gods themselves.

The Dark Apostles sit high in the esteem of their brethren, and their intense charisma and burning conviction inspires men to great and terrible acts. The yoke of the Imperium fosters festering resentment in those of weak character, and Dark Apostles are experts at fanning those sparks into raging blazes. When these preachers of horrific truths infiltrate an Imperial world, hidden cults are brought together and long-fostered alliances are brought to terrible fruition. It is never long before the bodies of Adeptus Arbites, Judges and aristocrats alike are strung from spire and cable. Mutants and madmen boil out into the populace, infecting those around them with the touch of Chaos. Just as the hysterical citizenry are on the brink of devouring themselves, the Dark Apostle will draw them together into an army and lead a great crusade against the Imperium's forces.

A Dark Apostle arrayed for war is an imposing sight. His battle-scarred power armour is emblazoned with forbidden texts and hung with parchments of human skin covered in potent invocations. The Apostle's own skin is tattooed with runic prayers to Chaos, and in his clenched fist he carries a defiled crozius arcanum, an evil corruption of the Chaplain's badge of office. But the Dark Apostle's most powerful weapon is his voice – a tool with which wars can be started and the gifts of the gods bestowed.

Dark Apostles are often accompanied into battle by twisted sycophants drawn from the most fervent Chaos Cultists. These Dark Disciples carry profane accoutrements of their masters' worship and parrot the fell words spoken in his baleful prayers. Many such disciples have been augmented to better serve in their role – their skin stretched out and inked with grim litanies, or their mouths fitted with Daemon-touched vox-grilles to project their voices into the warp. Amidst the din of combat they join their Dark Apostle's chants, crying out for the Chaos Gods to manifest their blessings.

THE LOST AND THE DAMNED

The forces of Chaos include a multitude of lesser hosts. Amongst them are hordes of bestial mutants, lumbering tribes of corrupted Ogryns and ad hoc warbands of renegade Imperial Knights. The most deadly of these armies are perhaps the least outlandish, those able to bypass the defences of the Corpse Emperor's armies and conquer the Imperium from within. The Dark Apostles take especial pleasure in corrupting the soldiery of the Astra Militarum. Throughout the Imperium there are those who wear the Aquila upon their breasts, but harbour resentment in their hearts. Ground down by the futility of the Imperium's wars and the callous inhumanity of the Departmento Munitorum, these warriors embrace whatever freedom from tyranny they can find. In heeding the false promises of the agents of Chaos, they exchange the endless grind of a decrepit dystopia for a short and bloody existence in thrall to the lords of hatred.

MASTERS OF EXECUTIONS

Amidst the thunderous tumult of battle, a Master of Executions strides unflinchingly forwards, his mind focused on the gruesome decapitations he will soon administer. He is a being of singular purpose, a brutal weapon in the arsenal of the Heretic Astartes, and his existence is driven by an unquenchable desire to take as trophies the heads of mighty champions and charismatic leaders. When he reaches the lines of the foe he lofts his enormous cleaver. Lowly soldiers are hacked apart with contemptible swiftness, their deaths providing only the most fleeting moments of joy to the executioner – hot sprays of blood feel cold against his skin, and the screams of terror that come as his blade makes its descent ring hollow in his ears. Yet every body through which he cleaves brings him nearer to his quarry.

As the Master of Executions draws closer to the enemy's champion he bellows his fatal decree, proclaiming the warrior's life forfeited to the Dark Gods. With a terrifying burst of speed, he closes upon his declared victim, crushing whatever defence they offer with blow after sweeping blow. A final unerring swing sees the energy-wreathed axe blade carve through armour, flesh and spine without slowing. As he watches the opponent's severed flesh spinning

through the air and the gushes of arterial blood that jet from the toppling corpse, the executioner feels the gaze of the Chaos Gods fall upon him. A jolt of exaltation runs through his body, his veins crackle with empyric power and his hunger for death grows even stronger. He claims the disembodied remains of his enemy as his trophies, then looks for the next foe worthy of his fury.

Only the most single-minded become Masters of Executions. It is a calling that comes in many forms – a Chaos Space Marine may hear a ceaseless stream of whispers telling them to seek out and behead the mightiest of their enemies, or they may see visions of disembodied skulls from which a deluge of blood drips onto the battlefield. Others perceive the heads of their foes as repositories of knowledge that need to be prised open, or as sheaves of flesh and bone that are ripe for the harvest. Regardless of how they are called, these warriors cast aside all other pursuits of glory and dedicate themselves solely to murder.

Through sorcerous rituals Masters of Executions attune their murderous senses to the currents of the warp, granting them the ability to see the souls of their foes. Some even go so far as to gouge out one of their eyes to allow the empyric currents to coalesce in the raw and empty socket. Even on the most anarchic battlefields an executioner can pick out his targets, looking through the clouds of choking smoke and ranks of lesser foes towards the bright burning spirits of the mightiest enemies, marking them for death.

The deadly expertise of each Master of Executions is evident in their gruesome array of trophies. Their collection of heads speaks to the manifold enemies they have slaughtered, with skulls and helms of different foes lashed to their armour or skewered on spiked racks. The most impressive trophies are given places of prominence, while from lesser foes sometimes only a tooth or fragment of jawbone is added to the panoply. It is not only heads, but other body parts that an executioner displays as the spoils of his labour. He might string the eyes, ears and tongue of a powerful mystic around his neck, fuse the shattered bones of a previously undefeated warrior to his wargear or drape the peeled skin of a charismatic leader over his armour. Some Masters of Executions find themselves compelled to butcher enemies from a specific race, and their trophy collections comprise the grim remnants of that species' greatest champions. Others feel the urge to slaughter a wide variety of foes, resulting in grisly displays that contain all manner of cadaverous specimens.

Within a warband, a Master of Executions is often used to mete out punishment to those who seek to usurp the rule of a Chaos Lord. The wayward Chaos Space Marine is corralled by his brethren into a gore-stained arena and forced to face the executioner in a duel to the death. Such contests are brutally swift, and serve to sate the murder-lust of both the warband and the Master of Executions. But a Chaos Lord must be ever wary, for while this practice helps thin out those warriors who have delusions of grandeur, the Master of Executions' axe may also come for him one day if there are no enemy champions to slaughter.

LORDS DISCORDANT

To Lords Discordant, showers of sparks and the flapping of loosed wiring are as pleasing as the jets of blood that gush from an open wound. These machine-obsessed heretics scuttle across the battlefield atop Helstalker mounts, a palpable aura of anarchy exuding from their very being. Upon sighting the enemy, they take stock of the war machines that have been brought to bear against them and plot their paths of destruction. A Lord Discordant is able to cut his way swiftly through the infantry on the front line, roasting them alive or riddling them with hails of shot, while his metallic steed crushes them to bloody paste beneath its blade-like limbs. But this rent flesh is merely an appetiser for the feast of suffering to come.

A Lord Discordant continues to spur his Helstalker onwards until he has reached the foe's tanks and towering walkers. As he charges, he bellows profane litanies in a tongue that is vile and incomprehensible to mortal ears, and causes comm systems, vox-grilles and laud hailers to crackle as though screaming in agony. His mere presence short-circuits machinery not riddled with daemonic entities – actuators and servos whir erratically, and targeting augurs cease to function. Once in range, the Lord's Helstalker pounces upon the nearest enemy vehicle, its massive forelimbs stabbing into the hull of its machine prey, piercing through ablative plating and tearing at gun turrets. Some Helstalkers use magma cutters to slice open the vehicle they have pinned, while others have enormous hypo-armour syringes that – after piercing the outer shell of their prey – inject scrapcode and daemonic dataphages directly into the machine's circuitry.

The Lord Discordant himself lunges forwards with his impaler chainglaive, its whirring blade gouging into metal and exposing the vehicle's internal workings, while his mechatendrils rip at its panelling. He hears the machine's pain, he feels it struggle to reroute vital functions to maintain system integrity, and his Helstalker feeds on this suffering. The Daemon Engine parasitically devours the motive force that powers its prey, be it a machine spirit or some other esoteric data-sentience employed in xenos technology. As it does so, its own metallic frame swells with ingested code and subroutines, while

rents in its casing crackle with warp energy and seal closed. The Lord Discordant siphons off the pained spirit of the dying vehicle, his mechatendrils lapping up the spasmodic electrical discharges and corrupting their information signatures. This harvested energy is then used to reinvigorate other Daemon Engines, or is released as a screaming beam to infect the systems of other enemy vehicles.

After their foe has been annihilated, Lords Discordant continue to prowl the battlefield, searching through the wreckage and piles of scrap for machinery in which some glimmer of motive force remains.

When such vehicle remnants are found, their energy is swiftly cannibalised and corrupted. Lords Discordant ceaselessly experiment with these machine sentiences, twisting them into myriad data configurations for different horrific effects, finding new ways to sow the seeds of disruption. Those Lords devoted to Khorne make motivators seethe with burning rage and transmute lubricating oils to viscous blood. Tzeentchian Lords Discordant cause vehicles to twist themselves through unseen folded dimensions, crumpling them into impossibly small heaps of slag. The techno-imperatives crafted by Nurglesque Lords cause vehicles to vent internal gasses, while their outer plating sloughs off like a diseased scab. Perhaps most disturbing are the Slaaneshi Lords Discordant, who are able to rewire machines to feel constant and excruciating pain.

CHAOS SPACE MARINES

The Adeptus Astartes were created as the Emperor's ultimate fighting force. Implanted with the gene-seed of the Primarchs, the Space Marines stand seven feet tall, with thickened bones, two hearts, hyper-dense muscles and all manner of special organs that allow them to survive and fight in the most hostile conditions. They feel little pain and heal wounds at a remarkable rate. Their will is hardened by constant training and fighting, and they battle with dedication and zeal, brooking no hesitation, mercy or cowardice. All of these things combine with the best weaponry and armour in the galaxy to make the Space Marines the most fearsome warriors of the Imperium.

The Chaos Space Marines have all of these strengths and skills, to which are added the power of Chaos and a brutal devotion to the Dark Gods. Ever since the Horus Heresy, Space Marines have been tempted by the path of Chaos, whether for selfish reasons or great ideals. Sundered from the Imperium, having turned their backs on the Emperor, these warriors know that there can be no peace for them, neither forgiveness nor absolution. They are wholly committed to the path they now tread, for good or ill, and they can expect no quarter from former battle-brothers.

The armament of the Chaos Space Marines differs little from that of their loyalist counterparts, for the weapons of the Adeptus Astartes are built to last. Boltguns, in various marks dating back ten thousand years, are their primary weapon, though squads that glorify close assaults and personal combat often favour bolt pistols and ritual knives, chainswords or axes. There is little uniformity between squads; much of the organisation and structure of the force's former Legion or Chapter falls by the wayside as they turn to the path of Chaos. In place of appointed sergeants, the Chaos Space Marines follow the strongest, boldest and most merciless of their brothers. These blood-soaked soldiers seek to become the favoured of the gods and eventually become mighty champions themselves. Their wargear varies dramatically and may include weapons taken as trophies from slain foes as well as arcane equipment carefully maintained since the Horus Heresy. It is the champions of these units that strive the hardest to gain recognition amongst the ranks of the Chaos Space Marines, spilling the blood of mighty foes in single combat in order to draw the gaze of the gods.

HAVOCS

Some Chaos Space Marine squads carry a high proportion of heavy weapons, the better to annihilate the hated foe. Known as Havocs, these squads provide devastating anti-infantry and anti-armour firepower, dominating large swathes of the battlefield with volley after punishing volley.

Such is the blood-pounding thrill of pouring heavy fire into the enemy ranks that many Havocs become obsessed by the power their weapons afford them. They see themselves as gods of the battlefield, blasting the insect vermin of the enemy into oblivion with each twitch of the finger. Over time, a Havoc squad that lingers within the warp may find their weapons becoming physically part of them, extensions of their own body that can

never be laid down or relinquished. Casings blend with flesh, blood plasma becomes highly volatile, and ammunition hoppers become hungry second mouths that snap and growl for more bullets. Eventually, Chaos Space Marine and weapon become one and the same. This is the way of Chaos – where the warp bleeds into realspace, it is not nature that defines form but deadly compulsion – the ugliness in a Havoc's soul is made flesh for all to see.

CHOSEN

The most experienced and dedicated Chaos Space Marines are known as Chosen. Even at a glance, it is obvious that they are favoured amongst the bitter brotherhood of Chaos, for their baroque armour is embellished with forbidden runes and their grimacing helmets give them the aspect of raging Daemons. Equipped with the finest wargear the warband can provide, the Chosen are even more hard-bitten and callous than other Chaos Space Marines, and think nothing of sacrificing the lives of their comrades to increase their own standing with the gods.

Squads of Chosen have many centuries of combat experience to draw upon and are typically found in the vanguard of any attack, fighting from the front where they can earn the most glory and take the greatest spoils. Confident in the extreme, and contemptuous even of those that march to war alongside them, the Chosen bow only to the gods themselves and to the Chaos champions who command their allegiance.

BIKERS

Well armed and highly mobile, Biker squads are mounted on bladed bikes that are possessed of a sinister, mechanical sentience. Even amongst the Chaos Space Marines, their Biker squads have a reputation for cruelty. They are tireless in pursuit of an enemy and will follow a foe night and day to kill or capture them – or in the hope that they will be led to fresh victims. Some have even melded physically with their metal steeds, balefire jetting from their exhausts and oil flowing in their veins.

Bikers are excellent for reconnaissance and launching deadly raids behind enemy lines. Like those of their loyalist counterparts, Chaos bikes are rugged and well-suited to dense terrain, though they have often been twisted by Chaos into something far more unsettling than a simple machine. They are fitted with built-in boltguns that can be fired by the rider without him needing to relinquish control of his steed, and they are often festooned with blades and spurs that dismember opponents as the rider crashes past.

CHAOS POWER ARMOUR

At the time of the Heresy, Crusade-pattern armour was in the process of disappearing from the Legions and being replaced by much-improved iterations of Space Marine power armour. Even so, over the fierce battles to come, both sides were forced to reinstate older marks of armour to replace their losses, as well as scavenging and cannibalising from their fallen brethren.

The armour of the Traitor Legions reflects these turbulent times, often featuring distinctive studded and riveted plasteel plates rather than the smooth ceramite of later designs. Exposed power cables blend with sinew and vein and many Chaos Space Marines individualise their armour with crests, horns, skulls chains and spikes. Space Marines who have only recently turned renegade may have armour that is almost untouched from their Chapter's standard wargear, except for the defilement or removal of symbols of allegiance to the Emperor. Often, though, a Chaos Space Marine's armour will have been changed by long exposure to the warp. It might sprout spines or bony ridges, be covered in a layer of scales or flicker with coruscating energy.

TERMINATORS

Chaos Terminators are heavily armoured veterans clad in debased suits of Tactical Dreadnought armour. They form the elite of their masters' warbands, for though they are ponderous compared to their power armour-clad comrades, nothing short of a dedicated anti-tank laser can stop a Terminator in full stride. These seasoned killers often act as the personal guards of an esteemed champion of Chaos, enforcing the commands of their leader with pitiless efficiency and taking their pick of the spoils after each victory. They tend to be egotistical, brutish and crude, using their physical prowess and the favour of their lord to intimidate other members of their warband. Far from resenting such

behaviour, most Chaos Space Marines simply plot to bring about the day when they can abuse such power for themselves.

As any Space Marine will recount, a suit of Terminator armour is an ancient and sacred artefact to be reverently maintained. The armour is massively bulky and contains a full array of fibre bundles and adamantine rods to support the heavy-gauge plasteel and ceramite plates that form the outer carapace. Legend has it that the Crux Terminatus emblazoned on each suit's shoulder incorporates a fragment of the Emperor's own blessed armour. Each Chapter can muster only a hundred or so of these suits, and not all of their systems are

properly understood, as their workmanship is from a bygone age. Nonetheless, those veterans given the honour of wearing one of these masterpieces to war are the most formidable foot soldiers in the Imperium.

The war suit worn by a Chaos Terminator, on the other hand, is as corrupt and twisted as the traitor within. Where once Imperial insignia were emblazoned upon its pauldrons and greaves, leering death's heads and the eye of Horus now stare accusingly at those brave enough to look upon them. Spiked trophy racks protrude from massive shoulders, the skulls of the enemy a barbaric testament to their wearer's martial prowess. Helmets have grown into bestial masks that sprout great tusks and razored horns, many of which have fused directly into the skulls of their wearers. When twinned with the stomping, heavy gait typical of all Terminators, these adornments conspire to give the impression of a slab-muscled, predatory hulk searching for its next meal.

Terminators are not the swiftest of troops when it comes to ground assault. To counter this, they frequently go to war in smoke-belching Land Raiders that can smash open the fortifications of the enemy. This allows their murderous passengers to reach the foe without having to first navigate the fierce bombardments so often arrayed against them. Much like their loyalist counterparts, Chaos Terminators can also be teleported directly into battle from the vaulted halls of their warships, though they are as likely to use sorcery for such a strike as they are science. The sudden appearance of a unit of Terminators within the enemy's headquarters has spelled the bloody end of many a protracted campaign.

POSSESSED

For some Chaos Space Marines, simply dedicating their souls to the service of the gods is not enough. Those who thirst for power at any cost will offer themselves wholly to Chaos, becoming willing hosts to the immaterial creatures of the warp. Such possession is a lengthy and agonising experience, as the Daemons within them infest their physical forms, moulding them to better suit their peculiar needs.

Those who offer themselves up for possession spend months in rituals of debasement and scarification, preparing their bodies to harbour a daemonic entity. Though the personalities of these half-mad supplicants are subsumed forever, mass possessions are nonetheless great celebrations of the union between the mortal and the daemonic. For the mortal host, a shortcut to exceptional power has been achieved. For the Daemon, the flesh and bone of the host acts as an anchor to the material realm that allows them to exist outside of warp-saturated environments; instead of fading away over time, as with their kin, they remain whole almost indefinitely.

Possessed are easily identified by their grotesque features and mutated bodies; they may have vicious claws, outlandishly warped limbs, tentacles, wings, extra mouths and eyes, or razored talons that can gouge through ceramite and steel. In battle they sometimes appear to flicker in and out of reality or even take different forms from one moment to the next, bounding along in the manner of predatory beasts only to erupt into howling tornadoes of teeth and claws that seem more ethereal storm than mortal man. They are superb trackers, able to perceive the material realm and the empyrean at the same time – they can see fear, taste doubt and feel the greasy psychic stain of despair. Using these uncanny senses, they can even guide the fleets of the Chaos Space Marines through the shifting tides of the warp should they deign to help their mortal allies. However, their primary role – and that which they most relish – is tearing apart their prey in frantic yet inventive displays of violence.

GREATER POSSESSED

Those mortal warriors who commit the most notable acts of monstrosity attract the attention of the most malefic warp beings – those named as Heralds by the Dark Gods. Towering over their fearsome kin, Greater Possessed are not only stronger and far more savage, but radiate an unholy charisma that even pure creatures of the warp recognise. Fellow Daemonkin look upon these deformed champions with great reverence, for they are living proof of the ultimate ascension that awaits them all. With gigantic pincer-claws and scythe-like talons of twisted bone, these malformed abominations slash and tear their prey apart, delighting in the gory carnage they wreak. Every Greater Possessed is a locus of empyric power in realspace, an instrument through which the fell corruptions of the warp are given form. Both mortal and daemonic warriors are driven to an exultant frenzy when they fight alongside these horrifying champions, desperate to claim such eternal honour for themselves with a worthy display of brutality. Yet the Greater Possessed themselves have little interest in the ascension of their allies – what mind they have is fixed on carnage.

RAPTORS

The cruel terror troops known as Raptors consider themselves the elite of the Chaos Space Marine warbands. Their murder squads epitomise what has become of the Assault Marines of the Traitor Legions. Though they were once rare and highly valued Imperial troops, the Raptors have fallen to their own pride and lust for violence. They now roam the galaxy as merciless hunters, relishing the fear they cause as they plummet screaming out of the skies.

Within the Space Marine Legions of old, jump pack troops were relatively rare. Horus knew well the value of the surprise attack, and such was his military genius that the arrival of his Assault Marines was the turning point in dozens of critical battles. They would be held in reserve until the enemy exposed a weakness in its battle line, whereupon entire jump pack companies would plunge into the fray, breaking the foe's defences wide open with meltagun, flamer, bolt pistol and chainsword.

Perhaps it was their habit of preying on lesser warriors that led to the slow corruption of the Assault companies that sided with Horus. Over time, those of their number who ventured in the Eye of Terror grew to love the exhilaration of soaring through the skies a little too much. They became addicted to the thrill of looking down upon the warriors beneath them, and as the rudimentary machine spirits of their jump packs also became corrupted, they melded with their wargear until the power of true flight became theirs. Now there are Raptors whose blood is high-octane fuel that runs through body and wargear alike, whose eyesight is so sharp they can pick out prey from several miles distant, or who can strike from above with the force of a meteor. The Chaos-tainted armour of a Raptor reflects his predatory nature, usually mimicking the appearance of a vicious bird of prey or swooping Daemon. Altered vox-casters protrude from helmet and plate, amplifying the raw hatred of their war cries and better enabling their wearers to terrify their enemies into submission before the final strike.

The Raptors' predilection for sadism and psychological warfare is a dark reflection of the Assault Marine's traditional role. Simple killing is no longer enough. The Raptors want not only to tear apart their prey, but to instil terror in them beforehand – they will go to great lengths to see their grovelling prey's face distorted with fear before the final blow is struck. Wherever the Raptors prowl, ghostly voices and horrific threats are broadcast into enemy comms networks, the skies are haunted by daemonic faces, and evil shrieks echo through the night so that their sleep-deprived quarry is driven to the edge of madness. Needless to say, the Night Lords, a Legion infamous for their terror tactics, attract a great many Raptors to their banner.

Raptors are seen as preening, self-indulgent egotists by many of their brethren, but their unquestionable skill in battle means that champions of Chaos will gladly enlist them nonetheless. There is no battle line or garrison that cannot be demoralised and subsequently shattered by a pack of Raptors. Only once the prey is at its most vulnerable will the Raptors take their grisly prize.

THE HOSTS RAPTORIAL

The thrill of false flight afforded by a jump pack can be addictive, especially to a Chaos Space Marine. Those who have delusions of godhood relish looking down on their prey as if they were little more than insects. As with all things that feel the caress of the warp, like attracts like, and the Raptors of the Traitor Legions only truly respect those who can lead from above. There exist amongst the armies of Chaos those warhosts that attack from on high without exception, a dark mirror of the Adeptus Astartes tactic of launching a planetstrike from low orbit to ensure the maximum impact.

Those Chaos Lords who go to war upon a jump pack's twin pillars of flame are often attended by large warbands of Raptors and Warp Talons. The most influential of these leaders marshal as many airborne Daemon Engines to their cause as they can, using Heldrake Fear Squadrons to eliminate the enemy's anti-air capabilities before the main strike descends. The Night Lords in particular make extensive use of such forces, for they revel in the terror caused by what their victims perceive as a dark flock of vengeful furies from myth come to rend their flesh and claim their souls.

WARP TALONS

When a pack of Warp Talons emerges from the warp, it appears to those on the battlefield below as if daemonic warriors have burst out from nothingness into fiery, vengeful life. Like the stuff of nightmares, they plummet downwards in an explosion of warp fire, tearing into the foe with murderous intent.

Warp Talon packs are comprised of tightly knit groups of horribly altered Chaos Space Marines who possess the ability to slice open the barriers between dimensions. Like their brothers-in-arms, the Raptors, they were once part of the Legiones Astartes Assault companies, though they have followed the path of the predator for so long that they live for nothing more than cutting, slashing and carving apart. This single-minded fixation with the act of severance has been wrought into the very substance of their bodies. In place of its hands and feet, each Warp Talon has a set of crackling swords with supernaturally sharp blades that can temporarily cut through the substance of reality itself.

Having fallen even further from their mortal origins than their Raptor allies, the Warp Talons have long since lost the means to speak, reason or create. The violence they wreak is eloquent enough. A pack of Warp Talons is not employed so much as set loose, for champions of Chaos know that these skyborne assassins respect only the hunt and the kill at hunt's end. Instead, the Warp Talons are given something important to their prey, such as a hank of hair, a loved one's finger bone or a piece of cloth from a favourite item of clothing. It is then that the hunt begins in earnest. Soaring into the skies on plumes of daemonic fire, the Warp Talons depart, already moving as one in their single-minded pursuit. They will not be seen again until their prey is located and battle is joined.

When the din of war resounds through the air, the Warp Talons are attracted to the ephemeral echoes of anger and pain that reverberate through the warp. These ripples in the aether are often refracted within the immaterium, where hunting packs of Warp Talons single out the psychic signature of their prey using senses that a mortal could not comprehend. Once the Warp Talons have closed in upon the emotional reflection of their victim's psyche, they will slice their spirit-sharp talons through the air above their quarry's location, cutting deep wounds in the veil between worlds with their energised claws. In this way, they force their way out from the swirling anarchy of the warp straight into the material dimension.

Though the lesion they slice in the fabric of realspace seals over as soon as the hunting pack has passed through, the mind-shattering nature of their attack is usually enough to stun their prey into inactivity. When the Warp Talons appear in reality they do so in an explosion of empyric flame, a flare of energy that is all colours and none at the same time, and accompanied by a cacophony of hellish cries that blasts all reason and thoughts of order from the mind. This moment of awestruck hesitation is often fatal, for as the Warp Talons hurtle into the ranks of the foe, their hellishly sharp claws part heads from necks and limbs from torsos.

THE FICKLE AEGIS OF THE WARP

Much like the daemonic entities made from the essences of the Ruinous Powers, those wholly claimed by Chaos have a kind of esoteric protection that can protect them from physical blows. A Chaos Space Marine who has sworn his soul to one of the Dark Gods may find an incoming bolt transmuted into scarlet liquid at the last moment, or see a volley of incoming bullets hit home as a shower of writhing grubs. A lascannon beam – potent enough to punch through the hull of a tank – might simply pass through a warp-claimed champion as if he was no more substantial than a phantasm. Similarly a plasma bolt might be caught in an outstretched gauntlet, twisted into a ball of fire, and then consumed by the target without harm.

Truly it is said that the favoured of the Ruinous Powers are part Daemon, for they are supernatural terrors to a man. However, it is just as likely that the empyric forces that protect them from the vagaries of fate will do precisely nothing at a critical moment, especially if the recipient has come to take them for granted. In such contradictions do the Chaos Gods find humour and justice alike.

CULT OF DESTRUCTION

OBLITERATORS

The monstrous warriors of the Obliterator cults are a blasphemy against nature and Machine God alike. Their forms are so altered, so thoroughly conjoined with the tools of war, that every cell in their bodies thrills with a spark of mechanical life. Only the Dark Mechanicum have mastered the complete fusion of metal and flesh, melding the inert and the animate together on a spiritual level in order to form something far greater than mere cybernetics. Because of their Chaos-born powers, Obliterators are capable of not only absorbing weaponry into themselves, but also of manifesting munitions from their titanium-laced flesh.

Each of their number is an inhuman arcano-cyborg whose blood can become roiling plasma, whose internal organs generate electricity, and whose brain is as much cognitive targeting engine as living tissue. In battle, fibre-bundle muscles split apart as blood-slicked gun barrels push through limbs and torsos. Oily fluids boil and drool out of exhaust valves as the crosshair eyes of the Obliterators settle over their prey. With a guttural roar of satisfaction, these lumbering gun-spawn let fly with devastating salvoes that annihilate man and machine alike.

Though cadres of the mysterious Obliterators are thankfully rare, they have an alarming tendency to suddenly appear wherever the fighting is thickest, manifesting in a storm of light before laying waste to their foes. Several theories have been put forward by agents of the Imperium regarding the exact nature of these abominations – some members of the Inquisition believe they are the by-product of a heretical Dark Mechanicum quest to embody the Omnissiah, whilst others proffer the notion that Obliterators are infected with some kind of Daemon-created technovirus. Opponents of the latter theory say that a technovirus could not exist in the way it is claimed, and that simple daemonic possession gives Obliterators their frighteningly powerful abilities. Only the truly learned realise that the term 'technovirus' is a misnomer; it is Chaos itself that mutates and corrupts the machine, just as it moulds and changes the flesh of men.

MUTILATORS

Mutilators are the high priests of the blade and the maul. It is believed that the first of their number were originally Traitor Legion Terminators who specialised in close-quarters fighting, but as with all who harbour an obsession within the warp, they grew to become the incarnation of the murderous desires in their hearts.

Those who dedicate themselves to the act of killing in a melee cannot help but be affected by it. The satisfying impact of a bludgeon smashing an unprotected head, the yielding of flesh to a honed blade, the axe's bloody bite – even the most faithful Space Marine cannot deny that these acts bring a rush to the mind and body alike. A lifetime of unrelenting battle can breed a dangerous need for such acts of violence, and when that period spans several centuries, the effects upon the psyche can be dramatic.

For those who seek refuge in the warp, this psychosis is magnified beyond all reason. Such warriors might begin their descent into madness by constant maintenance of their weapons in between battles, by chaining themselves to their wargear, or by outright refusing to let go of their favoured tools of war under any circumstances. These dangerously focused individuals are easy prey for the corruption of Chaos. Before long, a warrior who yearns too much for the visceral charms of battle may find that he has fused with his weapon, the blade becoming as much a part of him as a hand would be to a normal man. Over time, these assault specialists come to identify more with their weaponry than with their battle-brothers. Disillusioned by the fickle nature of Mankind, they instead strive for the simple purity of the blade. As the years take their toll, such individuals leave their humanity behind altogether.

Mutilators seek not only to commune with the war-spirits of their weapons, but to absorb them, assimilating the warp-spawned power of chainfists, power axes and lightning claws into their own souls and fleshmetal bodies so that they can manifest corrupted versions at will. However, the Mutilators are not content to stop there – eviscerators and bladed siege mauls whirr and clank into being at the ends of their grotesquely muscled arms, bringing death to the enemy. Each kill anoints and empowers the weapon-spirits that each Mutilator manifests, his dagger-sharp teeth bared in glee as he dismembers and crushes the bodies of his foes.

HELBRUTES

Helbrutes are twisted mockeries of the Space Marine Dreadnoughts they used to be, combining the firepower of a small tank with the mind of a frenzied maniac. Each Helbrute holds a living creature within its plated metal chest – a Chaos Space Marine driven over the edge of madness by a never-ending cycle of war.

A Helbrute is piloted by a warrior who has suffered extreme damage on the field of battle. The critically injured warrior is then bound into an amniotic sarcophagus at the walker's heart, connected by nervous system implants and mind impulse units to the controls of the battle engine. However, while loyalist members of the Adeptus Astartes consider it an honour to serve their Chapter for eternity as a Dreadnought, Chaos Space Marines consider such a fate to be little more than a living death – a torturous, mocking punishment from the Dark Gods. They abhor the thought of such a miserable half-life locked away in a dank and imprisoning womb, where they can no longer drink in the sights of battle with their own eyes or feel the kick of a boltgun in their fist. For them, it would be better to die and find final release in the maelstrom of the warp than to spend eternity locked in an adamantine shell.

As a result, most Helbrutes are completely psychotic, even before the warp melds the metal of their prison with the flesh inside. A creeping insanity, mingled with desperation and fury, eats away at them over the long millennia. Between battles, the sarcophagus containing the pilot is disconnected and dragged clear of its armoured shell to lie inert and seething in the darkness. The Helbrute is chained like a beast when it is not actually fighting, for fear that some residue of the pilot's soul may

send it into a berserk rampage. As the ships of a Chaos Space Marine fleet approach their prey, the Helbrute's heavy weapons are prepared and loaded, its power scourges and hammer-like fists are daubed in fresh blood, and its sarcophagus is installed. The madness of the Chaos Space Marine within burns ever fiercer as he rises from his dormancy. Once the fleet's warriors have landed, the Helbrute is unleashed, a lunatic beast of flesh and metal intent upon venting its rage on everything in its path.

> 'No. No! Not the sarcophagus… Khorne damn you, you disloyal curs, just kill me. JUST KILL ME!'
>
> *- Khalos the Ravager, last words prior to Helbrute interment*

CHAOS BATTLE TANKS

CHAOS RHINOS

The Rhino is the most common transport of the Space Marines, and the same can be said of the Heretic Astartes, for this machine is so ruggedly constructed it can see hundreds of years of warfare and still function at peak efficiency. The tank's chassis is based upon a Standard Template Construct, meaning that it is relatively simple to build, maintain and repair. Over the ten thousand years since the Long War began, the Rhino has seen continued use as the favoured transport of the Chaos Space Marines. They will even go so far as to loot them from defeated Imperial armies, though they will burn them clean of Imperial insignia as quickly as possible and festoon the stolen vehicles with spikes, blades and gory trophies taken from the dismembered bodies of their previous owners.

Over time, Chaos Rhinos become encrusted with the paraphernalia associated with their Legion or Renegade Chapter. The tanks of the Word Bearers are often hung with strips of parchment covered in the writings of Lorgar, and incorporate braziers filled with smouldering daemonbone incense, while those of the World Eaters may be ritually daubed with blood before each battle, until they accumulate a thick, multi-layered coat of dried gore.

The Black Legion and the Iron Warriors are particularly well known for launching massed Rhino assaults, bulling obstacles to the side as they close inexorably with their targets. At a single command, the tanks slew to a temporary halt, and the Chaos Space Marines within pile out to level storms of bolter fire at their enemies as their brothers in darkness drive home a killing charge.

CHAOS PREDATORS

The main battle tank of the Legiones Astartes, the Predator is such a versatile war machine that it can thrive in almost any theatre of war. It can be fitted with different weapon loadouts, allowing for anti-armour operations, anti-infantry firepower, or a mixed role depending on the enemy force's disposition. Based upon the tried and true Rhino chassis, the Predator has an armoured turret that can sport a long-barrelled autocannon or twin-linked lascannons, and it can be further armed with the addition of side sponsons mounting more heavy weaponry. By sacrificing all troop carrying capacity, the frontal chassis of the Predator can be reinforced, giving it far greater resilience than its personnel-carrier counterpart.

In a typical assault, Chaos Predators are used to provide fast-moving fire support. Capable of laying down punishingly accurate salvoes of firepower, the battle tank is used to eliminate enemy armour, pave the way for an infantry assault, or throw back enemy squads that attempt to counter-attack. When organised into squadrons, these tanks can change the course of a battle with a coordinated bombardment.

Frequently, the Predators used by the Chaos Space Marines have been in active service for longer than those who march alongside them. They have become embellished with horrific decorations, ragged pennants, leering gargoyles, beast-headed gun muzzles and icons of Chaos, making them as much a statement of their owners' hatred of the Imperium as weapons of war.

CHAOS LAND RAIDERS

The Chaos Land Raider is the heaviest ground vehicle in a Chaos Space Marine army. Its adamantine and ceramite plates can withstand all but the deadliest anti-tank weaponry, and the blessings of the Warpsmiths keep it at peak efficiency. The twin lascannons mounted in each sponson make short work of other vehicles that would dare to attempt to stop its rampage. Once in the thick of the enemy, this metal beast opens the jaws of its assault ramp and disgorges its cargo of bloodthirsty warriors.

The machine spirits that once dwelt inside the cogitators of these Chaos Land Raiders are distorted or forcibly supplanted by daemonic entities, giving these growling, snarling battle tanks a literal life of their own. Even should the driver and gunners of this graven idol of war meet an untimely end it will fight on, relishing its new-found freedom from the agendas of mortal men and pursuing a singular goal instead – the destruction of all order and harmony that falls under its crosshairs.

CHAOS VINDICATORS

Though it is based upon the hull of the Rhino, the Chaos Vindicator sacrifices its transport capacity in favour of reinforced armour and ammunition storage. Such heavy modifications are needed to allow for the massive demolisher cannon mounted on the front of its hull, a siege weapon so large that it occupies much of the area where the transport deck would be located. While it lacks the range of a standard battle cannon, the demolisher is far more potent and can breach a bunker or blast apart a tank with a single shell. Usually protected by an enormous metal siege shield that juts out from its front, the Chaos Vindicator can barge its way into position even under intense enemy fire, grinding towards the walls of a fortified stronghold until its devastating armament comes into range.

Vindicators were used extensively by the Traitor Legions during the Horus Heresy, most notably at the Siege of the Emperor's Palace, and have served the forces of Chaos continuously over the last ten millennia. The Iron Warriors, masters of siegecraft and heavy munitions, are infamous for fielding entire 'linebreaker squadrons' of Vindicators emblazoned with Chaos symbols and adorned with the defaced statuary of cities that have fallen to their assaults. When such tank formations combine their fire, it is as though the gods have spoken, and even a fully garrisoned Fortress of Redemption or Proteus-class battle bunker can be reduced to bloodstained rubble in a single catastrophic salvo.

Kog da Rekka could feel the ground shiver through his hobnailed boots. The spiky gitz were cheating by firing thick smoke from their wagons. The stinking clouds made it hard for his Tankbustaz to land a rokkit, and their aim was pretty bad in the first place. Da Rekka bared his teeth as the hulking black shapes nosed through the yellow-grey fug, engines growling like bad-tempered animals.

'Blow 'em up!' shouted Kog, his throat sore from one too many foul cigars. His fellow hunters let loose a volley, two rokkits engulfing the foremost wagon in a roaring fireball. The rest charged in whooping behind his twin Deff Dreads, their disc-like Tankbusta bombs primed and ready.

Then the Chaos tanks opened fire. The really big one, the one Kog had set his sights on, sent two columns of ruby light lancing through the mist. Each one hit a Dread in the midsection. One of the walkers went down flailing, the other started limping in a circle. Then the turreted wagons flanking the big tank opened fire, heavy weapons blowing apart the charging Tankbustas in welters of blood.

The ground was really shaking now. Kog felt much the same. He hefted his tankhammer as the big wagon opened its jaws, sponson guns mowing down the last of the Tankbustas. Then its passengers stormed out, all skulls and blades.

Time to win a new trophy, thought Kog. Or become one.

CHAOS CULTISTS

The teeming masses of the Imperium have colonised the galaxy from end to end. Trillions of souls labour night and day in an increasingly hostile universe. Miles-high hive cities boil with overpopulation, dense hab-complexes sprawl across continents, and industrial worlds grind and churn by the efforts of uncounted workers under the steely gaze of their high-handed overlords. But the adepts of the established order cannot be everywhere at once. A regime as restrictive and oppressive as the Imperium provides fertile ground for insurrection, and there are those that would foster this discontent for their own black ends. Rebellion festers in the foetid underbelly of almost every civilised world, a fire just waiting for a spark. Where the flames of heresy are given fuel, Chaos is quick to follow, turning desperate men into worshippers of the Dark Gods.

The cultists of Chaos can be found, in one form or another, almost anywhere the Imperium has spread. At first glance, they are indistinguishable from normal men, but under their clothes, their flesh is tattooed and branded with sigils that hurt the eyes of any faithful who look upon them. When the Chaos Space Marines come to a planet, the true colours of the cultists are revealed. The powers of darkness are ever quick to promise glory, and even the lowliest initiate knows that to fight alongside such legendary warriors is to court the gaze of the gods. Improvised armour is donned and long-hidden weapons are broken out as the cultists prepare to overthrow the Imperium one hab-block at a time. Rag-tag companies band together under the demagogues that arrive in their midst, for the everyday life of an Imperial citizen is usually so hopeless that even the hint of a new order can be intoxicating. When open war breaks out, screaming gangs of cultists rush into battle armed with primitive solid-shot weapons, the largest of their number toting heavy stubbers and industrial flamers. Despite their primitive wargear, Chaos Cultists are often able to drown a superior foe through sheer weight of numbers and a fierce desire to tear open the belly of the Imperium.

As the witch-hunting Ordo Hereticus is keen to point out, Chaos Cultists can come from almost any background. Psychotic soldiers, cut-throat hive gangers, decadent nobles, Guardsman deserters, persecuted abhumans and sewer-dwelling mutants all turn to Chaos in order to improve their lot. After all, even a man who has nothing can still barter away his soul. The gifts received by the most powerful cultists can be just as strange as those granted to their Chaos Space Marine masters; a favoured devotee might have muscles of living steel, flailing sucker-tentacles in place of a tongue, or the horned head of a mindless beast. Regardless of their station, each of these dangerous malcontents trains their mind and body for the day when the favoured of the gods will lead them to a darkly glorious future, when they can rise up against the hated order of the Imperium and set the galaxy aflame.

'An eternity of glory awaits you!' shouted Dar Kadran, his spined rod of office held high as if to catch the eye of some heavenly presence. 'Forwards, my immortal ones! Burn them with the fire that rages in your soul!'

Armandus let loose a fierce and joyful war cry. His fellow Brothers of Infinity followed suit, charging with their stolen autoguns blazing at the armoured giants silhouetted on the crest of the ridge. Muzzle flashes of amber flame lit the loyalists as they returned fire. Each hit was a fresh kill.

A bolt struck Koralodd, detonating with a loud thump to spray gore across all those nearby. Armandus spared the scattered bodies of the fallen Brothers little thought. They knew the risks. As Dar Kadran always said, glory was not won without sacrifice.

Taking a deep breath of demi-frenzon from his rebreather, Armandus stormed up the blood-thick mud of the ridge. His legs felt like tireless pistons powered by faith and hatred, his heirloom blade like his bloodlust given form. Soon he would cut down one of these giants himself, cut off his head, and offer it up to the Dark Lords.

Something huge and invisible hit Armandus in the shoulder. He lurched back. Then everything went red, his head ringing as agony blossomed with mind-shattering intensity. Through a haze of pain, he saw Dar Kadran stride past, the fleshy wreck that used to be Koralodd held before him as a human shield.

'You promised glory,' gasped Armandus, his vision fading fast.

'On the other side, you shall witness it,' spat Dar Kadran, his aura crackling black around him. 'Just wait and see.'

CHAOS SPAWN

Although physically powerful and extremely resilient, Chaos Spawn are insane, mewling creatures with no mental powers or self-awareness. Their former intelligence has been sacrificed to their failed ambition. Many a champion of great promise has ended up as a seething mound of bone and blubber, monstrous and screaming with lunatic rage.

The Ruinous Powers are generous but erratic with their favours. When blessing one of their followers, a Dark God might make them stronger, tougher, faster, astonishingly beautiful, hyper-intelligent or otherwise improve their lot in the world. Just as likely, the Chaos God may feel their loyal subject would benefit from their toes falling off, having an eye sprout in their navel or being transformed into a dribbling and imbecilic mountain of flesh. Most Gifts of Chaos take the form of some physical mutation. The more of these gifts a champion receives, the more potentially disastrous their cumulative effects can be – even the body of a Chaos Space Marine can only withstand so many mutations before he passes the point of no return.

Any champion of Chaos, regardless of prestige, can find himself one step ahead to becoming a Chaos Spawn, for the gods are fickle. A champion who does not earn himself the ultimate reward of daemonhood will surely become a Spawn unless he dies by some other means first.

Such is the fate of the Chaos champion – those that survive are destined either for everlasting, diabolical glory or an ignominious end as a slavering heap of limbs and protrusions.

The outward appearance of a Chaos Spawn is utterly unpredictable and frequently changes over the course of a battle. No two are alike, and their make-up owes as much to the capricious energies of Chaos as it does to functionality. A Spawn may have several sets of limbs, crab claws or tentacles, armour that bulges beneath the skin, tattered and useless wings, clumps of eye-stalks that wave like grass in a wind, a sinewy prehensile neck or a gaping maw of needle-thin teeth. Some Spawn have insectoid bodies or heads, others resemble featureless quivering mounds of inverted muscle covered with spines that drip acidic pus. All, however, are hideous to behold and deadly to face in battle.

DAEMON ENGINES

Daemon Engines are gigantic battle machines that prowl on mighty piston-driven limbs. To compare a Daemon Engine to an ordinary vehicle is folly, for each of these beasts has its own malevolent sentience rather than a crew. Bound within the battle-scarred metal of each Daemon Engine is the essence of a raging warp entity, imprisoned in a physically indomitable body in order to better serve the Chaos Space Marines in their long and bitter war.

The Imperium has little concept of how these affronts to sanity came into being. Even amongst the ranks of the Chaos Space Marines, there are few who understand how these monsters are created. Only the brotherhood of the Warpsmiths can bind a Daemon into a machine. Using corrupt rituals and forbidden alchemy, adepts of the dark arts can force immaterial spirits into a physical shell. It is the Warpsmiths that bring Daemon Engines into being, from minor gunbeasts to Chaos Titans. Beyond the soul forges of the immaterium, creatures of the warp are bound in nooses of rope woven from the hair of murderers or with chains fashioned of scrimshawed bone. These captive Daemons are dragged screaming into the flame-hearted citadels of the Dark Mechanicum. In the molten heat of the forges, Warpsmiths trap these Daemons within the rune-bound hulls of the giant metal abominations they have created. The screaming fiends must then be bludgeoned into submission until the time of battle is at hand. Dozens of machine-thralls are lost with the creation of each beast – a minor setback given the raw power these monsters provide.

FORGEFIENDS

The Forgefiend was originally devised to sow death amongst enemy forces from afar. Roughly centauroid in form, the torso of this Daemon Engine boasts twin weapon-mounts that carry hell-forged parodies of Imperial armaments. The most common Forgefiends are created with pairs of hades autocannons in place of their primary limbs, rotary gun-clusters that allow them to scythe down masses of enemy troops and even lightly armoured vehicles with contemptuous ease.

When a Daemon Engine is forged in the citadels of the warp, part of the fire that burns there is transferred into the heart of the engine itself. It is this brimstone-scented furnace that powers the engine's mechanical motion, but also that provides the baleful energies it pours into the ranks of its foe. It is not normal bullets that fly from the muzzles of the Forgefiend's guns. Instead, it spits out red-hot phosphor shells that are extruded from the twisting, convoluted cables that churn and writhe inside. Hidden intestinal tracts feed steaming, large-bore ammunition into each autocannon's chambers, each projectile bearing the taint of daemonic flame. Forgefiends can devour metal just as easily as flesh; when well fed, they can maintain a glowing salvo of shells for several minutes before stopping to gorge-load more raw materials into their interior feed-hoppers. The pulsing energies of a Forgefiend's furnace are not always employed to produce solid ammunition. Some sport flex-sheathed plasma weapons of ancient

design, weapons so large they would look more at home on a light aircraft than a land-bound walker. Those Daemon-beasts the Imperium have nicknamed Cerberites bear no less than three of these ectoplasma cannons, one mounted on each weapon-limb and one jutting out from their maws. These cannons were once prized artefacts, dating back to before the Heresy, but the Warpsmiths have perverted them into something far worse. Gargoyle-mouthed and drizzling balefire, the searing energies these devastating weapons hurl outwards are a hybrid of plasma and burning ectoplasm channelled straight from the Forgefiend's tainted heart.

MAULERFIENDS

The Daemon Engines known as Maulerfiends thunder towards the foe like monstrous attack dogs loosed from the leash. Their eyes glow with balefire as ectoplasmic drool drizzles from their fanged maws. Their thick front limbs end in articulated claws powerful enough to tear a Dreadnought limb from limb. Should they catch a squad of infantry, they will scissor them apart or crush them into paste with a flex of their massive talons.

Also known as Stalkers or Scalers, Maulerfiends have strength and agility enough to climb sheer surfaces – nowhere is safe from these Daemon Engines once they have the scent of their prey in their olfactory vents. If even a single Maulerfiend makes it to the walls of an enemy emplacement, it will clamber across the vertical faces, tapping with its claw-pincers until it finds a weak point before peeling open a large section and forcing its way inside. Because of their utility in siege warfare, Maulerfiends are used extensively by the Warpsmiths of the Iron Warriors. Even the most redoubtable Imperial strongholds will fall into deathly silence

once a Maulerfiend has breached the walls and set upon the fleshy bounty within.

Some Warpsmiths and Chaos Lords see their Maulerfiends as a feudal king might see his fiercest war hounds, and set them loose on heavily armoured targets with much the same sense of prideful satisfaction. When a Maulerfiend has latched onto its quarry, its destruction is all but assured. The magma cutters that protrude from the Maulerfiend's torso can focus the anger that burns inside it into a white-hot jet of flame that can melt through the thick rockcrete of a bastion wall. Many an Imperial Titan has been felled by a pair of Maulerfiends clambering up its legs and shearing through its joints with pinpoint energy blasts and raking adamantine claws.

Some Maulerfiends serve their masters as daemonic battering rams that barrel headlong through the enemy lines. They defend themselves from counter-attacks with segmented tendrils that whip out from their midsections to crush and confound those who would attempt to stay their advance. These 'Lashers' gorge themselves on the hot flesh of their victims until their blunt muzzles drip with blood, even though they can take no sustenance from the flesh of mortals.

HELDRAKES

Heldrakes are winged Daemon Engines that plummet out of the skies like living comets, hurtling towards enemy aircraft and crashing claws-first into them from above. Each is a vicious, hell-forged predator; a Heldrake takes cruel joy in diving down upon the unsuspecting air support of the enemy in order to shred them to pieces with its scything wings and rune-carved talons.

Heldrakes were once noble fighter craft flown by Space Marine pilots, though they have become something far more hideous. The energies of the warp have granted them a form better suited to the predatory role their twisted spirits savour. Though Heldrakes have the sweeping wings and powerful engines common to all Chaos fighter craft, the resemblance ends there, for their aspect is one of flying daemonic reptiles more than any ordinary aircraft.

The miasma of wrongness that surrounds these fell creatures is due not only to their monstrous hybridisation, but also to the keening anguish of what remains of the individuals that used to pilot the machines. The steersmen inside the Heldrakes, having become consumed by the power and independence granted them by their fighter craft, have literally become one with their vehicles. At first, the transformation is of the body – the pilots shrink back into the interiors of their machines until they see with the craft's auto-senses and speak with its vox-grilles. Eventually, as the machines themselves achieve daemonic sentience, the transformation affects the pilots' souls. After so many centuries swooping through the warp as pitiless hunters, the steersmen's spirits meld with that of their war engines until they are entirely subsumed. The pilots' physical forms become atrophied, foetal balls that burn deep in the cores where natural beasts would keep their hearts. Trapped and subservient to the murderous desires of the Daemons with which they share their prisons, the withered, blackened pilots scream in the darkness, their trauma and rage magnified by the vox-arrays of the Heldrakes into haunting cries.

Often, the first sign of a full-scale Chaos Space Marine invasion will come in the form of an attack by Heldrakes. These metallic monstrosities traverse the void between worlds by clinging to the underside of Chaos Space Marine attack ships, wings folded protectively around themselves in the manner of bats and piston-driven claws clamped onto the fuselage above. Umbilical cables, sheathed in organic webbing, probe outward from each Heldrake's body to burrow through the host warship's outer surface, drawing away energy as leeches draw blood. When the warships near low orbit, the Heldrakes detach themselves, unfurling their wings as they plummet towards the airspace of the victim planet. Some will soar through the skies as heralds of the destruction to come, retractable weapons pushing out from their gullets and spitting volleys of red-hot bullets that cut down the scrambling, earthbound defenders below. Others prefer to plunge through the clouds into the crucible of battle, screaming in savage joy as they crash headlong into the fight.

THE HELSCOURGE 'ABOMINATION'

What daemonic essence drives the Heldrake known as *Abomination*, none can say, for the beast-machine broke its bonds and slaughtered its Warpsmith creators upon the very hour of its binding. It has been the terror of Imperial air crews for centuries, a nightmare creature shrouded in horror stories. From hollow Cerberos to the acid veils of Nachtghast, *Abomination* has torn its victims from the skies with unrestrained savagery and drawn other Heldrakes in its wake.

VENOMCRAWLERS

Pounding forwards upon bladed limbs come the horrors known as Venomcrawlers. Grotesque amalgams of metal, flesh and daemonic entities, these monstrosities hiss and snarl as they scuttle towards their prey. Fleshy tongues flap from snarling maws and soulflayer tendrils lash back and forth, all tasting the air for the scent of their enemies' fear. Upon locking onto their target the Venomcrawlers emit an ear-splitting screech. Pent-up warp energy is channelled into their excruciator cannons, coalescing into hails of solid shot that rip through entire ranks of armoured foes with ease. With their guns still screaming the Daemon Engines close ground on their victims, using their eviscerating claws to prise open vehicles and skewer those within. Soulflayer tendrils thrash frantically, mangling bodies and flensing them of their essence. As the Venomcrawlers continue to butcher, their fanged mouths gape ever wider, drawing the souls of those slain into their vast mechanical abdomens.

Like other Daemon Engines, Venomcrawlers are created by the Warpsmiths of the Dark Mechanicum. Their spider-like frames are wrought in unhallowed forge halls and profane flesh-factories, and through heretical ritual parasitic entities are drawn forth from the warp to infest these horrifying machines. During such a ritual, the strongest Daemon presence is bound to the structure of the Venomcrawler in a state of inseparable symbiosis, while lesser entities are simply devoured. As more Daemons are absorbed its metallic form distends hideously to accommodate them, creating a reservoir of empyric energy within its swollen body.

Upon completion, Venomcrawlers continue to haunt the cavernous halls of the creators' factories, burrowing into and nesting within the warp-drenched superstructures. From there they wait for the telltale scent of other daemonic entities that have been drawn into realspace by Warpsmiths and Masters of Possession. Should these empyric beings somehow escape the binding rituals or burst from their hosts, the Venomcrawlers emerge to hunt them down, devouring them whole and storing the raging spirits within their bulbous bodies. It is this daemonic energy that powers the Venomcrawlers' formidable weaponry, and when such wayward entities are in short supply the war machines will turn to other sources of sustenance, consuming Daemonkin, Chaos Sorcerers or Heretic Astartes to remain well fed.

Venomcrawlers are uniquely valued both off and on the battlefield. Not only can their repositories of stored warp energy be siphoned in order to create fresh Daemon Engines, but they can be used in the thick of combat to weaken the fabric of reality. Masters of Possession are particularly adept at drawing upon this reservoir to lure the daemonic servants of the Chaos Gods into existence. At battle's end these Daemons are hastily consumed by the Venomcrawler, their essences used to replenish its depleted warp stores.

DEFILERS

Defilers are truly massive beasts of war, twice the size of most other Daemon Engines and with a temperament to match. The ground shivers and melts as they stalk towards their foes on six massive, segmented legs, their great pincer-arms twitching and snipping with an impatient need to slice through warm flesh. The Defiler's crab-like body supports a daemonic torso that carries an array of deadly weaponry, ranging from reaper autocannons to racks of highly explosive missiles. It is the battle cannon mounted in its chest turret, however, that is undoubtedly its most potent armament. Each hell-forged shell that thunders out from its growling muzzle is capable of crippling a squad of Space Marines in a single earth-shaking blast.

The Warpsmiths who create these nightmarish constructions originally devised them to be walking artillery pieces, though their obsession with destruction soon saw their creations becoming ever more bestial and aggressive. Over time, the multi-legged chassis that bears the Defilers to war has been adapted to include shearing claws and spiked armour plates. Its extremities are often fitted with subsidiary weapons such as modified autocannons, heavy flamers and combi-weapons that spew firepower as the Daemon Engine storms forward.

Those foes fortunate enough to survive a Defiler's barrage of shells must then face its full fury at close quarters. Built with piston-driven claws to grab and crush the enemy, and boasting whirring blades or whip-like flails mounted on articulated limbs, the Defiler charges into the foe, crushing and grinding as it smashes aside all opposition. Its mechanical growls drown out the cries of the wounded and dying; trampled corpses and severed limbs are left scattered in a red path behind it as the Defiler rampages through the enemy's ranks.

Like many of the Warpsmiths' creations, a Defiler's animus is provided by a bound Daemon of Chaos. When the immortal ire of this imprisoned entity is raised, the Defiler powers forwards on its clanking legs, spewing death with its guns. The Defiler rejoices in battle, for only then can it enjoy the blissful release of slaughter – once the feeble warriors of the Corpse God have been crushed, the Defiler will once more be bound in runic chains by its masters and dragged hissing back to the forges until it is needed once more.

'Daemonic fury, bound into the shell of a metal beast and set loose upon the galaxy. Tell me, mortal – have you ever seen such a glorious sight?'
    - Warpsmith Vhostokh, Scourge of Diesos

LORDS OF SKULLS

Grinding across the battlefield on rumbling tracks, the Lord of Skulls towers over its terrified foes. The very ground cracks apart in its wake, yawning chasms gaping wide to vomit skulls and fire onto the battlefield. Given life by the raging spirit of a Bloodthirster bound within its hull, and powered by the boiling blood of murderers, this unholy engine of war is death to all who stand before it. Its devastating guns reduce swathes of victims to ruin, drowning them in jets of red-hot gore or burying them under rains of gnashing skulls. As it ploughs through the enemy ranks, the Daemon Engine wields its roaring cleaver with a speed and skill that is horrifying in something so huge. Entire ranks of enemy warriors are swept away with a single swing, tanks and monstrous beasts swatted through the air like toys. Even towering war engines such as Stompas or Titans are made to look clumsy and sluggish as the Lord of Skulls hacks off their limbs and tears open their armoured torsos amid blossoms of dirty flame. Few warriors can face the Lord of Skulls and live, for it is a machine of absolute destruction.

Being the brazen vessels of Bloodthirsters, many Lords of Skulls are worshipped by the Daemonkin, and followed into battle as living altars of Khornate worship. Their track guards will be heaped with skulls and runic fetishes, offerings made by the warriors who charge to war in their shadow. Their every deed is met by howls of adulation from the blood-mad throng, the Daemonkin inspired to new heights of fanatical devotion by the Lord of Skulls' unstoppable rampage. The renegades of the Wrath pay especial heed to rumours of a Lord of Skulls rampaging across the material dimension, seeking it out and fighting in its wake, the better to see one of Khorne's masterpieces in action. Most warp entities rage against their incarceration in a Daemon Engine, but there are those few that see their cage as the perfect weapon. This is most common amongst Bloodthirsters of the eighth rank, some of whom see the Lord of Skulls as a suit of armour within which they may wage war on the denizens of realspace.

KHORNE BERZERKERS

It was the gruesome experiments of Angron, Primarch of the World Eaters, that led to the creation of the first Berzerkers. By the ritual lobotomisation of his warriors, he removed all sense of fear and danger and then heightened the rush his soldiers experienced in combat. When the Legion swore itself to Khorne, the Berzerkers were no longer bound by Imperial battle doctrine and were given full rein to exercise their bloodthirsty skills. They have since become the ultimate close combat shock troops, entering an uncontrollable frenzy in the heat of battle.

Those who wish to fully dedicate themselves to Khorne usually join the World Eaters to undergo the complex psycho-surgery they employ. Once the procedure is complete, they are one with their angry god, feeling nothing but the desire to kill, maim and burn. After the World Eaters Legion disbanded during the fighting on Skalathrax, most Berzerkers formed separate warbands, and many bastardised practices of lobotomisation spread to other Chaos Space Marine forces with them. Abaddon, in particular, has recruited a number of highly skilled Berzerker-surgeons to his cause, and only the Black Legion is even close to the World Eaters in their perfection of this barbaric procedure.

Khorne Berzerkers are savage fighters who revel in the bloodiest hand-to-hand fighting they can find. In their perpetual quest to offer up blood and skulls to Khorne, they carry many vicious close combat weapons into battle. Many wield roaring, adamantine-bladed chainaxes, although the chainsword is equally favoured. The champions that lead each warband can sometimes be seen hefting heavy, baroque weapons lined with diamond-hard teeth that can chew through vehicles to get at the crew inside. Ritual knives and scimitars are often worn into battle, the blades of which are only ever used to hack heads from necks.

After they have decapitated every nearby enemy soldier, the warriors of Khorne will even take the skulls of their own fallen and offer them to their brazen god before plunging back into the fray. The stark truth is that the brethren of the Blood God care little how they spill the blood of those around them. As far as the Berzerkers are concerned, bare fists, a heavy rock or sharpened teeth will do if nothing else is available!

All Berzerkers of Khorne relish their role as the Blood God's sacred destroyers, and are fanatical in the extreme. The warp-fuelled anger of these psychopathic warriors drives them into an endless frenzy of action. Those who face them in battle disappear under a rain of heavy blows, each potent enough to shear limbs and shatter shields. Their delight in pain and death is so strong that they have been known to attack their comrades in a blind rage and, if no other opponent is present, even to fall upon their own weapons as sacrifices to Khorne.

PLAGUE MARINES

Plague Marines are Chaos Space Marines who have sworn themselves to Nurgle, the Chaos God of pestilence and entropy. The first Plague Marines were warriors of the Death Guard Legion, trapped in the warp upon their spaceships when the virulent Destroyer Plague struck their fleet. Mortarion and his Legion offered themselves up to the service of the Lord of Decay in return for their lives. Their bodies became bloated and swollen with the corruption festering within them, but they no longer felt the agony of the warp-pox and did not die from its horrific symptoms.

Since then, many Space Marines have dedicated themselves to Nurgle, though few achieve the vaunted ranks of the Death Guard. Those who truly wish to join this most foetid of cadres must first swear loyalty to the Primarch Mortarion – only then will Nurgle bestow upon them the corrupting ague that created the Plague Marines. Outside of the Death Guard, a favoured few Sorcerers of Nurgle know the secrets of the Plague Marines, and Abaddon of the Black Legion has won many of these spellcasters to his cause. In return for fealty and long service, these blight-mages will bestow their pestilent gifts in the Warmaster's name.

Regardless of allegiance, all Plague Marines have disgusting, rotted bodies that stink of decay. The putrescent slime that oozes from their many weeping sores corrodes their armour and burns their skin, but despite their horrific disfigurements, the Plague Marines are fearsome warriors indeed. Their rotting brains are inured to the agony of bodily corruption, making them all but immune to the pain or debilitation caused by the weapons of the enemy. Not for nothing are these repugnant footsoldiers considered the most resilient of all the Chaos Space Marines.

The Plague Marines prefer short-ranged firefights, where they can truly appreciate the festering carnage they inflict upon their enemies even as they laugh off the bolts and las-blasts directed back at them. The blessed reek of corruption, the sight of freshly suppurating flesh and the blossoming gore of an infected wound – these are things to be grateful for. Those who do not appreciate

Grandfather Nurgle's bounty are soon laid low. Should the enemy close to within arm's reach, the Plague Marines will attack with plague-riddled knives, and even hurl toxic blight grenades – vile inventions containing virulent toxins that eat away at armour and fill the air with thick clouds of blinding spores. The most ostentatious blight grenades are 'death's heads' made from the severed remains of fallen enemies, each cranium filled to the brim with a cocktail of disease before being sealed with ancient wax.

As well as fighting at the behest of the Lords of Chaos, the Plague Marines dedicate their lives to spreading corruption and decay across the galaxy. The fleets of Nurgle that spew from the warp spread contagion and pestilence across dozens of star systems. Once the plague ships are abandoned or their crews finally destroyed, the hulks float back to the warp and eventually, perhaps guided by the hand of Nurgle himself, find their way back to a plague planet, where they are re-crewed for a new wave of attacks.

THE CLOUD OF FLIES

During a plague ship's journey through the warp, the interior of the craft erupts with large, furry black flies that fill its holds with their decaying carcasses. When the plague ship reaches a world, the Plague Marines disembark to make planetfall. As soon as their transports' hatches open, a thick cloud of insects is released, ready to spread its foulness over a virgin planet. The fly is sacred to Nurgle, for it feasts upon the rotten and the foul. Even one such beast can carry upon its little limbs a cornucopia of infections and viruses, spreading the gifts of contagion to everything blessed by its visitations. When they come on in a great swarm, these diminutive creatures can spread a plague with incredible speed, infecting, infesting, hatching and multiplying in celebration of Nurgle's bounteous cycle with each new day. The symbol of the fly is therefore common amongst the Plague Marines, with elements of its form echoed on the mutant bodies of the Death Guard, Nurgle's chosen sons.

NOISE MARINES

The origin of the Noise Marines goes back to the days and nights when Fulgrim and his Emperor's Children first heeded the silky whispers of Slaanesh, just before the outbreak of the Horus Heresy. Claiming inspiration from the tribesmen of Davin, Horus introduced Fulgrim and his chief lieutenants to the practice of elaborate feasting and drinking, including the use of exotic narcotics and indulgence in other pleasurable diversions.

Entranced by the ecstatic celebrations, the officers of the Emperor's Children took these debased customs back to the rest of their warriors. In this way, the cult of Slaanesh took root in the Legion. Ever since then, the Emperor's Children have sought to indulge every excess and depravity they can imagine, pushing the boundaries of their minds as far as they can as they hone their bodies to the limit of blissful endurance.

As just one example of the rewards granted by the Prince of Pleasure to those who worship him, a Noise Marine's hearing is a thousand times more sensitive than normal. They can distinguish the subtlest pitch in tone and volume, but are only able to enjoy the most deafening of cacophonies. Such raucous sensory input electrifies the Noise Marine's brain, causing extreme emotional stimulation that makes all other sensations seem pale and worthless. The louder and more discordant the noise, the more extreme the emotional reaction provoked. Only the din of battle and screams of the dying can truly stir a Noise Marine's attention for long. On the battlefield, his mind ceases to function normally and instead becomes a mere receptacle for the sensations ignited by the music of the apocalypse, thrilling to hear the shrieks of the wounded as they dance upon the path of destruction.

Regardless of faction, Noise Marines wear armour painted in various bold colours, as their senses are so distorted that only the most extravagant shades and patterns register to their minds. Though the staccato bark and blast of the boltgun is music to the Noise Marine's ears, many specialise in the use of a variety of outlandish sound-based weapons. The most common of these is the sonic blaster. The champions of these twisted hedonists instead use the blastmaster and the doom siren, each of which produces a series of deafeningly loud attacks that disintegrate the target with extreme-frequency psychosonic waves

SONIC WEAPONRY

The weapons of the Noise Marines are surreal indeed, so peculiar that their energies can blast through solid walls without losing potency. They are not fired by the twitch of a trigger so much as played like hellish musical instruments, their bursts of psychically resonating noise sliding, thumping and screeching across a dizzying spectrum of sound. By holding his ground, a Noise Marine can coax a deeper, more sustained frequency, or a discordant wail that can literally shake its target apart. Alternatively, should the wielder be overcome with the need to taste the deathly results of his sonic barrages first hand, he can let fly a wave of crippling harmonics even as he strides towards his victims. These salvoes of killing noise hammer the enemy with explosive crescendos that can burst eyeballs and rupture internal organs no matter how well protected the target.

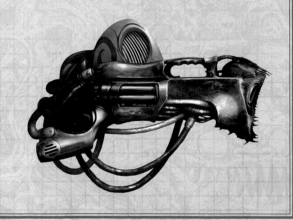

LUCIUS THE ETERNAL
BLADE OF AEONS

Many millennia ago, Lucius was a Space Marine of the Emperor's Children Legion, following his Primarch, Fulgrim, across the galaxy in the name of the Emperor. Forsaking all experience other than the art of combat, Lucius bore the scars of battle with pride and, over time, he began to equate pain with success. By the time the Emperor's Children had been seduced by Horus' rebellion, Lucius had cut deep lines across his face, head and chest, linking his scars in a maze of irregular patterns that distorted and deformed his features. Lucius slowly descended into madness. He was compelled by the whispers in his mind to commit ever more extreme acts, furthering an intense obsession with being the perfect swordsman.

Lucius continued to distinguish himself in the service of his Primarch as the Legion descended into Chaos worship. He fought with incredible speed and skill in the gladiatorial contests Fulgrim held when the Legion was travelling from world to world. Lucius was almost invincible, a force of nature that could not be bested. The champion remained undefeated until he was finally slain fighting the infamous Lord Commander Cyrius.

Slaanesh was loath to let such a promising protégé slip into oblivion. Over the next few weeks, the artificer armour Commander Cyrius wore began to warp and change. Cyrius' hair fell out in clumps, and dark lines appeared under his flesh, slowly pushing through his skin as a maze of scar tissue. Soon, Lucius had emerged completely. All that remained of his executioner was a screaming, writhing face, subsumed for eternity into Lucius' armour.

Lucius now stalks the galaxy as an arrogant slaughterer who can never truly be killed. Whoever slays him and takes even a moment of satisfaction from the act will find themselves transforming, slowly and painfully, into Lucius. The tortured visages of those who once killed him writhe within his armour, affording the swordsman endless gratification. His ornate sabre and sentient whip have tasted the blood of champions and kings across the galaxy, and he leads his debauched warhost with total confidence, welcoming death with as much passion as he inflicts it upon his foes.

'Brothers! Welcome to the feast!' screamed Lucius, the faces in his armour shrieking a dissonant echo. He watched hungrily as more silver-armoured Space Marines piled forwards into the breach, a tall-crested captain with a chainsword amongst them. Lucius' sword lashed out at the closest foes, arcs of ruby-red blood decorating the gnarled faces of his armour.

The path to the Captain was suddenly clear. The challenger lunged, but Lucius parried, laughing. The next blow was a feint. The buzzing chainsword sneaked beneath his guard, shrieking as it bit into Lucius' shin. Lucius hooted with mock fear as his whip swept down with blurring speed, snatching away the Captain's pistol as he raised it for a killing shot.

The shadows cast by the fortress coiled and writhed around Lucius as he dodged and blocked, the blows of his opponent coming hard and fast. Around them the breach was crammed with bodies; blood trickled from split ceramite, skulls were laid open to the air. As Noise Marines raced along the battlements towards them, Lucius tired of his sport. He turned a parry into a riposte, and the Captain fell, headless, amongst his men.

FABIUS BILE

THE PRIMOGENITOR

Fabius Bile is accursed throughout the galaxy and a renegade even from his own Legion. He claims to have unlocked the secrets of the Emperor's work in the creation of the Primarchs. Formerly of the Emperor's Children, Bile's fascination was always with the mysteries of life, not death. Amidst the carnage of the Heresy, Bile aided the Emperor's Children in their inexorable journey into the embrace of Slaanesh. He altered their brain chemistry to sharpen their senses and connected their pleasure centres more directly to their nervous systems so that every stimulus would bring them unholy joy.

Bile left Terra before Horus' defeat, accompanied by a retinue of altered followers. He moved through the war-torn Imperium like a shard of glass through an intestinal tract, selling his services to rebel commanders for prisoners, genetic samples and ancient technologies. Many ambitious overlords came to rue the day they let Bile experiment on their armies, until his acts of genocide and other atrocities sickened even the most deranged maniacs. He eventually found his way to the Eye of Terror, where he offered his services to the highest bidders, promising the champions of Chaos vile cures for their problems. There he set up a new base of operations upon a crone world. Once, it had been home to the best and brightest of the Eldar civilisation; now it was a darkened, twisted place of crawling madness.

Bile's knowledge of alchemy and genetic manipulation can be attested to by every planet he has had contact with, for he has left a trail of foul deviants and twisted abominations wherever his ships have landed. Most of Bile's experiments end with his subjects dead or so horribly deformed they might wish for death. Yet the altered specimens of Bile's efforts exhibit strength many times greater than the human norm. These are Bile's proudest creations, the New Man that forms the pinnacle of his foul art.

> 'If a man dedicates his life to good deeds and the welfare of others, he will die unthanked and unremembered. If he exercises his genius bringing misery and death to billions, his name will echo through the millennia for a hundred lifetimes. Infamy is always preferable to ignominy.'
>
> *- Fabius Bile*

THE CLONEFATHER

The shattered Traitor Legions making their home in the Eye of Terror have particular need of Fabius Bile's skills. His augmented warriors and bio-magicks can give a warband a vital edge, and cloned warriors and slaves are put to good use on a hundred battlefields. Yet it was the skills Bile once learned as an Apothecary of the Emperor's Children that are most precious to the lords of Chaos. The Traitor Legions need the ability to extract the progenoid glands of the fallen in order to create new Chaos Space Marines, and in this strange art Bile is undoubtedly pre-eminent. Without such skills, the Long War would slowly grind to a halt, and the fires that Horus had lit would go out forever. With so much influence at his behest, Fabius Bile has negotiated cunning if fragile bargains with the Daemon Primarchs, selling his secrets to each of them but refusing to aid one more than any other. In this way the Primogenitor ensures his position at the heart of a web of influence that spans across the Eye of Terror and beyond. Of late he has used his leverage to a singular end – the capture of the Primaris Space Marines sighted across the galaxy. His fondest desire is to harvest the genetic bounty of Primarch Guilliman himself.

HURON BLACKHEART
THE TYRANT OF BADAB

Huron Blackheart was once Chapter Master of the Astral Claws, though he has long turned his back on the Imperium. Now, he is better known as the Tyrant of Badab.

The rebel Space Marine warlord, Lugft Huron, was critically injured by a melta blast during the fighting inside the Palace of Thorns at the culmination of the Badab War. His Chapter, the Astral Claws, had sworn to fight to the death protecting their Chapter Master and their world, but when they saw that Badab was lost, they seized Huron's body and fought their way past the Imperial blockade in a handful of ships. Once away from the Badab System, they plunged into the warp rift known as the Maelstrom to evade pursuit.

The Tyrant lived. One side of his body had to be almost entirely reconstructed while the Astral Claws' ships hung in the Maelstrom. Within twelve days, Huron could stand, and he donned his power armour with grim determination. His followers hailed his recovery as a dark miracle. Huron's limited forces were still powerful enough to overwhelm the first pirate stronghold he found, slaughtering the corsairs in a matter of hours. The survivors soon learnt to fear his fury, swearing allegiance to the Tyrant and becoming his slaves. As he claimed the allegiance of ever more of the Maelstrom's denizens, Huron Blackheart was born. His power continued to grow, and he welded together a piratical empire of heretics and renegades. His Space Marines became the Red Corsairs, named for the blood-red colour they used to obliterate their old heraldries.

In recent years, the Red Corsairs' attacks have become less frequent, as though they are waiting for something. When Huron himself leads a raid, however, they are much more brazen, known to ambush well-protected convoys and relying on speed and overwhelming force to take their prizes. The strength of the Red Corsairs grows daily, and the name of Huron Blackheart is whispered fearfully across a score of sectors.

As a consummate raider with dozens of fleets at his disposal, Huron Blackheart has more material wealth that any warlord within a hundred light years of the Maelstrom. His Tyrant's Claw is a masterwork bionic that combines a set of serried talons, each swathed in a crackling disruption field, with an internal heavy flamer that can incinerate those who displease him. The strange quadruped that slinks in Blackheart's shadow is known as the Hamadrya, a bizarre and possibly daemonic familiar that bestows powerful psychic ability upon its master. No matter how rich and esoteric his trappings, however, the Tyrant can never escape the wracking pain that has haunted him since his fall during the Badab War. Perhaps it is this near-constant agony that adds fuel to the fires of wrath in Blackheart's soul; perhaps it is nothing more than pure hatred. Either way, this lord of mayhem is possibly the deadliest renegade in the annals of history.

THE MAELSTROM RAGES

The Eye of Terror is not the only wound in the galaxy to have become the lair of Chaos Space Marines. Raiders from the Maelstrom plague the void for light years in all directions, the worst of which are the Red Corsairs, led by Huron Blackheart. At the dawn of Abaddon's Thirteenth Black Crusade, Huron made his own simultaneous assaults upon the Imperium, draining the resources of the Adeptus Astartes who strive to hurl the Chaos Space Marines back to the hells from which they came. With the opening of the Great Rift, the Maelstrom has become but a part of a far larger empyric anomaly that spans the Imperium from one side to the other. Over the course of their near-constant pillaging of the Imperium's domains, Huron Blackheart and his raiders have become expert at negotiating those areas that are in the immaterium and on the fringes of realspace at the same time. Already the Red Corsairs have been sighted far further afield than the environs of the Maelstrom. It is all but certain that the Tyrant of Badab has struck some devil's bargain with the powers that dwell in the warp, for if the Imperium's after-action reports are to be believed, he has been seen in two different segmentums at the same time.

THE FALLEN

The Space Marines known as the Fallen are amongst the most enigmatic followers of the Chaos Gods, if indeed they are followers at all. Their origin has its roots in the dying days of the Horus Heresy, when Lion El'Jonson, Primarch of the Dark Angels Legion, returned to the beast-haunted forests of his home world, Caliban. As the unsuspecting ships of Jonson's fleet moved into orbit, they were met by a devastating barrage of defence laser fire. Ships exploded into flame and crashed to the surface like monstrous comets. Stunned by the attack, Jonson withdrew and attempted to find out what had happened on his home world.

A captured merchant ship soon provided the answer. When Lion El'Jonson had departed Caliban to take part in the Great Crusade, Luther, his second in command and lifelong battle-brother, had been left behind in charge of the remainder of the Dark Angels on Caliban. Despite the importance of Luther's position, it was not one that suited his ambitious personality, and soon his role as the planetary governor of some half-forgotten backwater world seemed more and more to him like an insult.

These seeds of jealousy grew until Luther had become a man obsessed, whose own neuroses had pushed him over the edge and made him dangerous beyond imagining. Using his renowned skills at oratory, Luther convinced the Dark Angels under his command that they had been shamed, that the Emperor had turned his face from them, instilling his own feelings of jealousy and rage in the Dark Angels who had been left on Caliban during the Great Crusade. When the Primarch returned, these feelings of betrayal erupted into open rebellion.

The fury that Jonson and the loyal Dark Angels felt at this terrible betrayal knew no bounds. They had fought from one end of the galaxy to the other and thought that the curse of Chaos had been cleansed from the planets of the Imperium. Now they found that their own home world, and their own brethren, had been corrupted and turned against them. Jonson immediately led an attack on the greatest of the Dark Angels' fortress monasteries himself. He knew that this was where he would find Luther, and so it was that the two former friends, now mortal enemies, faced each other. Even though the Primarch possessed superhuman powers, the two opponents were equally matched, for Luther's already considerable abilities had been enhanced by the Dark Gods of Chaos.

What followed was a duel of titanic proportions in which the adversaries landed blow after blow upon one another, tearing down the fortress monastery around them in the process until the whole massive edifice had been levelled by their battle. Meanwhile, the massed guns of the loyalist Dark Angels fleet pounded Caliban until its surface of began to crack and heave under the strain of the orbital bombardment. As the planet itself started to break apart, the battle between Luther and Jonson reached its climax. Luther, aided by the powers of Chaos, unleashed a furious psychic attack that knocked Jonson to his knees and left him mortally wounded. As the dying Primarch struggled to stand, his noble features wracked with pain, it was as if a curtain was lifted from Luther's eyes. He realised the full extent of what he had done. His was a triple betrayal – of his friend, of the Dark Angels, and of the Emperor. The truth shattered his sanity and he slumped down beside Jonson, no longer willing to fight.

Luther's psychic cry of pain and despair echoed through the warp. The Chaos Gods realised that they had been defeated, and lashed out in fury and frustration. A rent appeared in the fabric of realspace as a warp storm engulfed Caliban. In an uncontrollable, swirling flood of psychic energy the warp rushed into the physical universe. Those 'Fallen' Dark Angels who had served under Luther and his clandestine masters were sucked from the face of the planet into the warp and scattered throughout space and time. Caliban itself, already weakened by the loyal Dark Angels' bombardment, was ripped apart and destroyed, and much of the debris was sucked into the warp. The largest fragment of the planet, that which still bore massive architecture upon it, was refitted as a mobile fortress monastery and renamed the Rock. It serves as a reminder of the ruin visited upon the First Legion to this day.

This story of treachery and betrayal is the Dark Angels' secret shame. None know of it other than the Dark Angels themselves, their successor Chapters and, maybe, the Emperor on his Golden Throne. Even within the Chapter itself, very few Space Marines know exactly what happened during those fateful days. It is only when a Dark Angel reaches the ranks of the Deathwing that they learn the story of Luther's betrayal. More terrible still, they learn that many of the Dark Angels that followed Luther are still alive. These damned warriors are referred to by them as the Fallen Angels, or simply the Fallen.

Not all of the Fallen have succumbed to the power of Chaos to the same degree. A large number of the Fallen have embraced the ways of the Dark Gods completely, becoming true Chaos Space Marines. However, many others realise that their actions during the fall of Caliban were very wrong. Disgusted by the corrupting influence of the Chaos Gods and unable to reconcile themselves with the Dark Angels, they lead a solitary existence. Many become mercenaries or pirates, roaming the galaxy as masterless men. Others are willing to atone for their sins and in an attempt to do so have integrated themselves back into human societies, taking on the roles of mortal men.

However, whatever their subsequent actions, in the eyes of the Dark Angels the Fallen are the worst kind of sinners. The only way that they can rid themselves totally of their shame, and restore their honour and trust in the Emperor's eyes, is if all the Fallen are found and either made to repent or are slain. This is by no means an easy task. The Fallen are dispersed throughout space and time as either isolated individuals or in small warbands, and the Dark Angels can go for years without hearing any rumours that might lead them to one or more of the Fallen. When they do, however, and their mission is a success, those Fallen that are captured are taken back to the Rock. Deep inside its dungeons, Interrogator-Chaplains attempt to make the Fallen repent. Occasionally these captives do, and for their pains, die quickly. More frequently, the captured Fallen refuses and suffers a drawn-out and agonising death at the hands of those who would save their soul.

CYPHER

LORD OF THE FALLEN

There is one whom the Masters of the Dark Angels seek above all others. He is a being wrapped in shadow, an entity whose motives and methods are an enigma; even the name by which he is known alludes to concealment, although whether it is a metaphor or yet another conundrum is unknown. He is Cypher, and to the Dark Angels, he is nothing less than their most hated foe.

The Fall of Caliban was one of the last major catastrophes suffered by the Imperium during the bloody days of the Horus Heresy. Since that time, Cypher has been on the run, eluding capture for nearly ten thousand years. During that time, Cypher has appeared in each of the five segmentums, materialising as if from nowhere. Wherever he surfaces, he brings with him death and destruction, although whether he is the culprit or merely a herald of woe is unclear. Although the accounts are often tainted with bias, it appears that Cypher seldom instigates the violent acts that invariably occur when he is present; rather, he seems to act as a catalyst that fans the hatred and mistrust of those around him into a raging, uncontrollable fire. In each case, Cypher vanishes from the scene as abruptly as he arrived. Worlds burn in his wake, yet he leaves no clues as to where he will turn up next.

Besides havoc and ruin, there is another trail that Cypher leaves behind; legends and rumours abound after the passage of the mysterious robed figure. The intrigue over his rapid departure is further magnified by the inevitable wave of ensuing questions. Sometimes these interrogations will be conducted by Inquisitors or their agents, while at others Chaos Space Marines seek more knowledge about the cryptic figure that weaves in and out of their strongholds. Regardless of whether other factions arrive to ask questions, the Dark Angels always follow the trail. Grim-faced and taciturn as to their own purpose, they query any who were in contact or might have spoken with Cypher. Those who have some knowledge, or are suspected of having some, are taken away by a black-armoured Interrogator-Chaplain. Few return.

As to who or what Cypher truly is, none can say, but his possible ties to the Dark Angels are widely rumoured. Those who have witnessed him report that he wears simple ceremonial robes, much like many of the Dark Angels, and beneath his garment can be seen the thick plates of dark power armour. More damning still, however, is the fact that no matter where in the galaxy Cypher surfaces, the Dark Angels are never far behind. The Interrogator-Chaplains ask many questions, but give no answers themselves.

Despite the constant search for Cypher, none have yet been successful in capturing or destroying him. Or so it would seem. The Dark Angels have thought Cypher destroyed on numerous occasions, yet he always returns. Huron Blackheart's Red Corsairs, still seething after what they believe was their betrayal during the Escovan Campaign, thought they had cornered the elusive Cypher on the Strike Cruiser *Rapier*. In the deep emptiness of space, they halted the ship, yet when they boarded it they found only Chaos cultists. Before they were all slain, none of the cultists could verify the whereabouts of the mysterious Space Marine who had been in their midst, nor could they tell of how he had escaped.

It is obvious to those few Dark Angels Librarians who have studied the compiled data that Cypher's actions seem to follow some pattern or mission known only to himself. It is not even possible to deduce whether Cypher is for or against the Imperium, an ally or enemy to those who betrayed the Dark Angels. The only certainty is that disaster and strife follows in his wake.

HAARKEN WORLDCLAIMER

HERALD OF THE APOCALYPSE

Before every doom, there is a portent, before every apocalypse a sign. Haarken Worldclaimer is that dark omen given form, and the otherworldly destruction he heralds is the coming of the Warmaster himself – Abaddon the Despoiler, Lord of the Black Legion.

Haarken Worldclaimer takes a heinous joy in his role as the mouthpiece of Abaddon, for it is he that proclaims the death of worlds. He does so not with some quotidian threat or hollow boast, but by driving a spear of terror and confusion deep into the heart of citizen and soldier alike. In such a fashion, he prepares the way for the coming of the Black Legion, his Raptor hosts descending on tongues of flame to bring panic and despair with each murderous onslaught.

Long ago, the Traitor Legions learned the value of fear. A planet undermined by doubt – or better yet, paralysed by it – is one already half-conquered. Worldclaimer is a scholar and collector of dark knowledge as well as a leader of men, and he knows the power of words well chosen. He has studied the Grimoire Nostramo, that vilest of treatises written in kingsblood by the Primarch Curze. He has unearthed the Clotted Scrolls, learning well of the threats growled by Angron before he was consumed by those berzerker rages that gave his legion their reputation as Eaters of Worlds. He has even delved into the dread Book of Magnus, though it cost him a good part of his sanity to do so. In his studies, he has learned much. When he delivers his fell message – broadcast not only from his own laud hailer array but the vox-grilles and cankerous throats of a thousand acolytes – the raw and gloating hatred that drips from each syllable can shatter cohesion, cause mass surrenders, and even drive men to suicide.

Though many heralds would consider their duty done upon their lord's arrival, Haarken Worldclaimer revels in bringing destruction in person as well as from afar. He hastens to where the planet's denizens are coordinating their defences, to winding supply lines, secreted war rooms and remote command bunkers, and there he strikes. Descending from the skies alongside vast flocks of Raptors, Haarken

plunges towards the nerve centres of the enemy's war efforts. With thunderous bellows he proclaims to his foes below that the hour of their doom has arrived, and that the slaughter shall not cease until the earth has been anointed with every last drop of their blood. And this is no mindless bluster – while the foe scrabbles to intercept Worldclaimer, drawing forces from the front lines to drive back his assaults, the Chaos armies on the ground move in to capitalise on the confusion, tearing into disorganised flanks and crumpling re-forming battle formations.

Upon landing, Haarken is swift to join the slaughter. His cruel promises only ring louder as he slashes his way through the fray, sending waves of dread rippling across the enemy's tattered ranks. The assault on the foe's morale escalates as he singles out defiant generals and champions, launching

himself towards them and impaling them with practised efficiency. Such gruesome displays demonstrate the inevitability of Abaddon's will, and the wholesale butchery of the embattled world's greatest warriors eradicate any fragments of hope that remain on the planet.

Haarken's Daemon-touched relic, the Helspear, has tasted the blood of monarchs, xenos tyrants and even Chaos Lords over his long service as herald to the Despoiler, and each demoralising kill invigorates him, driving him to further acts of bloodshed. But it is not only the breasts of men and aliens into which this spear is plunged. It has become a symbolic act for Haarken, upon making planetfall, to drive his spear deep into the world's crust and roar out the fell promise that within eighty days and eighty nights, it will fall. He has yet to be proved false.

ABADDON THE DESPOILER
WARMASTER OF CHAOS

The name of Abaddon, Warmaster of Chaos, has become a bitter curse within the Imperium. During the Great Crusade, Abaddon rose to Captain of the First Company of the Luna Wolves Legion. Such was his tactical skill and physical prowess, it was rumoured that he may have been a clone-son of Horus. When the Heresy came to a head, it was clear that Abaddon's loyalty lay with his Primarch. He led the Terminators of the Sons of Horus across Isstvan, Yarant, and Terra itself. Abaddon's anguish at his master's death drove him deeper into madness and hatred than any mortal should ever sink. Before retreating, Abaddon took up the Warmaster's body and fought his way out of the quickly deteriorating battle. With their cadaverous prize, the Legion fled before the Emperor's armies.

When Abaddon returned, it was at the head of a diabolic horde ravaging star systems around the Eye of Terror. His Chaos Space Marines, now the Black Legion, were at the forefront of the attack, destroying all in their path. During this first Black Crusade, Abaddon formed many bloody pacts with the Chaos Gods. Below the Tower of Silence, he recovered a Daemon sword of prodigious power, making him nigh unstoppable. Since then, Abaddon has dreamed of forging an empire of Chaos upon the ruins of the Imperium. More Black Crusades have followed, each achieving some dark purpose that even the mightiest sages of the Imperium cannot discern. It is said that he alone has the power to unite the Traitor Legions and finish the treachery begun ten thousand years ago.

Now, as Abaddon's Thirteenth Black Crusade reaches its peak, Cadia has finally been overrun. Though the planet itself has fallen, possession of the Cadian Gate – the only stable path from the Eye of Terror – hangs in the balance. Should Abaddon triumph, the dark tide of Chaos will pour from the Eye of Terror along the length of the Crimson Path to strike at the most prized world of all – Holy Terra itself.

BLOODLETTERS

Acts of violent rage and deeds of bloody murder resound through the warp like a thunderous drumbeat, a booming echo that calls the Daemons of Khorne to war. Endless regiments of Bloodletters rush to answer the summons, their stooped forms eager to join in the slaughter. Filled with an insatiable desire for blood, these Lesser Daemons of Khorne are amongst the most aggressive creatures in the warp. Their unholy howls of triumph when spilling blood chill the hearts of all who hear them. Equally fearsome are their ceaseless screams of 'Blood for the Blood God! Skulls for the Skull Throne!'. Simply put, Bloodletters are violence and murder given physical form and purpose by the Blood God.

Bloodletters are Khorne's most numerous warriors, the foot soldiers of his daemonic legions. Their horrific appearance is an assault upon mortal sensibilities. Their skin is the colour of hot blood, and their angry eyes resemble burning coals.

Bloodletters are possessed of an inhuman strength; they can rip a mortal apart with cold-blooded ease, and in battle they carry long, jagged Hellblades that glow with the heinous energies of the warp. These vicious swords are said to be as sharp as Khorne's hatred. As they cut through flesh and bone, they become coated with the blood of the slain, glowing ever brighter as they slay, invigorated by the rich taste of death.

Bloodletters are ferocious Daemons that descend upon their foes in baying packs. The sight of spilt blood only drives them further into a frenzied rage, screaming with fury as they fall upon mortal flesh with dark blades, teeth and claws. Few soldiers can withstand such an onslaught, for the sight of their own comrades butchered by howling Bloodletters is enough to break even the stoutest soldiers.

Whilst Bloodletters are not the subtlest of creatures, they are not above subterfuge if it will lead to an even greater tally of skulls to offer the Blood God. However, where another Daemon may flatter and ensnare a mortal victim to torture them in perpetuity, a Bloodletter only ever resorts to persuasion or lies in order to stab a foe in the back. Bloodletters seek the blood of mortals to offer at the foot of the Skull Throne, ever hungry for fresh prey, ever willing to tear the warm red flesh from their victims with their talons and triumphantly smear the gore upon their curving horns.

DAEMONIC ALLIANCES

Being creatures of pure emotion that are native to the twisted mirror dimension of the empyrean, Daemons cannot survive for long in the cold reality of the material universe. They need some manner of focal point, some channel through which they can transfer their uncanny power from the immaterium and make themselves manifest in the worlds of flesh and blood. Over the span of the Imperium's history, the warp rifts that have led to a daemonic assault have usually been the result of untrained psykers opening their minds to the baleful whispers of the warp. Such an intrusion starts with the possession of the host, but can end with the psyker being turned body and soul into a hideous, shrieking gateway, a wound in reality that can allow hosts of Daemons to come pouring through.

Such small-scale invasions usually peter out as the flow of Chaos energy dries up, the Daemons fading away to nothing. The exceptions are when the Chaos Space Marines, having much the same goals as the Daemons of their patron gods, summon the legions of the warp into realspace. Through acts of voluntary possession, ritual sacrifice, psychic machination and sustained blasphemy, they weaken and shred the veil that holds the horrors of the warp hidden from the worlds of mortal men. All too often, when the Chaos Space Marines attack, hosts of Bloodletters, Horrors, Daemonettes and Plaguebearers burst from the ether to revel in the carnage.

HORRORS

Lesser Daemons of Tzeentch are literally magic made manifest. Pink Horrors, as they are known, frolic together in cheerful, brightly coloured mobs that caper and whirl, cackling insanely at their own incomprehensible jokes as they blur and cartwheel across the battlefield. As bright bolts of raw sorcery leap from their outstretched fingers, the Pink Horrors are filled with an increased joy, emitting squeals of laughter supplemented with many 'oohs' and 'ahhs' of delight as the magical light show screams overhead. These energies have a tendency to engulf the Pink Horrors' enemies in searing conflagrations of mutation, much to the joy of the Daemons themselves.

The principal weapon of the Lesser Daemon of Tzeentch is not its scrabbling claws or the gaping, fang-lined maw that sits amidst its rubbery torso, though one bitten or scratched by a Horror will be forever changed by the experience. Instead it is the raw warp energy that flows in the creature's veins. With a cackled word or gibbered phrase, the Horror throws balls of multicoloured flame at the enemy. Where these strike home they do not merely burn, but also wreak the most disturbing and peculiar changes, turning enemies to statues of screaming glass, to clouds of butterflies with anguished human faces, to strains of maddening music, mewling

infants or horrific mounds of tentacled flesh. Only Tzeentch can know what strange fate awaits those kissed by warpfire; even the Horrors themselves are oblivious, and take great joy in each sanity-shattering change as it is wrought.

The only way known way to end a Pink Horror's jubilant mood is to blow it to pieces or otherwise cut it apart. It is then that the Pink Horror undergoes a total transformation, splitting into halves that reshape themselves into smaller copies of the original. These new Daemons are different from their predecessor in two respects. The first is that their colour changes from pink to vivid blue, earning them the name of Blue Horrors. The second change is that the gleeful attitude of the Pink Horror is reversed – Blue Horrors are morose, whining and petty, eternally squabbling about whose fault it was that they lost their pink status once again. These replacement forms are miserable and sullen to the point of aggression, lurching after those who ruined their day to stab and throttle until they kill those with the temerity to have killed them first. Should a Blue Horror be killed before it can get its revenge, it will divide once more into two tiny Brimstone Horrors, blazing yellow manifestations of pure spite and bitterness that seek only to burn their enemies to scattering ash.

PLAGUEBEARERS

The dull knell of bells and the humming of flies herald the arrival of Nurgle's Plaguebearers. Forming the rank and file of his pestilent legions, the Lesser Daemons of Nurgle shuffle forwards, their ripe bodies swollen with contagion and rife with the stench of decay. Each Daemon has a single rheumy eye and a horn sprouting from its skull – the mark of Nurgle's Rot that each bears through eternity.

It is the Plaguebearers' role to keep stock of new diseases and symptoms, and to maintain some semblance of order amongst Nurgle's naturally mischievous hordes. The Plaguebearers' obsessive need to organise is characterised by their constant counting as they try to calculate every new outbreak of plague. However, this monotonous chanting achieves very little – it is practically impossible to catalogue anything amidst the ever-changing nature of Chaos. This in no way discourages them, however, for they are the embodiment of the need to impose order upon a meaningless and uncaring world. In battle, their corpulent forms resist all but the most fearsome weaponry, and they wield rusted blades that corrupt flesh and rust metal in an instant. Unfortunately for the Plaguebearers, they are prone to losing count during combat, and they stand above their dying foes groaning in frustration before starting their count all over again.

NURGLE'S ROT

Chief among the many gifts that the Lord of Plagues has granted an ungrateful galaxy is Nurgle's Rot. This perfect illness does not kill its host quickly; rather, it slowly turns the victim into a bloated living corpse teeming with the stuff of nightmares. Their blood curdles in their veins, their eyes grow together into a single globulous orb, and a horn sprouts from their head. The illness does not merely affect the body, however – it painfully corrupts the diseased mortal's soul to the point where the victim has to either end their own life or fully embrace the ways of Nurgle and become a Plaguebearer.

The longer an infected soul resists Nurgle's Rot, the more likely it is that they will survive the disgusting changes wrought upon them, and the more powerful a Plaguebearer they will become once the transformation is complete. Such individuals are sometimes possessed of a sheepish embarrassment that it took them so long to appreciate the blessings of their new existence. To one who has truly converted to Nurgle's cause, life as a bandy-legged mound of putrescent, boil-covered flesh and disgusting bodily functions is seen as the most fulsome of blessings rather than a despicable curse that will never end.

DAEMONETTES

Most numerous of Slaanesh's servants are his Lesser Daemons, the Daemonettes. They serve as courtiers and courtesans in the Palace of Pleasure, created to fulfil Slaanesh's every passing whim. They fill Slaanesh's throne room, lounging upon silken cushions, gossiping endlessly as they scheme to earn greater favour from their wilful master.

The Daemonettes are also Slaanesh's warriors and messengers beyond his realm. The Dark Prince is given to extreme changes of mood and when frustrated, he lashes out with his legions, sending his Daemonettes to tear down everything he finds repugnant and crude, and replace them with artistic vistas of destruction.

In battle, Daemonettes can be seen dancing across the blood-soaked ground, dead bodies forming a carpet beneath their feet. Their honeyed voices are raised in joyous songs of praise to Slaanesh as they slay and maim in the name of agony and pleasure. They are lithe, dexterous killers, gifting their victims with a mixture of excruciatingly painful caresses and the most delicate and tender of killing strokes. Even in the most gruesome of conflicts,

the Daemonettes smile in secret ecstasy as they go about their deadly work, delighting in the waves of emotion emanating from their enemies.

In appearance, the Daemonettes are both beautiful and revolting. They have an androgynous charm that is heightened by a permeating sense of beguilement. Though their true forms are repulsive and terrifying, this supernatural power makes them appear as the ultimate beauty and object of desire in the eyes of mortals, regardless of their race, gender or morality. None exposed to the Lesser Daemons of Slaanesh forget the tide of living sensuality; it evokes both loathing and a perverse longing that forever gnaws at the minds of those who see them.

Sometimes Slaanesh is more delicate in his machinations, seeking to undermine the will of his foes, tempting them from their chosen path and removing their opposition to his cause. Slaanesh will also despatch Daemonettes to corrupt those he wishes to enslave. Using their seductive spells, the Daemonettes whisper into the dreams and nightmares of their victims, fuelling their darkest desires with promises of glory and fulfilment. The warriors of the Chaos Space Marines are especially susceptible to this. Many a would-be conqueror has summoned a host of Slaanesh's handmaidens in the mistaken belief they will clinch a lasting victory, only to find it is he who is the pawn, and that his actions have a terrible cost…

Strange music skirled through the mists, repellent and inviting at the same time. Ellaria Moonspeaker's eyes opened wide, her hand closing protectively around her waystone by reflex. A cold caress of fear ran through the bone marrow of her arms and legs. Surely this nightmare was already over?

The slain Emperor's Children were already disappearing from sight, the heavy battle plate of the post-human warriors dragging their bodies into the marsh. The Ynnari strike force had lost seven Aspect Warriors in the fight, but they had killed three times that number, and the souls of the Aeldari's fallen were already being gathered so that they might live on.

Then, something moved in the mist, languid and graceful, and Ellaria knew their doom had come for them. It was a tapering claw at the end of a lithe limb. Suddenly, a crested head with too-large eyes burst from the mists to her right, hissing like a lizard. Ellaria shrieked, raising her shuriken catapult and opening fire. The Daemon was no longer there. Ellaria's fellow Guardians came in close, almost back to back. For a moment, she felt safer. Then she looked down.

Bursting out of the brackish liquid came six pale terrors. One of them wrapped its milk-white arms around Ellaria's legs, crawling bodily up her like some pallid spider. She felt its warmth, smelt its intoxicating musk, and felt both lust and dread consume her. The Daemon leered in close, and bit the waystone from her breast with its needle teeth. Then its claws closed around her throat, and Ellaria knew no more.

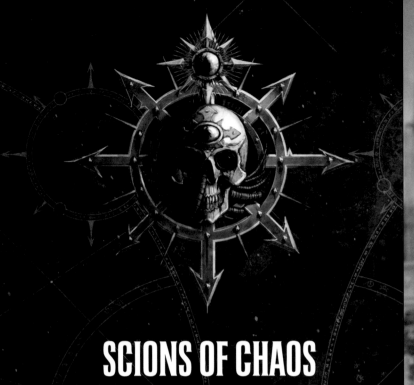

SCIONS OF CHAOS

A force of Chaos Space Marines is a terrifying vision of a dark future. Baroque armour twisted by the malefic energies of the warp is illuminated by the muzzle flares of gargoyle gun barrels. Bleached skulls, flayed skin and severed limbs adorn warrior and vehicle, grim trophies of the slain and loci for unholy power. At his corrupted core, however, each Chaos Space Marine is a soldier forged for war, and so bears the colours and icon of his Legion or Renegade Chapter.

Abaddon the Despoiler, Warmaster of Chaos, wielding the Talon of Horus and the Daemon sword Drach'nyen

Upon a war-ravaged battlefield deep within the Imperium Nihilus, Abaddon and his Black Legionnaires meet Roboute Guilliman and the Ultramarines head-on in an embittered battle to the death.

Black Legion Chaos Lord in
Terminator armour

Night Lords Terminator with
lightning claws

Word Bearers Terminator with
combi-bolter and power maul

Black Legion Terminator with reaper
autocannon and power fist

Black Legion Terminator with
combi-melta and power fist

Black Legion Terminator Champion
with power sword and combi-plasma

The Genestealer Cult uprising on Chalimnus V is brought to a sudden and bloody halt by the onslaught of the Word Bearers who tear
through the xenos cultists, bellowing that this world belongs not to alien filth, but to the Dark Gods of Chaos.

Emerging from amidst the swirling smoke of battle, a squad of Alpha Legion Chaos Space Marines guns down their Cadian enemies with callous disdain, their Cultist followers falling upon the shell-shocked survivors with vicious glee.

Black Legion Aspiring Champion
with plasma pistol and power axe

Black Legion Chaos Space
Marine with boltgun

Black Legion Chaos Space
Marine with heavy bolter

Black Legion Aspiring Champion with bolt
pistol and chainsword

Alpha Legion Chaos Space Marine
with plasma gun

Iron Warriors Chaos Space Marine
with missile launcher

Amidst the crash of bolter fire and the crackle of energised blades a mighty warband of Heretic Astartes warriors tears through the battle lines of a Genestealer Cult, leaving naught but mangled corpses and flaming wreckage in their wake.

Black Legion Dark Apostle

Dark Disciples follow their masters into battle, bearing corrupted tomes of dark lore and smoke-belching censers.

Black Legion Chaos Lord with thunder hammer and plasma pistol

Black Legion Master of Executions

Black Legion Greater Possessed   Black Legion Master of Possession   Black Legion Greater Possessed

Crimson Slaughter Possessed   Black Legion Possessed   Black Legion Possessed

Upon the ice-locked world of Nimboru, the fanatical Word Bearers overrun the Ultramarines' defences, their attack spearheaded by waves of Possessed Chaos Space Marines and rampaging Daemon Engines.

Haarken Worldclaimer, Herald of the Apocalypse

Black Legion Raptor with chainsword and bolt pistol

Black Legion Raptor with meltagun

Black Legion Raptor with chainsword and bolt pistol

Bursting from the shadows with spine-chilling shrieks of murder-lust, the Night Lords fall upon the outnumbered Dark Angels and tear their prey to bloody tatters.

Lord Discordant of the Black Legion armed with a baleflamer, mounted on a Helstalker equipped with a techno-virus injector

Powerful engines bellow like enraged beasts and hellish Daemonforges billow brimstone flames as the Iron Warriors advance upon their despised Imperial Fists foes. No amount of stubborn courage will hold back this hate-fuelled onslaught!

Black Legion Venomcrawler

A mailed fist of Black Legion battle tanks smashes into the machine-warriors of the Adeptus Mechanicus, a Lord Discordant leading the furious charge.

Animate abominations of malefically possessed adamantine and brass, the Daemon Engines of the Black Legion prowl, lumber and swoop into battle while Havocs provide supporting fire.

Black Legion Havoc with missile launcher

Black Legion Havoc with heavy bolter

Black Legion Havoc with reaper chaincannon

Black Legion Havoc Aspiring Champion with chainsword and plasma gun

Iron Warriors Havoc with lascannon

Night Lords Havoc with autocannon

Obliterators are armed with enormous crushing fists and rapidly adapting fleshmetal guns.

Grim and silent, the Fallen line the battlements of a captured Imperial fortress. The mysterious Cypher stands at their head, ready to lead them to battle once more.

Plague Marine with plasma gun

Plague Marine with boltgun and plague knife

Lucius the Eternal

Rubric Marine with warpflamer

Rubric Marine with inferno boltgun

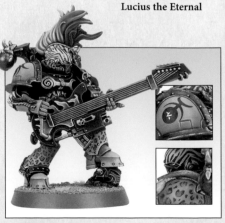

Noise Marine with sonic blaster

Berzerker Champion with plasma
pistol and chainaxe

Khârn the Betrayer

Khorne Berzerker bearing an Icon of Wrath

Khorne Berzerker with bolt
pistol and chainaxe

Berzerkers wear the skull-icon of Khorne.

Always at the forefront of any assault, Khârn the Betrayer charges headlong into a gun line of the Armageddon Steel Legion, eager to heap
more skulls at the foot of the Blood God's throne and carve the Red Path ever deeper into Imperial territory.

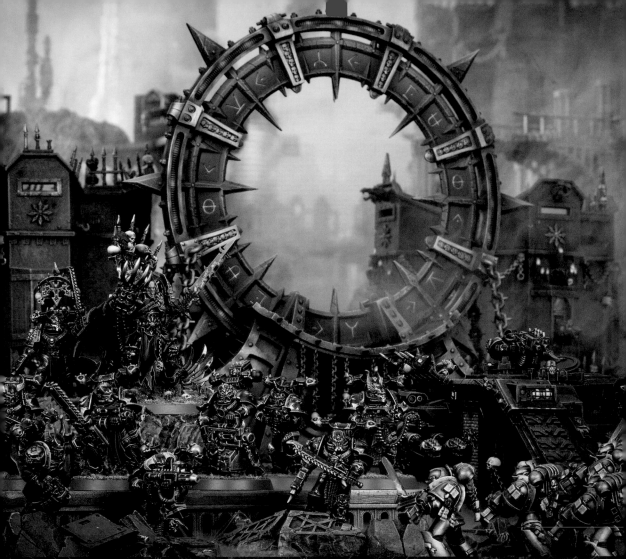

Wreathed in the fluctuating eldritch energies of a Noctilith Crown, Abaddon's veteran warriors unleash their fury upon the Grey Knights.

Brazen Beasts Terminator with chainaxe and combi-flamer

Sons of Vengeance Terminator with lightning claws

Flawless Host Havoc Aspiring Champion with chainsword and flamer

**Red Corsairs Chaos Space Marine
with bolt pistol and chainsword**

**Crimson Slaughter Chaos Space
Marine with plasma gun**

**Scourged Chaos Space Marine
with bolt pistol and chainsword**

**Blood Disciples Chaos Space Marine
with bolt pistol and chainsword**

**Aspiring Champion of the Cleaved
with plasma pistol and power fist**

**Invocators Chaos Space Marine
with boltgun**

**Corpus Brethren Chaos Space
Marine with flamer**

**Chaos Space Marine of the Purge
with bolt pistol and chainsword**

**Company of Misery Chaos
Space Marine with boltgun**

Bloodletters

Plaguebearers

Brimstone Horrors   **Blue Horrors**   **Pink Horrors**

Alluress   **Daemonettes**

THE PATH TO GLORY BECKONS

A warband of Chaos Space Marines is a versatile and hard-hitting group of warriors, levelling hails of explosive firepower as they close in for the kill. The starting forces below were picked to maximise these strengths.

The two warbands shown on this page represent different approaches to starting a Chaos Space Marines army. The first, Athkor's Destroyers, has been chosen to emphasise numbers and strategic versatility. Led by a Master of Possession and his Greater Possessed, the force has a solid core of Chaos Space Marines that allows the army to be fielded as a Patrol Detachment. With a Venomcrawler and

a pair of Obliterators to provide heavy firepower, this force can respond swiftly to any strategic challenge, and looks striking on the tabletop.

The second force is a tightly focused and utterly lethal collection of dark heroes and elite warriors themed around Abaddon the Despoiler and his chosen champions. The Warmaster, a Master

of Executions and a Dark Apostle with a sycophantic retinue fulfil the three HQ choices required for a Supreme Command Detachment, while the Terminators represent Abaddon's personal guard, the dreaded Bringers of Despair. This Detachment provides one extra Command Point with which to deploy powerful Stratagems, further augmenting the already elite force.

Bruakh Athkor, Master of Possession and Daemontwister of the Screaming Void, leads his warband of merciless killers into battle to reap souls for the Dark Gods' pleasure.

None can stand against Abaddon the Despoiler and the chosen champions who stand at his side, their weapons ever ready to strike down the Warmaster's many foes.

DEATH TO THE FALSE EMPEROR

As your collection of Chaos Space Marines grows, new warbands can be added and existing forces combined to create truly mighty tabletop armies like the one showcased here.

This army is led into battle by a truly terrifying band of mighty Chaos champions. Abaddon the Despoiler strides to war at its head, flanked by Ghordar Bann, Master of Executions, Uhlmak Doomspeaker the Dark Apostle, Master of Possession Bruakh Athkor and his monstrous Greater Possessed, the Worthy, and the ghastly Daemon Prince Sylathrax the Unbound. The Arch-Lord Discordant, Vex Machinator, rides his twisted mechanical steed into battle at the head of the army's unholy engines of war. So potent a gathering of dark might would be enough to shatter enemy armies by itself, yet this is only the beginning of this warband's strength.

The strategic core of the warband comprises two ten-man squads of Chaos Space Marines, Lorghan's Beasts and the Flayers. These post-human killers are equipped with a deadly array of ranged and close-combat weaponry, and one squad rides to battle aboard the Chaos Rhino *Fist of the Gods*. They are supported by the expendable mortal fools of the Chaos Cult known as the Risen.

Then come the elite warriors of Abaddon's warband. The hand-chosen Terminators of the Bringers of Despair mow down Abaddon's enemies without mercy. Meanwhile, the gibbering

Possessed abominations of Damnation's Slaves pounce upon their victims and tear them limb from limb. Heavy firepower for the force is provided by the Obliterators known as the Iron Butchers and Kyloth's Rain of Fire, a squad of Havocs. Finally, the warband has an unstoppable armoured fist in the form of the trio of monstrous Daemon Engines that Vex Machinator leads to war. *Spiteclaw* and *Soulbile* are a pair of scuttling Venomcrawlers, while the ectoplasma cannons of the Forgefiend *Hathkar's Revenge* annihilate another band of foes with every screaming salvo.

Not only is this army a powerful tabletop force in its own right, but it also fulfils all the requirements for a Battalion, Spearhead and Supreme Command Detachment, providing its player with a princely ten Command Points to spend on Stratagems that can turn the course of battle.

1. **Abaddon the Despoiler**
2. **Ghordar Bann, Master of Executions**
3. **Uhlmak, Dark Apostle**
4. **Bruakh Athkor, Master of Possession**
5. **Sylathrax the Unbound, Daemon Prince**
6. **The Worthy, Greater Possessed**
7. **Vex Machinator, Lord Discordant**
8. **Lorghan's Beasts, Chaos Space Marines**
9. **The Flayers, Chaos Space Marines**
10. *Fist of the Gods*, **Chaos Rhino**
11. **The Risen, Chaos Cultists**
12. **The Bringers of Despair, Terminators**
13. **Damnation's Slaves, Possessed**
14. **The Iron Butchers, Obliterators**
15. **Kyloth's Rain of Fire, Havocs**
16. *Spiteclaw*, **Venomcrawler**
17. *Soulbile*, **Venomcrawler**
18. *Hathkar's Revenge*, **Forgefiend**

SLAVES TO DARKNESS

This section contains all of the datasheets that you will need in order to fight battles with your Chaos Space Marine miniatures. Each datasheet includes the characteristics profiles of the unit it describes, as well as any wargear and abilities it may have. Some rules are common to several Chaos Space Marine units – these are described below and referenced on the datasheets.

KEYWORDS

Throughout this section you will come across keywords that are within angular brackets, specifically <LEGION> and <MARK OF CHAOS>. These are shorthand for a keyword of your own choosing, as described below.

<LEGION>

Chaos Space Marines belong to a Legion or Renegade Chapter. For simplicity we will refer to all of these as Legions, even though in truth Renegade Chapters have a different genesis.

Some datasheets specify what Legion the unit is from (e.g. Abaddon the Despoiler has the **BLACK LEGION** keyword, so is from the Black Legion). If a Heretic Astartes datasheet does not specify which Legion it is from, it will have the <LEGION> keyword. When you include such a unit in your army, you must nominate which Legion that unit is from. You then simply replace the <LEGION> keyword in every instance on that unit's datasheet with the name of your chosen Legion.

For example, if you were to include a Chaos Lord in your army, and you decided he was from the Alpha Legion, his <LEGION> Faction keyword is changed to **ALPHA LEGION** and his Lord of Chaos ability would then read: 'You can re-roll hit rolls of 1 made for friendly **ALPHA LEGION** units within 6" of this model.'

The Death Guard, Thousand Sons and Fallen deviate significantly in terms of organisation and fighting styles. As a result, you cannot choose one of these keywords when determining which Legion a unit in this codex is from. The rules and abilities for the Death Guard and Thousand Sons Legions are detailed in their own codexes, and both of the datasheets that describe the forces of the Fallen can be found later in this book.

<MARK OF CHAOS>

Many Heretic Astartes units dedicate themselves to a single Chaos God, whilst others worship the entire pantheon in all its dark glory. The Chaos God a unit is dedicated to is denoted by the Mark of Chaos that it bears.

Some datasheets specify the Mark of Chaos for a unit (e.g. Khârn the Betrayer has the **KHORNE** keyword). If a Heretic Astartes datasheet does not specify which Mark of Chaos a unit has, it will have the <MARK OF CHAOS> keyword. When you include such a unit in your army, you must nominate which Mark of Chaos that unit has. You then simply replace the <MARK OF CHAOS> keyword in every instance on that unit's datasheet with one of the following: **KHORNE**, **TZEENTCH**, **NURGLE** or **SLAANESH**. Note that **PSYKERS** cannot have the **KHORNE** keyword.

You do not have to choose a Mark of Chaos for a unit if you do not want to; if you do not, it is assumed that the unit has not dedicated itself to a specific Dark God. The exceptions are units from the World Eaters or Emperor's Children Legions: all **WORLD EATERS** units must have the **KHORNE** keyword if they are able to do so, and all **EMPEROR'S CHILDREN** units must have the **SLAANESH** keyword if they are able to do so. If a unit has the **TZEENTCH**, **NURGLE** or **SLAANESH** keywords, it cannot be from the World Eaters Legion, and if a unit has the **KHORNE**, **TZEENTCH** or **NURGLE** keywords, it cannot be from the Emperor's Children Legion. In addition, **PSYKERS** cannot be from the World Eaters Legion.

ABILITIES

The following ability is common to several Chaos Space Marine units:

DEATH TO THE FALSE EMPEROR

The seething hatred that Chaos Space Marines harbour for the Corpse Emperor and his weakling Imperium is a weapon unto itself.

Each time you roll a hit roll of 6+ for a model with this ability in the Fight phase, it can, if it was targeting an **IMPERIUM** unit, immediately make an extra attack against the same unit using the same weapon. These extra attacks cannot themselves generate any further attacks.

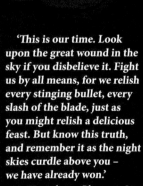

'This is our time. Look upon the great wound in the sky if you disbelieve it. Fight us by all means, for we relish every stinging bullet, every slash of the blade, just as you might relish a delicious feast. But know this truth, and remember it as the night skies curdle above you – we have already won.'

- Hyperlogus Phaevra, Lord Sensorium of the Silken Death

CHAOS SPACE MARINES WARGEAR LISTS

Many of the units you will find on the following pages reference one or more of the following wargear lists (e.g. Special Weapons). When this is the case, the unit may take any item from the appropriate list below. The profiles for the weapons in these lists can be found in the Forbidden Armoury section (pg 156-159).

CHAMPION EQUIPMENT

The champion can take up to two weapons chosen from the following list:

- Bolt pistol
- Chainaxe
- Chainsword
- Lightning claw
- Plasma pistol
- Power axe
- Power fist
- Power maul
- Power sword

One of the champion's weapons can be chosen from the following list:

- Boltgun
- Combi-bolter
- Combi-flamer
- Combi-melta
- Combi-plasma

COMBI-WEAPONS

- Combi-bolter
- Combi-flamer
- Combi-melta
- Combi-plasma

PISTOLS

- Bolt pistol
- Plasma pistol

HEAVY WEAPONS

- Autocannon
- Heavy bolter
- Lascannon
- Missile launcher
- Reaper chaincannon*

*Cannot be taken by Fallen.

SPECIAL WEAPONS

- Flamer
- Meltagun
- Plasma gun

MELEE WEAPONS

- Chainaxe
- Chainsword
- Lightning claw
- Power axe
- Power fist
- Power maul
- Power sword
- Thunder hammer

TERMINATOR MELEE WEAPONS

- Chainaxe
- Chainfist
- Lightning claw
- Power axe
- Power fist
- Power maul
- Power sword

DAEMONIC RITUAL

Through dark pacts and blasphemous rituals, a champion of Chaos weakens the fabric of reality, opening a gateway to the warp through which daemonic allies can pour to rend and tear the enemies of the Dark Gods.

Instead of moving in their Movement phase, any **CHAOS CHARACTER** can, at the end of their Movement phase, attempt to summon a unit with this ability by performing a Daemonic Ritual (the character cannot do so if they arrived as reinforcements this turn, or if they themselves have been summoned to the battlefield this turn).

If they do so, first choose one of the four Chaos Gods – **KHORNE**, **TZEENTCH**, **NURGLE** or **SLAANESH**. A **CHARACTER** who owes allegiance to one of the Dark Gods can only attempt to summon the units of their patron – for example, a **KHORNE CHARACTER** could only attempt to summon a **KHORNE** unit.

Roll up to three D6 – this is your summoning roll. You can summon one new unit with the Daemonic Ritual ability to the battlefield that has a Power Rating equal to or less than the total result so long as it has the same Chaos God keyword you chose at the start. This unit is treated as reinforcements for your army and can be placed anywhere on the battlefield that is wholly within 12" of the character and more than 9" from any enemy model. If the total rolled is insufficient to summon any unit, the ritual fails and no new unit is summoned.

If your summoning roll included any doubles, your character then suffers 1 mortal wound. If it contained any triples, it instead suffers D3 mortal wounds.

ABADDON THE DESPOILER

NAME	M	WS	BS	S	T	W	A	Ld	Sv
Abaddon the Despoiler	6"	2+	2+	5	5	8	6	10	2+

Abaddon the Despoiler is a single model armed with Drach'nyen and the Talon of Horus. Only one of this model may be included in your army.

WEAPON	RANGE	TYPE	S	AP	D	ABILITIES
Talon of Horus (shooting)	24"	Rapid Fire 2	4	-1	D3	-
Drach'nyen	Melee	Melee	+1	-3	3	Roll a D6 each time the bearer fights. On a 1 they suffer 1 mortal wound and cannot use this weapon further during this phase. On a 2+ they can make that many additional attacks with this weapon.
Talon of Horus (melee)	Melee	Melee	x2	-4	D3	-

ABILITIES	
Death to the False Emperor (pg 118) **The Warmaster:** If your army is Battle-forged and Abaddon the Despoiler is your Warlord, you receive 2 additional Command Points. **Dark Destiny:** Abaddon the Despoiler has a 4+ invulnerable save. In addition, all damage suffered by Abaddon the Despoiler is halved (rounding up). **Lord of the Black Legion:** You can re-roll hit rolls for friendly **BLACK LEGION** units while they are within 6" of Abaddon the Despoiler.	**Mark of Chaos Ascendant:** Friendly **HERETIC ASTARTES** units automatically pass Morale tests while they are within 12" of Abaddon the Despoiler. **Teleport Strike:** During deployment, you can set up Abaddon in a teleportarium chamber instead of placing him on the battlefield. At the end of any of your Movement phases he can use a teleport strike to arrive on the battlefield – set him up anywhere on the battlefield that is more than 9" away from any enemy models.

FACTION KEYWORDS	CHAOS, KHORNE, NURGLE, SLAANESH, TZEENTCH, HERETIC ASTARTES, BLACK LEGION
KEYWORDS	CHARACTER, INFANTRY, CHAOS LORD, TERMINATOR, ABADDON THE DESPOILER

HAARKEN WORLDCLAIMER

NAME	M	WS	BS	S	T	W	A	Ld	Sv
Haarken Worldclaimer	12"	2+	2+	4	4	5	5	9	3+

Haarken Worldclaimer is a single model armed with the Helspear and a lightning claw. Only one of this model may be included in your army.

WEAPON	RANGE	TYPE	S	AP	D	ABILITIES
Helspear	12"	Assault 1	+1	-3	D3	-
Lightning claw	Melee	Melee	User	-2	1	You can re-roll failed wound rolls for this weapon. If a model is armed with two lightning claws, each time it fights it can make 1 additional attack with them.

ABILITIES	
Death to the False Emperor (pg 118) **Lord of the Raptors:** You can re-roll hit rolls for attacks made with melee weapons used by friendly **RAPTOR** units within 6" of this model. **Sigil of Corruption:** This model has a 4+ invulnerable save. **Herald of the Apocalypse:** Enemy units within 18" of this model must subtract 1 from their Leadership characteristic.	**Raptor Strike:** During deployment, you can set up this model in low orbit instead of placing it on the battlefield. At the end of any of your Movement phases, this model can use a Raptor strike to arrive on the battlefield – set it up anywhere on the battlefield that is more than 9" from any enemy models. **Head-claimer:** Each time an enemy **CHARACTER** is slain by an attack made by this model, add 1 to this model's Attacks characteristic.

FACTION KEYWORDS	CHAOS, HERETIC ASTARTES, BLACK LEGION
KEYWORDS	CHARACTER, INFANTRY, RAPTOR, JUMP PACK, FLY, HAARKEN WORLDCLAIMER

DAEMON PRINCE

NAME	M	WS	BS	S	T	W	A	Ld	Sv
Daemon Prince	8"	2+	2+	7	6	8	4	10	3+

A Daemon Prince is a single model armed with a hellforged sword and a set of malefic talons.

WEAPON	RANGE	TYPE	S	AP	D	ABILITIES
Warp bolter	24"	Assault 2	4	-1	2	-
Daemonic axe	Melee	Melee	+1	-3	3	When attacking with this weapon, you must subtract 1 from the hit roll.
Hellforged sword	Melee	Melee	User	-2	3	-
Malefic talons	Melee	Melee	User	-2	2	Each time this model fights, it can make 1 additional attack with this weapon. A model armed with two sets of malefic talons can make 3 additional attacks with them instead.

WARGEAR OPTIONS	
	• This model may replace its hellforged sword with a daemonic axe or second set of malefic talons. • This model may take a warp bolter. • This model may have wings (**Power Rating +1**). If it does, its Move characteristic is increased to 12" and it gains the **FLY** keyword.

ABILITIES	
	Death to the False Emperor (pg 118) **Daemonic:** This model has a 5+ invulnerable save. **Daemonic Allegiance:** When you include a Daemon Prince in your army, you must choose which of the four Chaos Gods it owes its allegiance to: **KHORNE**, **TZEENTCH**, **NURGLE** or **SLAANESH**. It then gains the appropriate keyword.	**Prince of Chaos:** You can re-roll hit rolls of 1 made for friendly <**LEGION**> units within 6" of this model. This ability also affects friendly **DAEMON** units within 6", but only if they owe their allegiance to the same Chaos God e.g. **KHORNE DAEMON** units are only affected by **KHORNE** Daemon Princes. **Might over Magic:** A Daemon Prince of **KHORNE** increases its Attacks characteristic by 1.

PSYKER	
	A Daemon Prince of **TZEENTCH**, **NURGLE** or **SLAANESH** gains the **PSYKER** keyword. It can attempt to manifest one psychic power in each friendly Psychic phase, and attempt to deny one psychic power in each enemy Psychic phase. It knows the *Smite* psychic power and one psychic power from the Dark Hereticus discipline (pg 168).

FACTION KEYWORDS	**CHAOS, HERETIC ASTARTES, <LEGION>**
KEYWORDS	**CHARACTER, MONSTER, DAEMON, DAEMON PRINCE**

A mighty Daemon Prince stands tall over the battlefield, spurring the Heretic Astartes on with his blood-curdling bellows.

KHÂRN THE BETRAYER

NAME	M	WS	BS	S	T	W	A	Ld	Sv
Khârn the Betrayer	6"	2+	2+	5	4	5	6	9	3+

Khârn the Betrayer is a single model armed with Gorechild, a unique plasma pistol, frag grenades and krak grenades. Only one of this model may be included in your army.

WEAPON	RANGE	TYPE	S	AP	D	ABILITIES
Khârn's plasma pistol	12"	Pistol 1	8	-3	2	Each time you roll a hit roll of 1 when firing this weapon, the bearer suffers 1 mortal wound.
Gorechild	Melee	Melee	+1	-4	D3	This weapon always hits on a roll of 2+, regardless of any modifiers.
Frag grenade	6"	Grenade D6	3	0	1	-
Krak grenade	6"	Grenade 1	6	-1	D3	-

ABILITIES	**Death to the False Emperor** (pg 118)	**Sigil of Corruption:** Khârn the Betrayer has a 4+ invulnerable save.
	The Betrayer: You cannot re-roll or modify hit rolls of 1 made for Khârn the Betrayer in the Fight phase. Instead, those attacks automatically hit a friendly unit within 1". Randomly determine which unit is hit if there is more than one. If there are no friendly units within 1" of Khârn, the hits are discarded.	**Blood for the Blood God:** Khârn the Betrayer can fight twice in each Fight phase, instead of only once. **Kill! Maim! Burn!:** You can re-roll failed hit rolls made for friendly WORLD EATERS units within 1" of Khârn the Betrayer.

FACTION KEYWORDS	CHAOS, KHORNE, HERETIC ASTARTES, WORLD EATERS
KEYWORDS	CHARACTER, INFANTRY, CHAOS LORD, KHÂRN THE BETRAYER

Khârn the Betrayer charges forwards to be first into the fray, his chainaxe Gorechild roaring in anticipation of the slaughter to come.

FABIUS BILE

NAME	M	WS	BS	S	T	W	A	Ld	Sv
Fabius Bile	6"	2+	3+	5	4	5	6	9	3+

Fabius Bile is a single model armed with the Xyclos Needler, the Rod of Torment, frag grenades and krak grenades. Only one of this model may be included in your army.

WEAPON	RANGE	TYPE	S	AP	D	ABILITIES
Xyclos Needler	18"	Pistol 3	*	0	1	This weapon wounds on a 2+, unless it is targeting a **Vehicle**, in which case it wounds on a 6+.
Rod of Torment	Melee	Melee	User	-1	D3	When attacking a **Vehicle**, this weapon has a Damage of 1.
Frag grenade	6"	Grenade D6	3	0	1	-
Krak grenade	6"	Grenade 1	6	-1	D3	-

ABILITIES	**Death to the False Emperor** (pg 118) **The Chirurgeon:** At the start of your turn, Fabius Bile regains up to D3 lost wounds.	**Enhanced Warriors:** Fabius Bile can enhance one unit of **Heretic Astartes Infantry** (but not **Characters** – they refuse the dubious honour of Bile's gifts) that is within 1" of him at the end of any Movement phase. Roll a D6 for each model in the unit; the unit suffers 1 mortal wound for each roll of 6 (only the strong survive Bile's experimental cocktails). Then roll a D3 and refer to the table below to see what bonus the survivors gain for the rest of the battle. A unit can only be enhanced once per game: **D3 Bonus** 1 **Swollen Musculature:** +1 Strength 2 **Calcific Growths:** +1 Toughness 3 **Berserk Rage:** +1 Attack
FACTION KEYWORDS	**Chaos, Heretic Astartes**	
KEYWORDS	**Character, Infantry, Fabius Bile**	

LUCIUS THE ETERNAL

NAME	M	WS	BS	S	T	W	A	Ld	Sv
Lucius the Eternal	6"	2+	2+	4	4	5	5	9	3+

Lucius the Eternal is a single model armed with the Lash of Torment, a master-crafted power sword, a doom siren, frag grenades and krak grenades. Only one of this model may be included in your army.

WEAPON	RANGE	TYPE	S	AP	D	ABILITIES
Doom siren	8"	Assault D6	5	-2	1	This weapon automatically hits its target. Units do not receive the benefit of cover to their saving throws for attacks made with this weapon.
Lash of Torment	6"	Assault 2	User	-1	2	This weapon can be fired within 1" of an enemy unit, and can target enemy units within 1" of friendly units.
Master-crafted power sword	Melee	Melee	User	-3	2	-
Frag grenade	6"	Grenade D6	3	0	1	-
Krak grenade	6"	Grenade 1	6	-1	D3	-

ABILITIES	**Death to the False Emperor** (pg 118) **Armour of Shrieking Souls:** Lucius the Eternal has a 5+ invulnerable save. Whenever you make a successful saving throw for Lucius in the Fight phase, roll a D6. On a roll of 4+, the unit that made the attack suffers 1 mortal wound after all of its attacks have been made.	**Duellist's Pride:** If Lucius the Eternal directs all of his attacks against a single enemy **Character**, roll an extra 2 attacks. These extra attacks must also be directed at that character. **Lord of Slaanesh:** You can re-roll all hit rolls of 1 made for friendly **Emperor's Children** units within 6" of Lucius the Eternal.
FACTION KEYWORDS	**Chaos, Slaanesh, Heretic Astartes, Emperor's Children**	
KEYWORDS	**Character, Infantry, Chaos Lord, Lucius the Eternal**	

CYPHER

4 POWER

NAME	M	WS	BS	S	T	W	A	Ld	Sv
Cypher	7"	2+	2+	4	4	5	4	9	3+

Cypher is a single model armed with his unique pistols – a bolt pistol and a plasma pistol – frag grenades and krak grenades. Only one of this model may be included in your army.

WEAPON	RANGE	TYPE	S	AP	D	ABILITIES
Cypher's bolt pistol	16"	Pistol 3	4	-1	1	-
Cypher's plasma pistol	12"	Pistol 2	8	-3	2	-
Frag grenade	6"	Grenade D6	3	0	1	-
Krak grenade	6"	Grenade 1	6	-1	D3	-

ABILITIES	
Mysterious Protection: Cypher has a 4+ invulnerable save. In addition, roll a D6 if Cypher is slain. On a roll of 2+, Cypher's model is still removed from play, but he is not considered to have been slain for the purposes of any mission victory conditions. **Lord Cypher:** You can re-roll hit rolls of 1 made for friendly **FALLEN** units within 6" of Cypher.	**Blazing Weapons:** Cypher can use his pistols in your Shooting phase even if he has Advanced or Fallen Back in the same turn. **No-one's Puppet:** Cypher cannot use the Daemonic Ritual ability, even though he has the **CHAOS** and **CHARACTER** keywords.

FACTION KEYWORDS	**IMPERIUM, CHAOS, FALLEN**
KEYWORDS	**CHARACTER, INFANTRY, CYPHER**

HURON BLACKHEART

6 POWER

NAME	M	WS	BS	S	T	W	A	Ld	Sv
Huron Blackheart	6"	2+	2+	4	4	5	5	9	3+
Hamadrya	6"	6+	-	2	4	1	1	9	3+

Huron Blackheart and his Hamadrya are a single unit. Huron is armed with the Tyrant's Claw, a power axe, frag grenades and krak grenades. Only one of this unit may be included in your army.

WEAPON	RANGE	TYPE	S	AP	D	ABILITIES
Tyrant's Claw (shooting)	9"	Assault D6	5	-1	1	This weapon automatically hits its target.
Power axe	Melee	Melee	+1	-2	1	-
Tyrant's Claw (melee)	Melee	Melee	x2	-3	D3	When attacking with this weapon, you must subtract 1 from the hit roll.
Frag grenade	6"	Grenade D6	3	0	1	-
Krak grenade	6"	Grenade 1	6	-1	D3	-

ABILITIES	
Death to the False Emperor (pg 118) **The Tyrant of Badab:** If your army is Battle-forged and Huron Blackheart is your Warlord, you receive 1 additional Command Point. **Sigil of Corruption:** Huron Blackheart has a 4+ invulnerable save.	**The Hamadrya:** After Huron Blackheart has manifested a psychic power, his Hamadrya can lend him additional power if it is still alive. When it does so, Huron Blackheart can immediately attempt to manifest an additional psychic power. **Lord of the Red Corsairs:** You can re-roll hit rolls of 1 for friendly **RED CORSAIRS** units within 6" of Huron Blackheart.

PSYKER	Huron Blackheart can attempt to manifest one psychic power in each friendly Psychic phase, and attempt to deny one psychic power in each enemy Psychic phase. He knows the *Smite* psychic power and one psychic power from the Dark Hereticus discipline (pg 168).

FACTION KEYWORDS	**CHAOS, HERETIC ASTARTES, RED CORSAIRS**
KEYWORDS	**CHARACTER, INFANTRY, CHAOS LORD, PSYKER, HURON BLACKHEART**

CHAOS LORD

NAME	M	WS	BS	S	T	W	A	Ld	Sv
Chaos Lord	6"	2+	2+	4	4	5	4	9	3+

A Chaos Lord is a single model armed with a chainsword, a bolt pistol, frag grenades and krak grenades.

WEAPON	RANGE	TYPE	S	AP	D	ABILITIES
Bolt pistol	12"	Pistol 1	4	0	1	-
Chainsword	Melee	Melee	User	0	1	Each time the bearer fights, it can make 1 additional attack with this weapon.
Frag grenade	6"	Grenade D6	3	0	1	-
Krak grenade	6"	Grenade 1	6	-1	D3	-

WARGEAR OPTIONS	• This model may replace its bolt pistol with one item from the *Pistols*, *Combi-weapons* or *Melee Weapons* list. • This model may replace its chainsword with one item from the *Pistols* or *Melee Weapons* list. • This model may take a jump pack (**Power Rating +1**). If it does, its Move characteristic is increased to 12" and it gains the **JUMP PACK** and **FLY** keywords.

ABILITIES	**Death to the False Emperor** (pg 118) **Lord of Chaos:** You can re-roll hit rolls of 1 made for friendly **<LEGION>** units within 6" of this model. **Sigil of Corruption:** This model has a 4+ invulnerable save.	**Jump Pack Assault:** During deployment, if this model has a jump pack, you can set it up high in the skies instead of placing it on the battlefield. At the end of any of your Movement phases this model can assault from above – set it up anywhere on the battlefield that is more than 9" away from any enemy models.

FACTION KEYWORDS	CHAOS, <MARK OF CHAOS>, HERETIC ASTARTES, <LEGION>
KEYWORDS	CHARACTER, INFANTRY, CHAOS LORD

CHAOS LORD
IN TERMINATOR ARMOUR

NAME	M	WS	BS	S	T	W	A	Ld	Sv
Chaos Lord in Terminator Armour	5"	2+	2+	4	4	6	4	9	2+

A Chaos Lord in Terminator Armour is a single model armed with a power sword and combi-bolter.

WEAPON	RANGE	TYPE	S	AP	D	ABILITIES
Combi-bolter	24"	Rapid Fire 2	4	0	1	-
Power sword	Melee	Melee	User	-3	1	-

WARGEAR OPTIONS	• This model may replace its combi-bolter with one item from the *Combi-weapons* or *Terminator Melee Weapons* list. • This model may replace its power sword with one item from the *Terminator Melee Weapons* list.

ABILITIES	**Death to the False Emperor** (pg 118) **Lord of Chaos:** You can re-roll hit rolls of 1 made for friendly **<LEGION>** units within 6" of this model. **Sigil of Corruption:** This model has a 4+ invulnerable save.	**Teleport Strike:** During deployment, you can set up a Chaos Lord in Terminator armour in a teleportarium chamber instead of placing him on the battlefield. At the end of any of your Movement phases he can use a teleport strike to arrive on the battlefield – set him up anywhere on the battlefield that is more than 9" away from any enemy models.

FACTION KEYWORDS	CHAOS, <MARK OF CHAOS>, HERETIC ASTARTES, <LEGION>
KEYWORDS	CHARACTER, INFANTRY, TERMINATOR, CHAOS LORD

MASTER OF POSSESSION

NAME	M	WS	BS	S	T	W	A	Ld	Sv
Master of Possession	6"	3+	3+	4	4	4	3	9	3+

A Master of Possession is a single model armed with a force stave, bolt pistol, frag grenades and krak grenades.

WEAPON	RANGE	TYPE	S	AP	D	ABILITIES
Bolt pistol	12"	Pistol 1	4	0	1	-
Force stave	Melee	Melee	+2	-1	D3	-
Frag grenade	6"	Grenade D6	3	0	1	-
Krak grenade	6"	Grenade 1	6	-1	D3	-

ABILITIES	Death to the False Emperor (pg 118)	Rite of Possession: PSYKERS suffer Perils of the Warp on any Psychic test roll of a double that is made for them, instead of just double 1 or 6, while they are within 12" of any enemy models with this ability.
	Daemonkin: This model has a 5+ invulnerable save.	
PSYKER	This model can attempt to manifest two psychic powers in each friendly Psychic phase, and attempt to deny one psychic power in each enemy Psychic phase. It knows the *Smite* psychic power and two psychic powers from the Malefic discipline (pg 169).	
FACTION KEYWORDS	CHAOS, <MARK OF CHAOS>, HERETIC ASTARTES, <LEGION>	
KEYWORDS	CHARACTER, INFANTRY, PSYKER, MASTER OF POSSESSION	

SORCERER

NAME	M	WS	BS	S	T	W	A	Ld	Sv
Sorcerer	6"	3+	3+	4	4	4	3	9	3+

A Sorcerer is a single model armed with a force sword, a bolt pistol, frag grenades and krak grenades.

WEAPON	RANGE	TYPE	S	AP	D	ABILITIES
Bolt pistol	12"	Pistol 1	4	0	1	-
Force axe	Melee	Melee	+1	-2	D3	-
Force stave	Melee	Melee	+2	-1	D3	-
Force sword	Melee	Melee	User	-3	D3	-
Frag grenade	6"	Grenade D6	3	0	1	-
Krak grenade	6"	Grenade 1	6	-1	D3	-

WARGEAR OPTIONS	• This model may replace its bolt pistol with one item from the *Pistols*, *Combi-weapons* or *Melee Weapons* list. • This model may replace its force sword with a force stave or force axe. • This model may take a jump pack (**Power Rating +1**). If it does, its Move characteristic is increased to 12" and it gains the **JUMP PACK** and **FLY** keywords.
ABILITIES	Death to the False Emperor (pg 118) Jump Pack Assault: During deployment, if this model has a jump pack, you can set it up high in the skies instead of placing it on the battlefield. At the end of any of your Movement phases this model can assault from above – set it up anywhere on the battlefield that is more than 9" away from any enemy models.
PSYKER	This model can attempt to manifest two psychic powers in each friendly Psychic phase, and attempt to deny one psychic power in each enemy Psychic phase. It knows the *Smite* psychic power and two psychic powers from the Dark Hereticus discipline (pg 168).
FACTION KEYWORDS	CHAOS, <MARK OF CHAOS>, HERETIC ASTARTES, <LEGION>
KEYWORDS	CHARACTER, INFANTRY, PSYKER, SORCERER

SORCERER
IN TERMINATOR ARMOUR

NAME	M	WS	BS	S	T	W	A	Ld	Sv
Sorcerer in Terminator Armour	5"	3+	3+	4	4	5	3	9	2+

A Sorcerer in Terminator Armour is a single model armed with a force stave and combi-bolter.

WEAPON	RANGE	TYPE	S	AP	D	ABILITIES
Combi-bolter	24"	Rapid Fire 2	4	0	1	-
Force axe	Melee	Melee	+1	-2	D3	-
Force stave	Melee	Melee	+2	-1	D3	-
Force sword	Melee	Melee	User	-3	D3	-

WARGEAR OPTIONS	• This model may replace its combi-bolter with one item from the *Combi-weapons* or *Terminator Melee Weapons* list. • This model may replace its force stave with a force axe or force sword.
ABILITIES	**Death to the False Emperor** (pg 118) **Terminator Armour:** This model has a 5+ invulnerable save.	**Teleport Strike:** During deployment, you can set up a Sorcerer in Terminator armour in a teleportarium chamber instead of placing him on the battlefield. At the end of any of your Movement phases he can use a teleport strike to arrive on the battlefield – set him up anywhere on the battlefield that is more than 9" away from any enemy models.
PSYKER	This model can attempt to manifest two psychic powers in each friendly Psychic phase, and attempt to deny one psychic power in each enemy Psychic phase. It knows the *Smite* psychic power and two psychic powers from the Dark Hereticus discipline (pg 168).
FACTION KEYWORDS	**CHAOS, <MARK OF CHAOS>, HERETIC ASTARTES, <LEGION>**
KEYWORDS	**CHARACTER, INFANTRY, TERMINATOR, PSYKER, SORCERER**

EXALTED CHAMPION

NAME	M	WS	BS	S	T	W	A	Ld	Sv
Exalted Champion	6"	2+	3+	4	4	4	4	8	3+

An Exalted Champion is a single model armed with a chainsword, a bolt pistol, frag grenades and krak grenades.

WEAPON	RANGE	TYPE	S	AP	D	ABILITIES
Bolt pistol	12"	Pistol 1	4	0	1	-
Chainsword	Melee	Melee	User	0	1	Each time the bearer fights, it can make 1 additional attack with this weapon.
Frag grenade	6"	Grenade D6	3	0	1	-
Krak grenade	6"	Grenade 1	6	-1	D3	-

WARGEAR OPTIONS	• This model may replace its bolt pistol with one item from the *Pistols*, *Combi-weapons* or *Melee Weapons* list. • This model may replace its chainsword with one item from the *Pistols* or *Melee Weapons* list.
ABILITIES	**Death to the False Emperor** (pg 118) **Aspire to Glory:** You can re-roll failed wound rolls in the Fight phase for friendly **<LEGION>** units that are within 6" of an Exalted Champion. **For the Dark Gods:** You can re-roll failed hit rolls for this model if the target is an enemy **CHARACTER**.
FACTION KEYWORDS	**CHAOS, <MARK OF CHAOS>, HERETIC ASTARTES, <LEGION>**
KEYWORDS	**CHARACTER, INFANTRY, EXALTED CHAMPION**

LORD DISCORDANT
ON HELSTALKER

DAMAGE
Some of this model's characteristics change as it suffers damage, as shown below:

REMAINING W	M	ADDITIONAL ATTACKS
7-12+	12"	5
4-6	9"	4
1-3	6"	3

NAME	M	WS	BS	S	T	W	A	Ld	Sv
Lord Discordant on Helstalker	*	2+	2+	4	6	12	4	9	2+

A Lord Discordant on Helstalker is a single model armed with an autocannon, bolt pistol, impaler chainglaive, mechatendrils, frag grenades and krak grenades. His Helstalker is armed with bladed limbs and tail and a techno-virus injector.

WEAPON	RANGE	TYPE	S	AP	D	ABILITIES
Lord Discordant						
Autocannon	48"	Heavy 2	7	-1	2	-
Baleflamer	18"	Assault D6	6	-2	2	This weapon automatically hits its target.
Bolt pistol	12"	Pistol 1	4	0	1	-
Impaler chainglaive	Melee	Melee	+2	-2	2	If the bearer made a charge move or performed a Heroic Intervention this turn, attacks with this weapon are made with a Strength characteristic of x2 instead of +2.
Mechatendrils	Melee	Melee	User	0	1	Each time the bearer fights, it can make 2 additional attacks with this weapon.
Frag grenade	6"	Grenade D6	3	0	1	-
Krak grenade	6"	Grenade 1	6	-1	D3	-
Helstalker						
Magma cutter	6"	Pistol 1	8	-4	3	-
Bladed limbs and tail	Melee	Melee	+3	-2	D3	After the Lord Discordant makes his close combat attacks, you can attack with his Helstalker. Make a number of additional attacks as shown in the damage table above, using this weapon profile.
Techno-virus injector	Melee	Melee	+4	-4	D3	After the Lord Discordant makes his close combat attacks, you can attack with his Helstalker. Make a single attack using this weapon profile in addition to the Helstalker's bladed limbs and tail. Each time a wound roll for an attack made with this weapon is successful when targeting a **VEHICLE** unit, that unit suffers D3 mortal wounds in addition to any normal damage.

WARGEAR OPTIONS	• The Lord Discordant can replace his autocannon with a baleflamer. • The Helstalker can replace its techno-virus injector with a magma cutter.

ABILITIES	**Death to the False Emperor** (pg 118) **Daemonic:** This model has a 5+ invulnerable save. **Infernal Regeneration:** At the start of your turn, this model regains 1 lost wound. **Aura of Discord:** Subtract 1 from hit rolls for attacks made by **VEHICLE** units while they are within 6" of any enemy models with this ability. In addition, add 1 to hit rolls for attacks made by **<LEGION> DAEMON ENGINE** units while they are within 6" of any friendly **<LEGION>** models with this ability.	**Spirit Thief:** Each time this model destroys an enemy **VEHICLE** unit in the Fight phase, this model can either repair a friendly Daemon Engine or release a beam of energy. If you choose to repair a friendly Daemon Engine, pick a friendly **<LEGION> DAEMON ENGINE** (other than models that can **FLY**) within 3" of this model. That **DAEMON ENGINE** regains D3 lost wounds. If you choose to release a beam of energy, pick an enemy **VEHICLE** within 12" of this model and roll a D6. On a 2+ that **VEHICLE** suffers D3 mortal wounds.

FACTION KEYWORDS	**CHAOS, <MARK OF CHAOS>, HERETIC ASTARTES, <LEGION>**

KEYWORDS	**CHARACTER, VEHICLE, DAEMON, DAEMON ENGINE, WARPSMITH, HELSTALKER, LORD DISCORDANT**

WARPSMITH

4 POWER

NAME	M	WS	BS	S	T	W	A	Ld	Sv
Warpsmith	6"	3+	2+	4	4	4	3	9	2+

A Warpsmith is a single model armed with a power axe, mechatendrils, a meltagun, a flamer, a bolt pistol, frag grenades and krak grenades.

WEAPON	RANGE	TYPE	S	AP	D	ABILITIES
Bolt pistol	12"	Pistol 1	4	0	1	-
Flamer	8"	Assault D6	4	0	1	This weapon automatically hits its target.
Meltagun	12"	Assault 1	8	-4	D6	If the target is within half range of this weapon, roll two dice when inflicting damage with it and discard the lowest result.
Mechatendrils	Melee	Melee	User	0	1	Each time the bearer fights, it can make 2 additional attacks with this weapon.
Power axe	Melee	Melee	+1	-2	1	-
Frag grenade	6"	Grenade D6	3	0	1	-
Krak grenade	6"	Grenade 1	6	-1	D3	-

WARGEAR OPTIONS	• This model may replace its bolt pistol with one item from the *Pistols* or *Combi-weapons* list.

ABILITIES	**Death to the False Emperor** (pg 118) **Master of Mechanisms:** At the end of your Movement phase, a Warpsmith can repair a single friendly \<LEGION\> VEHICLE (other than models that can FLY) within 1". That model regains D3 lost wounds. A Warpsmith can instead curse a single enemy VEHICLE within 18". Roll a D6; on a roll of 2+, that vehicle suffers 1 mortal wound. A VEHICLE cannot be repaired or cursed by more than one Warpsmith in the same turn.
FACTION KEYWORDS	CHAOS, \<MARK OF CHAOS\>, HERETIC ASTARTES, \<LEGION\>
KEYWORDS	CHARACTER, INFANTRY, WARPSMITH

MASTER OF EXECUTIONS

4 POWER

NAME	M	WS	BS	S	T	W	A	Ld	Sv
Master of Executions	6"	2+	3+	4	4	4	5	9	3+

A Master of Executions is a single model armed with an axe of dismemberment, bolt pistol, frag grenades and krak grenades.

WEAPON	RANGE	TYPE	S	AP	D	ABILITIES
Bolt pistol	12"	Pistol 1	4	0	1	-
Axe of dismemberment	Melee	Melee	x2	-3	D3	Each time you make a wound roll of 6+ for this weapon, the target unit suffers 1 mortal wound in addition to any other damage.
Frag grenade	6"	Grenade D6	3	0	1	-
Krak grenade	6"	Grenade 1	6	-1	D3	-

ABILITIES	**Death to the False Emperor** (pg 118) **Trophy-taker:** Once per Fight phase, you can re-roll one hit roll, wound roll or damage roll for an attack made by this model that targets a CHARACTER.	**Warp-sighted Butcher:** After the enemy has completed all of their charge moves, this model can perform a Heroic Intervention if it is within 3" of any enemy models, or 6" of any enemy CHARACTERS. If this model is within 6" of any enemy CHARACTERS, it can move up to 6" when performing a Heroic Intervention instead of 3", as long as it finishes this move within 1" of the nearest enemy CHARACTER.
FACTION KEYWORDS	CHAOS, \<MARK OF CHAOS\>, HERETIC ASTARTES, \<LEGION\>	
KEYWORDS	CHARACTER, INFANTRY, MASTER OF EXECUTIONS	

DARK APOSTLE

NAME	M	WS	BS	S	T	W	A	Ld	Sv
Dark Apostle	6"	2+	3+	4	4	4	3	9	3+

A Dark Apostle is a single model armed with an accursed crozius, bolt pistol, frag grenades and krak grenades.

WEAPON	RANGE	TYPE	S	AP	D	ABILITIES
Bolt pistol	12"	Pistol 1	4	0	1	-
Accursed crozius	Melee	Melee	+1	-1	2	-
Frag grenade	6"	Grenade D6	3	0	1	-
Krak grenade	6"	Grenade 1	6	-1	D3	-

ABILITIES	**Death to the False Emperor** (pg 118) **Sigil of Corruption:** This model has a 4+ invulnerable save.	**Demagogue:** Friendly <Legion> units within 6" of this model in the Morale phase can use this model's Leadership instead of their own.

PRIEST	This model can chant prayers. It knows the Dark Zealotry prayer (below) and one prayer from the Prayers to the Dark Gods (pg 167). At the start of each battle round, you can pick one of the prayers this model knows and roll a D6. On a 3+, the prayer is heard. That prayer takes effect until the end of that battle round. The same prayer cannot be chanted more than once per battle round by any model in your army, whether it is heard or not. **Dark Zealotry:** If this prayer is heard, you can re-roll hit rolls in the Fight phase for attacks made by friendly <Legion> units while they are within 6" of this priest.

FACTION KEYWORDS	**Chaos, <Mark of Chaos>, Heretic Astartes, <Legion>**
KEYWORDS	**Character, Infantry, Priest, Dark Apostle**

DARK DISCIPLES

NAME	M	WS	BS	S	T	W	A	Ld	Sv
Dark Disciple	6"	4+	5+	3	3	1	1	6	5+

This unit contains 2 Dark Disciples. Each model is armed with a close combat weapon.

WEAPON	RANGE	TYPE	S	AP	D	ABILITIES
Close combat weapon	Melee	Melee	User	0	1	-

ABILITIES	**Followers:** Only one unit of Dark Disciples can be included in your army for each Dark Apostle in your army. <Legion> Dark Disciples units do not take up slots in a Detachment that includes any <Legion> Dark Apostles. While this unit is within 2" of any friendly <Legion> Dark Apostles, enemy models can only shoot this unit if it is the closest enemy unit (ignore **Characters** with a Wounds characteristic of less than 10 when determining if this unit is the closest enemy unit to the firing model). **Relic of Corruption:** While any <Legion> Dark Disciples units are within 2" of a friendly <Legion> Dark Apostle, add 1 to dice rolls to see if a prayer chanted by that Dark Apostle is heard.

FACTION KEYWORDS	**Chaos, <Mark of Chaos>, Heretic Astartes, <Legion>**
KEYWORDS	**Infantry, Dark Disciples**

CHAOS SPACE MARINES

NAME	M	WS	BS	S	T	W	A	Ld	Sv
Chaos Space Marine	6"	3+	3+	4	4	1	1	7	3+
Aspiring Champion	6"	3+	3+	4	4	1	2	8	3+

This unit contains 1 Aspiring Champion and 4 Chaos Space Marines. It can include up to 5 additional Chaos Space Marines (**Power Rating +4**), up to 10 additional Chaos Space Marines (**Power Rating +7**) or up to 15 additional Chaos Space Marines (**Power Rating +10**). Each model is armed with a boltgun, bolt pistol, frag grenades and krak grenades.

WEAPON	RANGE	TYPE	S	AP	D	ABILITIES
Bolt pistol	12"	Pistol 1	4	0	1	-
Boltgun	24"	Rapid Fire 1	4	0	1	-
Plasma pistol	When attacking with this weapon, choose one of the profiles below.					
- Standard	12"	Pistol 1	7	-3	1	-
- Supercharge	12"	Pistol 1	8	-3	2	On a hit roll of 1, the bearer is slain.
Chainsword	Melee	Melee	User	0	1	Each time the bearer fights, it can make 1 additional attack with this weapon.
Frag grenade	6"	Grenade D6	3	0	1	-
Krak grenade	6"	Grenade 1	6	-1	D3	-

WARGEAR OPTIONS	
	• The Aspiring Champion may replace his bolt pistol and boltgun with items from the *Champion Equipment* list.
	• Any Chaos Space Marine may replace his boltgun with a chainsword.
	• One Chaos Space Marine may replace his bolt pistol with a plasma pistol, or replace his boltgun with one item from the *Special Weapons* or *Heavy Weapons* list.
	• If the unit numbers ten or more models, an additional Chaos Space Marine may replace his boltgun with one item from the *Special Weapons* or *Heavy Weapons* list.
	• One model may take a Chaos Icon (pg 159).

ABILITIES	**Death to the False Emperor** (pg 118)
FACTION KEYWORDS	**CHAOS, <MARK OF CHAOS>, HERETIC ASTARTES, <LEGION>**
KEYWORDS	**INFANTRY, CHAOS SPACE MARINES**

With weapons and armour emblazoned with profane iconography, Chaos Space Marines stride boldly across the field of battle, howling promises of death to all who would dare stand in their path.

CHAOS CULTISTS

NAME	M	WS	BS	S	T	W	A	Ld	Sv
Chaos Cultist	6"	4+	4+	3	3	1	1	5	6+
Cultist Champion	6"	4+	4+	3	3	1	2	6	6+

This unit contains 1 Cultist Champion and 9 Chaos Cultists. It can include up to 10 additional Chaos Cultists (**Power Rating +3**) or up to 20 additional Chaos Cultists (**Power Rating +6**). Each model is armed with an autogun.

WEAPON	RANGE	TYPE	S	AP	D	ABILITIES
Autogun	24"	Rapid Fire 1	3	0	1	-
Autopistol	12"	Pistol 1	3	0	1	-
Flamer	8"	Assault D6	4	0	1	This weapon automatically hits its target.
Heavy stubber	36"	Heavy 3	4	0	1	-
Shotgun	12"	Assault 2	3	0	1	If the target is within half range, add 1 to this weapon's Strength.
Brutal assault weapon	Melee	Melee	User	0	1	Each time the bearer fights, it can make 1 additional attack with this weapon.

WARGEAR OPTIONS	• Any Chaos Cultist may replace their autogun with an autopistol and brutal assault weapon. • For every ten models in the unit, one Chaos Cultist may replace their autogun with a heavy stubber or a flamer. • The Cultist Champion may replace their autogun with a shotgun or a brutal assault weapon and autopistol.
FACTION KEYWORDS	**CHAOS, <MARK OF CHAOS>, HERETIC ASTARTES, <LEGION>**
KEYWORDS	**INFANTRY, CHAOS CULTISTS**

Chaos Cultists charge in teeming throngs towards the enemy in the hope of earning the favour of the Dark Gods.

BLOODLETTERS

NAME	M	WS	BS	S	T	W	A	Ld	Sv
Bloodletter	6"	3+	3+	4	3	1	1	7	6+
Bloodreaper	6"	3+	3+	4	3	1	2	7	6+

This unit contains 1 Bloodreaper and 9 Bloodletters. It can include up to 10 additional Bloodletters (**Power Rating +4**) or up to 20 additional Bloodletters (**Power Rating +8**). Each model is armed with a hellblade.

WEAPON	RANGE	TYPE	S	AP	D	ABILITIES
Hellblade	Melee	Melee	User	-3	1	Each time you make a wound roll of 6+ for this weapon, that hit is resolved with a Damage of 2.

WARGEAR OPTIONS	
	• For every ten models in the unit, one Bloodletter may take an Instrument of Chaos. • For every ten models in the unit, one Bloodletter may take a Daemonic Icon.

ABILITIES

Daemonic Ritual (pg 119)

Daemonic: Models in this unit have a 5+ invulnerable save.

Unstoppable Ferocity: If this unit charges or is charged, add 1 to the Strength and Attacks characteristics of all models in the unit until the end of the turn.

Murderous Tide: Bloodletters attacking en masse are a terrifying prospect, swarming forwards to eviscerate foes with their hellblades. You can add 1 to hit rolls made for each model in this unit while it contains 20 or more models.

Daemonic Icon: If you roll a 1 when taking a Morale test for a unit with any Daemonic Icons, reality blinks and the daemonic horde is bolstered. No models flee and D6 slain Bloodletters are instead added to the unit.

Instrument of Chaos: A unit that includes any Instruments of Chaos adds 1 to their Advance and charge rolls.

FACTION KEYWORDS	**CHAOS, KHORNE, DAEMON**
KEYWORDS	**INFANTRY, BLOODLETTERS**

HORRORS

NAME	M	WS	BS	S	T	W	A	Ld	Sv
Pink Horror	6"	4+	4+	3	3	1	1	7	6+
Blue Horror	6"	5+	-	2	3	1	1	7	6+
Pair of Brimstone Horrors	6"	5+	-	1	3	1	2	7	6+

This unit contains 10 Pink, Blue or pairs of Brimstone Horrors, in any combination. It can include up to 10 additional Horrors (**Power Rating +4**) or up to 20 additional Horrors (**Power Rating +8**). Pink Horrors attack with coruscating flames, while Blue Horrors and Brimstone Horrors simply scrabble at anyone who comes too close.

WEAPON	RANGE	TYPE	S	AP	D	ABILITIES
Coruscating flames	18"	Assault 2	User	0	1	-

WARGEAR OPTIONS	• For every ten models in the unit, one Pink Horror may take an Instrument of Chaos. • For every ten models in the unit, one Pink Horror may take a Daemonic Icon.

ABILITIES	**Daemonic Ritual** (pg 119) **Daemonic Icon:** If you roll a 1 when taking a Morale test for a unit with any Daemonic Icons, reality blinks and the daemonic horde is bolstered. No models flee and D6 slain Pink Horrors are instead added to the unit. **Split:** Each time a Pink Horror is slain, you can add up to two Blue Horrors to its unit before you remove the slain model. Each time a Blue Horror is slain, you can add one pair of Brimstone Horrors to its unit before you remove the slain model. The replacement models cannot be placed within 1" of an enemy model. Note that Horrors that flee do not generate any extra models for their unit. *Matched Play: In matched play you must pay reinforcement points for each and every Blue and Brimstone Horror model that you add to a unit of Horrors, but the additional models can take the unit above its starting strength.* **Instrument of Chaos:** A unit that includes any Instruments of Chaos adds 1 to their Advance and charge rolls.	**Iridescent Horror:** When you set up this unit for the first time, you may select a single Pink Horror in the unit – that model has an Attacks characteristic of 2, instead of 1. **Magic Made Manifest:** A unit of Horrors can attempt to manifest one psychic power in each friendly Psychic phase, and attempt to deny one psychic power in each enemy Psychic phase. However, when you do so, only roll a single D6 for the Psychic test or Deny the Witch test, and use the result to determine the outcome. Note that this means the Horrors cannot roll a double 1 or 6 to suffer Perils of the Warp. In addition, if the unit manifests the *Smite* psychic power while it contains less than 10 Pink Horror models, it only inflicts 1 mortal wound rather than D3. **Ephemeral Daemons:** Pink Horrors have an invulnerable save of 4+. Blue Horrors have an invulnerable save of 5+. Pairs of Brimstone Horrors have an invulnerable save of 6+. **Magical Horde:** Change the Type of this unit's coruscating flames to Assault 3 while the unit contains 20 or more Pink Horrors.

PSYKER	This unit can attempt to manifest one psychic power in each friendly Psychic phase, and attempt to deny one psychic power in each enemy Psychic phase. It knows the *Smite* power. When manifesting or denying a psychic power, first select a model in the unit – measure range, visibility etc. from this model. If a Brimstone Horror is selected, it is slain after the psychic power has been attempted and, if successful, resolved.

FACTION KEYWORDS	**CHAOS, TZEENTCH, DAEMON**
KEYWORDS	**INFANTRY, PSYKER, HORRORS**

'Butcher your enemy's warriors without mercy. Crush his armies and leave none alive. But do not stop there. Burn his cities. Bomb his worlds from orbit. Slaughter everything and everyone until he kneels in the ashes of those he sought to protect. Only then will he understand the true fury of the Dark Gods.'

- *Haakor of the Black Legion*

PLAGUEBEARERS

NAME	M	WS	BS	S	T	W	A	Ld	Sv
Plaguebearer	5"	4+	4+	4	4	1	1	7	6+
Plagueridden	5"	4+	4+	4	4	1	2	7	6+

This unit contains 1 Plagueridden and 9 Plaguebearers. It can include up to 10 additional Plaguebearers (**Power Rating +4**) or up to 20 additional Plaguebearers (**Power Rating +8**). Each model is armed with a plaguesword.

WEAPON	RANGE	TYPE	S	AP	D	ABILITIES
Plaguesword	Melee	Melee	User	0	1	You can re-roll failed wound rolls for this weapon.

WARGEAR OPTIONS	• For every ten models in the unit, one Plaguebearer may take an Instrument of Chaos. • For every ten models in the unit, one Plaguebearer may take a Daemonic Icon.

ABILITIES

Daemonic Ritual (pg 119)

Daemonic: Models in this unit have a 5+ invulnerable save.

Disgustingly Resilient: Each time a model in this unit loses a wound, roll a D6; on a roll of 5 or 6, the model does not lose that wound.

Instrument of Chaos: A unit that includes any Instruments of Chaos adds 1 to their Advance and charge rolls.

Cloud of Flies: Large groups of Plaguebearers attract great clouds of flies that buzz about them, obscuring them from view. If this unit contains 20 or more models at the start of a phase, your opponent must subtract 1 from all hit rolls for attacks that target them.

Daemonic Icon: If you roll a 1 when taking a Morale test for a unit with any Daemonic Icons, reality blinks and the daemonic horde is bolstered. No models flee and D6 slain Plaguebearers are instead added to the unit.

FACTION KEYWORDS	CHAOS, NURGLE, DAEMON
KEYWORDS	INFANTRY, PLAGUEBEARERS

DAEMONETTES

NAME	M	WS	BS	S	T	W	A	Ld	Sv
Daemonette	7"	3+	3+	3	3	1	2	7	6+
Alluress	7"	3+	3+	3	3	1	3	7	6+

This unit contains 1 Alluress and 9 Daemonettes. It can include up to 10 additional Daemonettes (**Power Rating +4**) or up to 20 additional Daemonettes (**Power Rating +8**). Each model attacks with piercing claws.

WEAPON	RANGE	TYPE	S	AP	D	ABILITIES
Piercing claws	Melee	Melee	User	-1	1	Each time you make a wound roll of 6+ for this weapon, that hit is resolved with an AP of -4.

WARGEAR OPTIONS	• For every ten models in the unit, one Daemonette may take an Instrument of Chaos. • For every ten models in the unit, one Daemonette may take a Daemonic Icon.

ABILITIES

Daemonic Ritual (pg 119)

Daemonic: Models in this unit have a 5+ invulnerable save.

Graceful Killers: Increase the Attacks characteristic of each model in this unit by 1 while it contains 20 or more models.

Instrument of Chaos: A unit that includes any Instruments of Chaos adds 1 to their Advance and charge rolls.

Quicksilver Swiftness: This unit always fights first in the Fight phase even if it didn't charge. If the enemy has units that have charged, or that have a similar ability, then alternate choosing units to fight with, starting with the player whose turn is taking place.

Daemonic Icon: If you roll a 1 when taking a Morale test for a unit with any Daemonic Icons, reality blinks and the daemonic horde is bolstered. No models flee and D6 slain Daemonettes are instead added to the unit.

FACTION KEYWORDS	CHAOS, SLAANESH, DAEMON
KEYWORDS	INFANTRY, DAEMONETTES

CHOSEN

NAME	M	WS	BS	S	T	W	A	Ld	Sv
Chosen	6"	3+	3+	4	4	1	2	8	3+
Chosen Champion	6"	3+	3+	4	4	1	3	9	3+

This unit contains 1 Chosen Champion and 4 Chosen. It can include up to 5 additional Chosen (**Power Rating +5**). Each model is armed with a boltgun, a bolt pistol, frag grenades and krak grenades.

WEAPON	RANGE	TYPE	S	AP	D	ABILITIES
Bolt pistol	12"	Pistol 1	4	0	1	-
Boltgun	24"	Rapid Fire 1	4	0	1	-
Plasma pistol	When attacking with this weapon, choose one of the profiles below.					
- Standard	12"	Pistol 1	7	-3	1	-
- Supercharge	12"	Pistol 1	8	-3	2	On a hit roll of 1, the bearer is slain.
Chainsword	Melee	Melee	User	0	1	Each time the bearer fights, it can make 1 additional attack with this weapon.
Lightning claw	Melee	Melee	User	-2	1	You can re-roll failed wound rolls for this weapon. If a model is armed with two lightning claws, each time it fights it can make 1 additional attack with them.
Frag grenade	6"	Grenade D6	3	0	1	-
Krak grenade	6"	Grenade 1	6	-1	D3	-

WARGEAR OPTIONS	• Any Chosen may take one item from the *Melee Weapons* list. • Up to four Chosen may choose one of the following options: - Replace his bolt pistol with a plasma pistol. - Replace his boltgun with one item from the *Combi-weapons* or *Special Weapons* list. - Replace his boltgun and bolt pistol with a lightning claw. • An additional Chosen may replace his boltgun with one item from the *Special Weapons* or *Heavy Weapons* list. • The Chosen Champion may either take one item from the *Melee Weapons* list, or replace his boltgun and bolt pistol with items from the *Champion Equipment* list. • One model may take a Chaos Icon (pg 159).
ABILITIES	**Death to the False Emperor** (pg 118)
FACTION KEYWORDS	**CHAOS, <MARK OF CHAOS>, HERETIC ASTARTES, <LEGION>**
KEYWORDS	**INFANTRY, CHOSEN**

TERMINATORS

NAME	M	WS	BS	S	T	W	A	Ld	Sv
Terminator	5"	3+	3+	4	4	2	2	8	2+
Terminator Champion	5"	3+	3+	4	4	2	3	9	2+

This unit contains 1 Terminator Champion and 4 Terminators. It can include up to 5 additional Terminators (**Power Rating +10**). Each model is armed with a combi-bolter and chainaxe.

WEAPON	RANGE	TYPE	S	AP	D	ABILITIES
Combi-bolter	24"	Rapid Fire 2	4	0	1	-
Heavy flamer	8"	Heavy D6	5	-1	1	This weapon automatically hits its target.
Reaper autocannon	36"	Heavy 4	7	-1	1	-
Chainaxe	Melee	Melee	+1	-1	1	-
Lightning claw	Melee	Melee	User	-2	1	You can re-roll failed wound rolls for this weapon. If a model is armed with two lightning claws, each time it fights it can make 1 additional attack with them.

WARGEAR OPTIONS	• Any model may replace its combi-bolter with one item from the *Combi-weapons* list. • Any model may replace its chainaxe with one item from the *Terminator Melee Weapons* list. • Any model may replace its combi-bolter and chainaxe with a pair of lightning claws. • For every five models in the unit, one Terminator may replace his combi-bolter with a heavy flamer or reaper autocannon. • One model may take a Chaos Icon (pg 159).
ABILITIES	**Death to the False Emperor** (pg 118) **Terminator Armour:** Models in this unit have a 5+ invulnerable save. **Teleport Strike:** During deployment, you can set up this unit in a teleportarium chamber instead of placing it on the battlefield. At the end of any of your Movement phases the unit can use a teleport strike to arrive on the battlefield – set it up anywhere on the battlefield that is more than 9" away from any enemy models.
FACTION KEYWORDS	**CHAOS, <MARK OF CHAOS>, HERETIC ASTARTES, <LEGION>**
KEYWORDS	**INFANTRY, TERMINATORS**

Though ponderous compared to their heretical brethren, Terminators are capable of weathering hails of incoming fire as they close the ground to slaughter their next victims.

GREATER POSSESSED

NAME	M	WS	BS	S	T	W	A	Ld	Sv
Greater Possessed	7"	2+	3+	5	5	5	5	8	3+

This unit contains 1 Greater Possessed. It can include 1 additional Greater Possessed (**Power Rating +4**). Each model attacks with daemonic mutations.

WEAPON	RANGE	TYPE		S	AP	D	ABILITIES
Daemonic mutations	Melee	Melee		User	-2	D3	-

ABILITIES	**Death to the False Emperor** (pg 118)	**Daemonic:** Models in this unit have a 5+ invulnerable save.
	Champions of the Host: The first time this unit is set up, all models in this unit must be set up at the same time, though they do not need to be set up in unit coherency. From that point onwards, each Greater Possessed is treated as a separate unit.	**Locus of Power:** Add 1 to the Strength characteristic of <MARK OF CHAOS> <LEGION> DAEMON units while they are within 6" of any friendly models with this ability.

FACTION KEYWORDS	CHAOS, <MARK OF CHAOS>, HERETIC ASTARTES, <LEGION>
KEYWORDS	CHARACTER, INFANTRY, DAEMON, GREATER POSSESSED

POSSESSED

NAME	M	WS	BS	S	T	W	A	Ld	Sv
Possessed	7"	3+	3+	5	4	2	*	8	3+

This unit contains 5 Possessed. It can include up to 5 additional Possessed (**Power Rating +5**), up to 10 additional Possessed (**Power Rating +10**) or up to 15 additional Possessed (**Power Rating +15**). Each model attacks with horrifying mutations.

WEAPON	RANGE	TYPE		S	AP	D	ABILITIES
Horrifying mutations	Melee	Melee		User	-2	1	-

WARGEAR OPTIONS	• One model may take a Chaos Icon (pg 159).

ABILITIES	**Death to the False Emperor** (pg 118)	**Writhing Tentacles:** Roll a D3 when a unit of Possessed is selected to attack in the Fight phase. The result is the Attacks characteristic of each model in the unit.
	Daemonic: Models in this unit have a 5+ invulnerable save.	

FACTION KEYWORDS	CHAOS, <MARK OF CHAOS>, HERETIC ASTARTES, <LEGION>
KEYWORDS	INFANTRY, DAEMON, POSSESSED

HELBRUTE

NAME	M	WS	BS	S	T	W	A	Ld	Sv
Helbrute	8"	3+	3+	6	7	8	4	8	3+

A Helbrute is a single model equipped with a multi-melta and a Helbrute fist.

WEAPON	RANGE	TYPE	S	AP	D	ABILITIES
Combi-bolter	24"	Rapid Fire 2	4	0	1	-
Heavy flamer	8"	Heavy D6	5	-1	1	This weapon automatically hits its target.
Helbrute plasma cannon	36"	Heavy D3	8	-3	2	For each hit roll of 1, the Helbrute suffers 1 mortal wound after all of this weapon's attacks have been resolved.
Missile launcher	When attacking with this weapon, choose one of the profiles below.					
- Frag missile	48"	Heavy D6	4	0	1	-
- Krak missile	48"	Heavy 1	8	-2	D6	-
Multi-melta	24"	Heavy 1	8	-4	D6	If the target is within half range of this weapon, roll two dice when inflicting damage with it and discard the lowest result.
Reaper autocannon	36"	Heavy 4	7	-1	1	-
Twin heavy bolter	36"	Heavy 6	5	-1	1	-
Twin lascannon	48"	Heavy 2	9	-3	D6	-
Helbrute fist	Melee	Melee	x2	-3	3	-
Helbrute hammer	Melee	Melee	x2	-4	D6	When attacking with this weapon, you must subtract 1 from the hit roll.
Power scourge	Melee	Melee	+2	-2	2	Each time the bearer fights, it can make 3 additional attacks with this weapon.

WARGEAR OPTIONS	• This model may replace its multi-melta with a second Helbrute fist, or a twin heavy bolter, twin lascannon, Helbrute plasma cannon, or reaper autocannon. • This model may replace one Helbrute fist with a missile launcher. • This model may replace each Helbrute fist with a Helbrute hammer or power scourge. • This model may incorporate a combi-bolter or heavy flamer into each Helbrute fist.

ABILITIES	**Crazed:** At the end of any phase in which this model suffers any unsaved wounds or mortal wounds, roll a D6. On a roll of 6, this model immediately makes a shooting attack as if it were your Shooting phase if there are no enemies within 1", or piles in and fights as if it were the Fight phase if there are enemies within 1". If there is no visible target within range, nothing happens.	**Battering Onslaught:** Add 1 to this model's Attacks characteristic if it is equipped with two melee weapons. **Explodes:** If this model is reduced to 0 wounds, roll a D6 before removing the model from the battlefield; on a 6 it explodes, and each unit within 3" suffers D3 mortal wounds.

FACTION KEYWORDS	**CHAOS, <MARK OF CHAOS>, HERETIC ASTARTES, <LEGION>**
KEYWORDS	**VEHICLE, HELBRUTE**

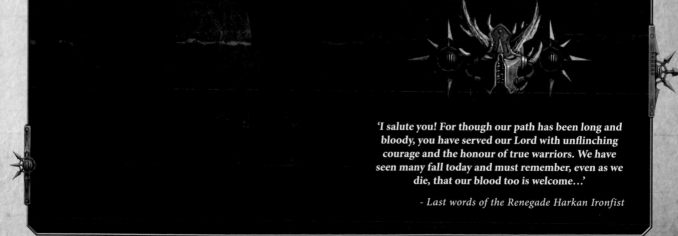

'I salute you! For though our path has been long and bloody, you have served our Lord with unflinching courage and the honour of true warriors. We have seen many fall today and must remember, even as we die, that our blood too is welcome…'

- *Last words of the Renegade Harkan Ironfist*

Khorne Berzerkers are vicious butchers driven to slaughter every living thing they find in the name of the Blood God.

KHORNE BERZERKERS

5 POWER

NAME	M	WS	BS	S	T	W	A	Ld	Sv
Khorne Berzerker	6"	3+	3+	5	4	1	2	7	3+
Berzerker Champion	6"	3+	3+	5	4	1	3	8	3+

This unit contains 1 Berzerker Champion and 4 Khorne Berzerkers. It can include up to 5 additional Khorne Berzerkers (**Power Rating +4**), up to 10 additional Khorne Berzerkers (**Power Rating +8**) or up to 15 additional Khorne Berzerkers (**Power Rating +12**). Each model is armed with a chainsword, bolt pistol, frag grenades and krak grenades.

WEAPON	RANGE	TYPE	S	AP	D	ABILITIES
Bolt pistol	12"	Pistol 1	4	0	1	-
Plasma pistol	When attacking with this weapon, choose one of the profiles below.					
- Standard	12"	Pistol 1	7	-3	1	-
- Supercharge	12"	Pistol 1	8	-3	2	On a hit roll of 1, the bearer is slain.
Chainaxe	Melee	Melee	+1	-1	1	-
Chainsword	Melee	Melee	User	0	1	Each time the bearer fights, it can make 1 additional attack with this weapon.
Frag grenade	6"	Grenade D6	3	0	1	-
Krak grenade	6"	Grenade 1	6	-1	D3	-

WARGEAR OPTIONS	• Any Khorne Berzerker may replace his chainsword or bolt pistol with a chainaxe.
	• Up to two Khorne Berzerkers may replace their bolt pistol with a plasma pistol.
	• The Berzerker Champion may replace his bolt pistol and chainsword with items from the *Champion Equipment* list.
	• One Khorne Berzerker in the unit may take an Icon of Wrath (pg 159).

ABILITIES	**Death to the False Emperor** (pg 118)	**Berzerker Horde:** The Battlefield Role of **WORLD EATERS** Khorne Berzerkers is Troops instead of Elites.
	Blood for the Blood God: This unit can fight twice in each Fight phase, instead of only once.	

FACTION KEYWORDS	**CHAOS, KHORNE, HERETIC ASTARTES, <LEGION>**
KEYWORDS	**INFANTRY, KHORNE BERZERKERS**

RUBRIC MARINES

6 POWER

NAME	M	WS	BS	S	T	W	A	Ld	Sv
Rubric Marine	5"	3+	3+	4	4	1	1	7	3+
Aspiring Sorcerer	6"	3+	3+	4	4	1	2	8	3+

This unit contains 1 Aspiring Sorcerer and 4 Rubric Marines. It can include up to 5 additional Rubric Marines (**Power Rating +5**), up to 10 additional Rubric Marines (**Power Rating +11**) or up to 15 additional Rubric Marines (**Power Rating +16**).
• Each Rubric Marine is armed with an inferno boltgun.
• The Aspiring Sorcerer is armed with a force stave and an inferno bolt pistol.

WEAPON	RANGE	TYPE	S	AP	D	ABILITIES
Inferno bolt pistol	12"	Pistol 1	4	-2	1	-
Inferno boltgun	24"	Rapid Fire 1	4	-2	1	-
Plasma pistol	When attacking with this weapon, choose one of the profiles below.					
- Standard	12"	Pistol 1	7	-3	1	-
- Supercharge	12"	Pistol 1	8	-3	2	On a hit roll of 1, the bearer is slain.
Soulreaper cannon	24"	Heavy 4	5	-3	1	-
Warpflame pistol	6"	Pistol D6	3	-2	1	This weapon automatically hits its target.
Warpflamer	8"	Assault D6	4	-2	1	This weapon automatically hits its target.
Force stave	Melee	Melee	+2	-1	D3	-

WARGEAR OPTIONS	• The Aspiring Sorcerer may replace his inferno bolt pistol with a plasma pistol or warpflame pistol. • Any Rubric Marine may replace his inferno boltgun with a warpflamer. • For every ten models in the unit, one Rubric Marine may replace his inferno boltgun with a soulreaper cannon. • One Rubric Marine may take an Icon of Flame (pg 159).
ABILITIES	**Death to the False Emperor** (pg 118) **Favoured of Tzeentch:** Models in this unit have a 5+ invulnerable save. **All is Dust:** Add 1 to saving throws for Rubric Marines if the attack has a Damage characteristic of 1. In addition, the -1 modifier to hit rolls for moving and shooting with a Heavy weapon does not apply to Rubric Marines.
PSYKER	An Aspiring Sorcerer can attempt to manifest one psychic power in each friendly Psychic phase, and attempt to deny one psychic power in each enemy Psychic phase. He knows the *Smite* psychic power. When an Aspiring Sorcerer manifests the *Smite* psychic power, he inflicts 1 mortal wound instead of D3, or D3 mortal wounds instead of D6 if the result of the Psychic test is more than 10.
FACTION KEYWORDS	**CHAOS, TZEENTCH, HERETIC ASTARTES, <LEGION>**
KEYWORDS	**INFANTRY, PSYKER, RUBRIC MARINES**

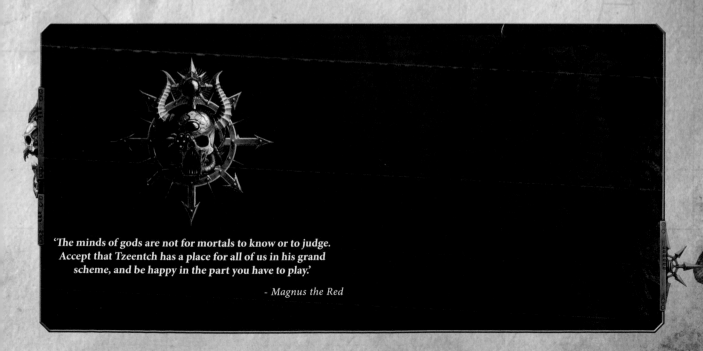

'The minds of gods are not for mortals to know or to judge. Accept that Tzeentch has a place for all of us in his grand scheme, and be happy in the part you have to play.'

- Magnus the Red

PLAGUE MARINES

NAME	M	WS	BS	S	T	W	A	Ld	Sv
Plague Marines	5"	3+	3+	4	5	1	1	7	3+
Plague Champion	5"	3+	3+	4	5	1	2	8	3+

This unit contains 1 Plague Champion and 4 Plague Marines. It can include up to 2 additional Plague Marines (**Power Rating +2**), up to 5 additional Plague Marines (**Power Rating +5**), up to 10 additional Plague Marines (**Power Rating +9**) or up to 15 additional Plague Marines (**Power Rating +14**). Each model is armed with a plague knife, boltgun, blight grenades and krak grenades.

WEAPON	RANGE	TYPE	S	AP	D	ABILITIES
Blight launcher	24"	Assault 2	6	-2	D3	Plague weapon (see below).
Bolt pistol	12"	Pistol 1	4	0	1	-
Boltgun	24"	Rapid Fire 1	4	0	1	-
Meltagun	12"	Assault 1	8	-4	D6	If the target is within half range of this weapon, roll two dice when inflicting damage with it and discard the lowest result.
Plague belcher	9"	Assault D6	4	0	1	Plague weapon (see below). This weapon automatically hits its target.
Plague spewer	9"	Heavy D6	5	-1	1	Plague weapon (see below). This weapon automatically hits its target.
Plasma gun		When attacking with this weapon, choose one of the profiles below.				
- Standard	24"	Rapid Fire 1	7	-3	1	-
- Supercharge	24"	Rapid Fire 1	8	-3	2	On a hit roll of 1, the bearer is slain after all of this weapon's attacks have been resolved.
Plasma pistol		When attacking with this weapon, choose one of the profiles below.				
- Standard	12"	Pistol 1	7	-3	1	-
- Supercharge	12"	Pistol 1	8	-3	2	On a hit roll of 1, the bearer is slain.
Bubotic axe	Melee	Melee	+1	-2	1	Plague weapon (see below).
Flail of corruption	Melee	Melee	+2	-2	2	Plague weapon (see below). Make D3 hit rolls each time you attack with this weapon. Excess damage from this weapon is not lost; instead, keep allocating damage to another model in the target unit until either all the damage has been allocated or the target is destroyed.
Great plague cleaver	Melee	Melee	x2	-3	D6	Plague weapon (see below). When attacking with this weapon, you must subtract 1 from the hit roll.
Mace of contagion	Melee	Melee	+2	-1	3	Plague weapon (see below). When attacking with this weapon, you must subtract 1 from the hit roll.
Plague knife	Melee	Melee	User	0	1	Plague weapon (see below).
Plaguesword	Melee	Melee	User	0	1	You can re-roll failed wound rolls for this weapon.
Power fist	Melee	Melee	x2	-3	D3	When attacking with this weapon, you must subtract 1 from the hit roll.
Blight grenade	6"	Grenade D6	3	0	1	Plague weapon (see below).
Krak grenade	6"	Grenade 1	6	-1	D3	-

WARGEAR OPTIONS	• The Plague Champion may replace his plague knife with a plaguesword. • The Plague Champion may replace his boltgun with a bolt pistol, a plasma pistol or a plasma gun. • The Plague Champion may take a power fist. • Up to two Plague Marines can each replace their boltgun with either a plague spewer, a plague belcher, a blight launcher, a meltagun or a plasma gun. • Any Plague Marine can replace their boltgun with either a bubotic axe or a second plague knife. • Up to two Plague Marines can each replace their boltgun with a mace of contagion and a bubotic axe. • Up to two Plague Marines can each replace their boltgun with either a great plague cleaver or a flail of corruption. • One Plague Marine with a boltgun or with two plague knives may also take an Icon of Despair (pg 159).

ABILITIES	**Death to the False Emperor** (pg 118) **Vectors of Death and Disease:** A Plague Marine equipped with two plague knives, a plague knife and a bubotic axe, or a mace of contagion and a bubotic axe, has an Attacks characteristic of 2 instead of 1.	**Disgustingly Resilient:** Each time a model in this unit loses a wound, roll a D6; on a roll of 5 or 6, the model does not lose that wound. **Plague Weapon:** You can re-roll wound rolls of 1 for this weapon.

FACTION KEYWORDS	CHAOS, NURGLE, HERETIC ASTARTES, <LEGION>
KEYWORDS	INFANTRY, PLAGUE MARINES

NOISE MARINES

NAME	M	WS	BS	S	T	W	A	Ld	Sv
Noise Marine	6"	3+	3+	4	4	1	2	7	3+
Noise Champion	6"	3+	3+	4	4	1	3	8	3+

This unit contains 1 Noise Champion and 4 Noise Marines. It can include up to 5 additional Noise Marines (**Power Rating +5**), up to 10 additional Noise Marines (**Power Rating +9**) or up to 15 additional Noise Marines (**Power Rating +13**). Each model is armed with a boltgun, a bolt pistol, frag grenades and krak grenades.

WEAPON	RANGE	TYPE	S	AP	D	ABILITIES
Blastmaster	When attacking with this weapon, choose one of the profiles below.					
- Single frequency	48"	Heavy D3	8	-2	D3	Units do not receive the benefit of cover to their saving throws for attacks made with this weapon.
- Varied frequency	36"	Assault D6	4	-1	1	
Bolt pistol	12"	Pistol 1	4	0	1	-
Boltgun	24"	Rapid Fire 1	4	0	1	-
Doom siren	8"	Assault D6	5	-2	1	This weapon automatically hits its target. Units do not receive the benefit of cover to their saving throws for attacks made with this weapon.
Sonic blaster	24"	Assault 3	4	0	1	Units do not receive the benefit of cover to their saving throws for attacks made with this weapon.
Chainsword	Melee	Melee	User	0	1	Each time the bearer fights, it can make 1 additional attack with this weapon.
Frag grenade	6"	Grenade D6	3	0	1	-
Krak grenade	6"	Grenade 1	6	-1	D3	-

WARGEAR OPTIONS	
	• Any model may replace its boltgun with a chainsword or sonic blaster.
	• One Noise Marine may replace his boltgun with a blastmaster. If the unit numbers ten or more models, a second Noise Marine may do this.
	• The Noise Champion may replace his bolt pistol and boltgun with items from the *Champion Equipment* list.
	• The Noise Champion may take a doom siren.
	• One Noise Marine may take an Icon of Excess (pg 159).

ABILITIES	
	Death to the False Emperor (pg 118)
	Music of the Apocalypse: Each time a model in this unit is slain, it is driven to make one last attack before succumbing to its injuries. Do not remove the slain model yet – after the attacking unit has finished making all its attacks, the slain model can make a shooting attack with one of its ranged weapons, or throw a grenade, even if the model's unit is within 1" of the enemy. The slain model is then removed as a casualty as normal.
	Masters of the Kakophoni: The Battlefield Role of EMPEROR'S CHILDREN Noise Marines is Troops instead of Elites.

FACTION KEYWORDS	CHAOS, SLAANESH, HERETIC ASTARTES, \<LEGION\>
KEYWORDS	INFANTRY, NOISE MARINES

The soul-blasting cacophony generated by sonic weaponry is as invigorating to the Noise Marines as it is lethal to their victims.

MUTILATORS

6 POWER

NAME	M	WS	BS	S	T	W	A	Ld	Sv
Mutilator	4"	3+	3+	5	4	3	3	8	2+

This unit contains 3 Mutilators. Each Mutilator is armed with fleshmetal weapons.

WEAPON	RANGE	TYPE	S	AP	D	ABILITIES
Fleshmetal weapons	Melee	Melee	+D3	-D3	D3	See below

ABILITIES	**Death to the False Emperor** (pg 118)	**Daemonic:** Models in this unit have a 5+ invulnerable save.

Fleshmetal Weapons: When a unit of Mutilators is chosen to fight, roll three D3, one after the other. For that fight, the first roll is added to the Mutilators' Strength for the unit's attacks, the second roll is the AP for the unit's attacks, and the third roll is the Damage for the unit's attacks. For example, if the rolls were a 1, followed by a 3, followed by a 2, then all of the unit's attacks for that fight would have a Strength of +1, an AP of -3, and a Damage of 2.

Teleport Strike: During deployment, you can set up this unit in a teleportarium chamber instead of placing it on the battlefield. At the end of any of your Movement phases the unit can use a teleport strike to arrive on the battlefield – set it up anywhere on the battlefield that is more than 9" away from any enemy models.

FACTION KEYWORDS	CHAOS, <MARK OF CHAOS>, HERETIC ASTARTES, <LEGION>
KEYWORDS	INFANTRY, DAEMON, CULT OF DESTRUCTION, MUTILATORS

FALLEN

6 POWER

NAME	M	WS	BS	S	T	W	A	Ld	Sv
Fallen	6"	3+	3+	4	4	1	2	8	3+
Fallen Champion	6"	3+	3+	4	4	1	3	9	3+

This unit contains 1 Fallen Champion and 4 Fallen. It can include up to 5 additional Fallen (**Power Rating +4**). Each model is armed with a boltgun, a bolt pistol, frag grenades and krak grenades.

WEAPON	RANGE	TYPE	S	AP	D	ABILITIES
Bolt pistol	12"	Pistol 1	4	0	1	-
Boltgun	24"	Rapid Fire 1	4	0	1	-
Plasma pistol	When attacking with this weapon, choose one of the profiles below.					
- Standard	12"	Pistol 1	7	-3	1	-
- Supercharge	12"	Pistol 1	8	-3	2	On a hit roll of 1, the bearer is slain.
Chainsword	Melee	Melee	User	0	1	Each time the bearer fights, it can make 1 additional attack with this weapon.
Lightning claw	Melee	Melee	User	-2	1	You can re-roll failed wound rolls for this weapon. If a model is armed with two lightning claws, each time it fights it can make 1 additional attack with them.
Frag grenade	6"	Grenade D6	3	0	1	-
Krak grenade	6"	Grenade 1	6	-1	D3	-

WARGEAR OPTIONS	• Any model may replace its boltgun with a chainsword.

• Up to four Fallen may choose one of the following options:
  - Replace bolt pistol with a plasma pistol.
  - Replace boltgun with one item from the *Combi-weapons* or *Special Weapons* list.
  - Replace bolt pistol and boltgun with two lightning claws.
  - Take one item from the *Melee Weapons* list.
• One additional Fallen may replace his boltgun with one item from the *Special Weapons* or *Heavy Weapons* list.
• The Fallen Champion may replace his boltgun and/or bolt pistol with one item from the *Champion Equipment* list.

ABILITIES	**Fallen Angels:** You can re-roll hit rolls of 1 for any Fallen unit when shooting (including when firing Overwatch) as long as the unit did not move in its last Movement phase. In addition, Fallen units can never lose more than one model as the result of any single failed Morale test; any additional casualties beyond the first are ignored.
FACTION KEYWORDS	IMPERIUM, CHAOS, FALLEN
KEYWORDS	INFANTRY

RAPTORS

5 POWER

NAME	M	WS	BS	S	T	W	A	Ld	Sv
Raptor	12"	3+	3+	4	4	1	1	7	3+
Raptor Champion	12"	3+	3+	4	4	1	2	8	3+

This unit contains 1 Raptor Champion and 4 Raptors. It can include up to 5 additional Raptors (**Power Rating +4**) or up to 10 additional Raptors (**Power Rating +8**). Each model is armed with a bolt pistol, chainsword, frag grenades and krak grenades.

WEAPON	RANGE	TYPE	S	AP	D	ABILITIES
Bolt pistol	12"	Pistol 1	4	0	1	-
Plasma pistol	When attacking with this weapon, choose one of the profiles below.					
- Standard	12"	Pistol 1	7	-3	1	-
- Supercharge	12"	Pistol 1	8	-3	2	On a hit roll of 1, the bearer is slain.
Chainsword	Melee	Melee	User	0	1	Each time the bearer fights, it can make 1 additional attack with this weapon.
Frag grenade	6"	Grenade D6	3	0	1	-
Krak grenade	6"	Grenade 1	6	-1	D3	-

WARGEAR OPTIONS
- Up to two Raptors may replace their bolt pistol and chainsword with a plasma pistol and chainsword, or with one item from the *Special Weapons* list.
- The Raptor Champion may replace his bolt pistol and chainsword with items from the *Champion Equipment* list.
- One model may take a Chaos Icon (pg 159).

ABILITIES

Death to the False Emperor (pg 118)

Fearsome Visage: Units within 1" of any enemy Raptors must subtract 1 from their Leadership characteristic.

Raptor Strike: During deployment, you can set up this unit in low orbit instead of placing it on the battlefield. At the end of any of your Movement phases the unit can use a Raptor strike to arrive on the battlefield – set it up anywhere on the battlefield that is more than 9" away from any enemy models.

FACTION KEYWORDS CHAOS, <MARK OF CHAOS>, HERETIC ASTARTES, <LEGION>

KEYWORDS INFANTRY, JUMP PACK, FLY, RAPTORS

WARP TALONS

6 POWER

NAME	M	WS	BS	S	T	W	A	Ld	Sv
Warp Talon	12"	3+	3+	4	4	1	1	8	3+
Warp Talon Champion	12"	3+	3+	4	4	1	2	8	3+

This unit contains 1 Warp Talon Champion and 4 Warp Talons. It can include up to 5 additional Warp Talons (**Power Rating +6**). Each model is armed with two lightning claws.

WEAPON	RANGE	TYPE	S	AP	D	ABILITIES
Lightning claw	Melee	Melee	User	-2	1	You can re-roll failed wound rolls for this weapon. If a model is armed with two lightning claws, each time it fights it can make 1 additional attack with them.

ABILITIES

Death to the False Emperor (pg 118)

Daemonic: Models in this unit have a 5+ invulnerable save.

Warpflame Strike: When you set up this unit during deployment, it can be set up in the warp, ready to strike, instead of being placed on the battlefield. If it is, it can use a Warpflame Strike to arrive on the battlefield at the end of any of your Movement phases; when it does so, set the unit up anywhere that is more than 9" from any enemy models. In addition, enemy units cannot fire Overwatch against units that arrived by warpflame strike in the same turn.

FACTION KEYWORDS CHAOS, <MARK OF CHAOS>, HERETIC ASTARTES, <LEGION>

KEYWORDS INFANTRY, DAEMON, JUMP PACK, FLY, WARP TALONS

2 POWER

CHAOS SPAWN

NAME	M	WS	BS	S	T	W	A	Ld	Sv
Chaos Spawn	7"	4+	-	5	5	4	D6	9	5+

This unit contains 1 Chaos Spawn. It can include up to 4 additional Chaos Spawn (**Power Rating +2 per model**). Each Chaos Spawn attacks with hideous mutations.

WEAPON	RANGE	TYPE	S	AP	D	ABILITIES
Hideous mutations	Melee	Melee	User	-2	2	-

ABILITIES	
Fearsome: Enemy units within 1" of any Chaos Spawn must subtract 1 from their Leadership.	**Mutated Beyond Reason:** When a unit of Chaos Spawn makes its close combat attacks, roll a D3 and consult the table below: **D3 Result** 1 **Razor Claws:** The hideous mutations of all Chaos Spawn in the unit have an AP of -4 until the end of the Fight phase. 2 **Grasping Pseudopods:** Each Chaos Spawn in the unit adds 2 to its Attacks characteristic until the end of the Fight phase. 3 **Toxic Haemorrhage:** You can re-roll failed wound rolls for this unit until the end of the Fight phase.

FACTION KEYWORDS	CHAOS, <MARK OF CHAOS>, HERETIC ASTARTES, <LEGION>
KEYWORDS	BEAST, CHAOS SPAWN

4 POWER

BIKERS

NAME	M	WS	BS	S	T	W	A	Ld	Sv
Biker	14"	3+	3+	4	5	2	1	7	3+
Biker Champion	14"	3+	3+	4	5	2	2	8	3+

This unit contains 1 Biker Champion and 2 Bikers. It can include up to 3 additional Bikers (**Power Rating +4**) or up to 6 additional Bikers (**Power Rating +7**). Each model is armed with a bolt pistol, frag grenades and krak grenades, and rides a bike equipped with a combi-bolter.

WEAPON	RANGE	TYPE	S	AP	D	ABILITIES
Bolt pistol	12"	Pistol 1	4	0	1	-
Combi-bolter	24"	Rapid Fire 2	4	0	1	-
Chainsword	Melee	Melee	User	0	1	Each time the bearer fights, it can make 1 additional attack with this weapon.
Frag grenade	6"	Grenade D6	3	0	1	-
Krak grenade	6"	Grenade 1	6	-1	D3	-

WARGEAR OPTIONS	
• Any Biker may replace his bolt pistol with a chainsword. • The Biker Champion may replace his bolt pistol with one item from the *Champion Equipment* list. • Up to two Bikers may either take one additional item from the *Special Weapons* list, or replace their bike's combi-bolter with one item from the *Special Weapons* list. • One model may take a Chaos Icon (pg 159).	

ABILITIES	**Death to the False Emperor** (pg 118) **Turbo-boost:** When this unit Advances, add 6" to its Move characteristic for that Movement phase instead of rolling a dice.

FACTION KEYWORDS	CHAOS, <MARK OF CHAOS>, HERETIC ASTARTES, <LEGION>
KEYWORDS	BIKER, BIKERS

HAVOCS

7 POWER

NAME	M	WS	BS	S	T	W	A	Ld	Sv
Havoc	6"	3+	3+	4	5	1	1	7	3+
Aspiring Champion	6"	3+	3+	4	5	1	2	8	3+

This unit contains 1 Aspiring Champion and 4 Havocs. The Aspiring Champion is armed with a flamer, chainsword, frag grenades and krak grenades. Each Havoc is armed with a heavy bolter or lascannon, and frag grenades and krak grenades.

WEAPON	RANGE	TYPE	S	AP	D	ABILITIES
Flamer	8"	Assault D6	4	0	1	This weapon automatically hits its target.
Heavy bolter	36"	Heavy 3	5	-1	1	-
Lascannon	48"	Heavy 1	9	-3	D6	-
Chainsword	Melee	Melee	User	0	1	Each time the bearer fights, it can make 1 additional attack with this weapon.
Frag grenade	6"	Grenade D6	3	0	1	-
Krak grenade	6"	Grenade 1	6	-1	D3	-

WARGEAR OPTIONS	• Any Havoc may replace their heavy bolter or lascannon with one item from the *Heavy Weapons* list. • The Aspiring Champion may replace his flamer with one item from the *Champion Equipment* or *Special Weapons* list. • The Aspiring Champion may replace his chainsword with one item from the *Champion Equipment* list.
ABILITIES	**Death to the False Emperor** (pg 118) **Stabilisation Talons:** This unit can move and fire Heavy weapons without suffering the penalty to their hit rolls.
FACTION KEYWORDS	CHAOS, <MARK OF CHAOS>, HERETIC ASTARTES, <LEGION>
KEYWORDS	INFANTRY, HAVOCS

OBLITERATORS

6 POWER

NAME	M	WS	BS	S	T	W	A	Ld	Sv
Obliterator	4"	3+	3+	5	5	4	3	8	2+

This unit contains 1 Obliterator. It can include up to 2 additional Obliterators (**Power Rating +6 per model**). Each Obliterator is armed with fleshmetal guns and crushing fists.

WEAPON	RANGE	TYPE	S	AP	D	ABILITIES
Fleshmetal guns	24"	Assault 6	6+D3	-D3	D3	See below
Crushing fists	Melee	Melee	+1	-1	D3	-

ABILITIES	**Death to the False Emperor** (pg 118) **Daemonic:** Models in this unit have a 5+ invulnerable save. **Teleport Strike:** During deployment, you can set up this unit in a teleportarium chamber instead of placing it on the battlefield. At the end of any of your Movement phases the unit can use a teleport strike to arrive on the battlefield – set it up anywhere on the battlefield that is more than 9" away from any enemy models.	**Fleshmetal Guns:** When this unit is chosen to shoot in the Shooting phase or fires Overwatch, roll three D3, one after the other, to determine the characteristics of the unit's fleshmetal guns for that Shooting phase or Overwatch attack. The first roll is added to 6 to determine the Strength, the second roll is the AP, and the third roll is the Damage. For example, if the rolls were a 1, followed by a 3, followed by a 2, then the weapon would have a Strength of 7, an AP of -3 and a Damage of 2.
FACTION KEYWORDS	CHAOS, <MARK OF CHAOS>, HERETIC ASTARTES, <LEGION>	
KEYWORDS	INFANTRY, DAEMON, CULT OF DESTRUCTION, OBLITERATORS	

CHAOS VINDICATOR

7 POWER

NAME	M	WS	BS	S	T	W	A	Ld	Sv
Chaos Vindicator	*	6+	*	6	8	11	*	8	3+

A Chaos Vindicator is a single model equipped with a demolisher cannon.

DAMAGE
Some of this model's characteristics change as it suffers damage, as shown below:

REMAINING W	M	BS	A
6-11+	10"	3+	3
3-5	5"	4+	D3
1-2	3"	5+	1

WEAPON	RANGE	TYPE	S	AP	D	ABILITIES
Demolisher cannon	24"	Heavy D3	10	-3	D6	When attacking units with 5 or more models, change this weapon's Type to Heavy D6.
Havoc launcher	48"	Heavy D6	5	0	1	-

WARGEAR OPTIONS
- This model may take a havoc launcher and/or one item from the *Combi-weapons* list.

ABILITIES

Smoke Launchers: Once per game, instead of shooting any weapons in the Shooting phase, this model can use its smoke launchers; until your next Shooting phase your opponent must subtract 1 from all hit rolls for ranged weapons that target this vehicle.

Explodes: If this model is reduced to 0 wounds, roll a D6 before removing the model from the battlefield; on a 6 it explodes, and each unit within 6" suffers D3 mortal wounds.

FACTION KEYWORDS CHAOS, <MARK OF CHAOS>, HERETIC ASTARTES, <LEGION>

KEYWORDS VEHICLE, CHAOS VINDICATOR

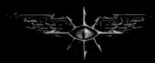

'It is the fate of the weak to die unknown, and the destiny of the strong to rule for eternity. Give me glory, or give me death!'

- Gauwe Psgas

CHAOS PREDATOR

9 POWER

NAME	M	WS	BS	S	T	W	A	Ld	Sv
Chaos Predator	*	6+	*	6	7	11	*	8	3+

A Chaos Predator is a single model equipped with a Predator autocannon.

DAMAGE
Some of this model's characteristics change as it suffers damage, as shown below:

REMAINING W	M	BS	A
6-11+	12"	3+	3
3-5	6"	4+	D3
1-2	3"	5+	1

WEAPON	RANGE	TYPE	S	AP	D	ABILITIES
Havoc launcher	48"	Heavy D6	5	0	1	-
Heavy bolter	36"	Heavy 3	5	-1	1	-
Lascannon	48"	Heavy 1	9	-3	D6	-
Predator autocannon	48"	Heavy 2D3	7	-1	3	-
Twin lascannon	48"	Heavy 2	9	-3	D6	-

WARGEAR OPTIONS
- This model may replace its Predator autocannon with a twin lascannon.
- This model may take either two heavy bolters or two lascannons.
- This model may take a havoc launcher and/or one item from the *Combi-weapons* list.

ABILITIES

Smoke Launchers: Once per game, instead of shooting any weapons in the Shooting phase, this model can use its smoke launchers; until your next Shooting phase your opponent must subtract 1 from all hit rolls for ranged weapons that target this vehicle.

Explodes: If this model is reduced to 0 wounds, roll a D6 before removing the model from the battlefield; on a 6 it explodes, and each unit within 6" suffers D3 mortal wounds.

FACTION KEYWORDS CHAOS, <MARK OF CHAOS>, HERETIC ASTARTES, <LEGION>

KEYWORDS VEHICLE, CHAOS PREDATOR

CHAOS LAND RAIDER

NAME	M	WS	BS	S	T	W	A	Ld	Sv
Chaos Land Raider	*	6+	*	8	8	16	*	9	2+

DAMAGE
Some of this model's characteristics change as it suffers damage, as shown below:

REMAINING W	M	BS	A
9-16+	10"	3+	6
5-8	5"	4+	D6
1-4	3"	5+	1

A Chaos Land Raider is a single model equipped with a twin heavy bolter and two twin lascannons.

WEAPON	RANGE	TYPE	S	AP	D	ABILITIES
Havoc launcher	48"	Heavy D6	5	0	1	-
Twin heavy bolter	36"	Heavy 6	5	-1	1	-
Twin lascannon	48"	Heavy 2	9	-3	D6	-

WARGEAR OPTIONS	• This model may take a havoc launcher and/or one item from the *Combi-weapons* list.
ABILITIES	**Smoke Launchers:** Once per game, instead of shooting any weapons in the Shooting phase, a Chaos Land Raider can use its smoke launchers; until your next Shooting phase your opponent must subtract 1 from all hit rolls for ranged weapons that target this vehicle. **Daemonic Machine Spirit:** Ignore the -1 to hit modifier for moving and shooting Heavy weapons for this model. **Explodes:** If this model is reduced to 0 wounds, roll a D6 before removing the model from the battlefield and before any embarked models disembark; on a 6 it explodes, and each unit within 6" suffers D6 mortal wounds.
TRANSPORT	This model can transport 10 <LEGION> INFANTRY models (each TERMINATOR and JUMP PACK model takes up the space of two other models, and each CULT OF DESTRUCTION model takes up the space of three other models).
FACTION KEYWORDS	CHAOS, <MARK OF CHAOS>, HERETIC ASTARTES, <LEGION>
KEYWORDS	VEHICLE, TRANSPORT, CHAOS LAND RAIDER

Eager to grind warm flesh beneath its tracks, a Chaos Land Raider ploughs towards the foe, its engine roaring for death.

FORGEFIEND

POWER 8

NAME	M	WS	BS	S	T	W	A	Ld	Sv
Forgefiend	✴	4+	✴	6	7	12	✴	8	3+

DAMAGE
Some of this model's characteristics change as it suffers damage, as shown below:

REMAINING W	M	BS	A
7-12+	8"	4+	4
4-6	6"	5+	3
1-3	4"	6+	2

A Forgefiend is a single model equipped with two hades autocannons and Daemon jaws.

WEAPON	RANGE	TYPE	S	AP	D	ABILITIES
Ectoplasma cannon	24"	Heavy D3	7	-3	D3	-
Hades autocannon	36"	Heavy 4	8	-1	2	-
Daemon jaws	Melee	Melee	User	-1	2	-

WARGEAR OPTIONS	• This model may replace both hades autocannons with ectoplasma cannons. • This model may replace its Daemon jaws with an ectoplasma cannon.

ABILITIES	**Daemonic:** This model has a 5+ invulnerable save. **Infernal Regeneration:** At the start of your turn, this model regains 1 lost wound.	**Explodes:** If this model is reduced to 0 wounds, roll a D6 before removing the model from the battlefield; on a 6 it explodes, and each unit within 6" suffers D3 mortal wounds.

FACTION KEYWORDS	CHAOS, <MARK OF CHAOS>, HERETIC ASTARTES, <LEGION>

KEYWORDS	VEHICLE, DAEMON, DAEMON ENGINE, FORGEFIEND

DEFILER

POWER 9

NAME	M	WS	BS	S	T	W	A	Ld	Sv
Defiler	✴	4+	✴	8	7	14	✴	8	3+

DAMAGE
Some of this model's characteristics change as it suffers damage, as shown below:

REMAINING W	M	BS	A
8-14+	8"	4+	4
4-7	6"	5+	3
1-3	4"	5+	2

A Defiler is a single model equipped with a battle cannon, a reaper autocannon, a twin heavy flamer and Defiler claws.

WEAPON	RANGE	TYPE	S	AP	D	ABILITIES
Battle cannon	72"	Heavy D6	8	-2	D3	-
Havoc launcher	48"	Heavy D6	5	0	1	-
Reaper autocannon	36"	Heavy 4	7	-1	1	-
Twin heavy bolter	36"	Heavy 6	5	-1	1	-
Twin heavy flamer	8"	Heavy 2D6	5	-1	1	This weapon automatically hits its target.
Twin lascannon	48"	Heavy 2	9	-3	D6	-
Defiler claws	Melee	Melee	x2	-3	D6	-
Defiler scourge	Melee	Melee	+4	-2	3	Each time the bearer fights, it can make 3 additional attacks with this weapon.

WARGEAR OPTIONS	• This model may replace its twin heavy flamer with a havoc launcher or Defiler scourge. • This model may replace its reaper autocannon with a twin heavy bolter or twin lascannon. • This model may take one item from the *Combi-weapons* list.

ABILITIES	**Daemonic:** This model has a 5+ invulnerable save. **Infernal Regeneration:** At the start of your turn, this model regains 1 lost wound. **Explodes:** If this model is reduced to 0 wounds, roll a D6 before removing it from the battlefield; on a 6 it explodes, and each unit within 6" suffers D3 mortal wounds.	**Smoke Launchers:** Once per game, instead of shooting any weapons in the Shooting phase, this model can use its smoke launchers; until your next Shooting phase your opponent must subtract 1 from all hit rolls for ranged weapons that target this vehicle.

FACTION KEYWORDS	CHAOS, <MARK OF CHAOS>, HERETIC ASTARTES, <LEGION>

KEYWORDS	VEHICLE, DAEMON, DAEMON ENGINE, DEFILER

MAULERFIEND

7 POWER

DAMAGE
Some of this model's characteristics change as it suffers damage, as shown below:

REMAINING W	M	S	A
7-12+	10"	6	4
4-6	8"	5	3
1-3	6"	4	2

NAME	M	WS	BS	S	T	W	A	Ld	Sv
Maulerfiend	*	4+	4+	*	7	12	*	8	3+

A Maulerfiend is a single model equipped with Maulerfiend fists and two magma cutters.

WEAPON	RANGE	TYPE	S	AP	D	ABILITIES
Magma cutter	6"	Pistol 1	8	-4	3	-
Lasher tendrils	Melee	Melee	User	-2	2	Each time the bearer fights, it can make 6 additional attacks with this weapon.
Maulerfiend fists	Melee	Melee	x2	-3	3	

WARGEAR OPTIONS	• This model may replace both magma cutters with lasher tendrils.

ABILITIES	**Daemonic:** This model has a 5+ invulnerable save. **Infernal Regeneration:** At the start of your turn, this model regains 1 lost wound.	**Explodes:** If this model is reduced to 0 wounds, roll a D6 before removing the model from the battlefield; on a 6 it explodes, and each unit within 6" suffers D3 mortal wounds.

FACTION KEYWORDS	**Chaos, <Mark of Chaos>, Heretic Astartes, <Legion>**
KEYWORDS	**Vehicle, Daemon, Daemon Engine, Maulerfiend**

VENOMCRAWLER

7 POWER

DAMAGE
Some of this model's characteristics change as it suffers damage, as shown below:

REMAINING W	M	S	A
6-10+	10"	6	4
3-5	8"	5	3
1-2	6"	4	2

NAME	M	WS	BS	S	T	W	A	Ld	Sv
Venomcrawler	*	4+	4+	*	7	10	*	8	3+

A Venomcrawler is a single model equipped with soulflayer tendrils, eviscerating claws and two excruciator cannons.

WEAPON	RANGE	TYPE	S	AP	D	ABILITIES
Excruciator cannon	36"	Assault D3	+2	-2	D3	-
Eviscerating claws	Melee	Melee	+2	-3	3	-
Soulflayer tendrils	Melee	Melee	User	-2	2	Each time the bearer fight, it can make 2 additional attacks with this weapon.

ABILITIES	**Daemonic:** This model has a 5+ invulnerable save. **Devourer of Souls:** At the start of your turn, this model regains 1 lost wound. In addition, at the end of a Fight phase in which this model destroyed any enemy models, this model regains 1 lost wound.	**Reservoir of Daemonic Energy:** Add 1 to the result of any Daemonic Ritual summoning rolls made for **<Legion> Masters of Possession** while they are within 6" of any friendly **<Legion> Venomcrawlers**. **Soul-shredding Explosion:** If this model is reduced to 0 wounds, roll a D6 before removing the model from the battlefield; on a 5+ it explodes, and each unit within 6" suffers D3 mortal wounds.

FACTION KEYWORDS	**Chaos, <Mark of Chaos>, Heretic Astartes, <Legion>**
KEYWORDS	**Vehicle, Daemon, Daemon Engine, Venomcrawler**

CHAOS RHINO

4 POWER

A Chaos Rhino is a single model equipped with a combi-bolter.

NAME	M	WS	BS	S	T	W	A	Ld	Sv
Chaos Rhino	*	6+	*	6	7	10	*	8	3+

DAMAGE

Some of this model's characteristics change as it suffers damage, as shown below:

REMAINING W	M	BS	A
6-10+	12"	3+	3
3-5	6"	4+	D3
1-2	3"	5+	1

WEAPON	RANGE	TYPE	S	AP	D	ABILITIES
Combi-bolter	24"	Rapid Fire 2	4	0	1	-
Havoc launcher	48"	Heavy D6	5	0	1	-

WARGEAR OPTIONS	• This model may take a havoc launcher and/or one item from the *Combi-weapons* list.
ABILITIES	**Self-repair:** Roll a D6 at the start of your turn; on a 6, this model regains 1 lost wound.
	Smoke Launchers: Once per game, instead of shooting any weapons in the Shooting phase, this model can use its smoke launchers; until your next Shooting phase your opponent must subtract 1 from all hit rolls for ranged weapons that target this vehicle.
	Explodes: If this model is reduced to 0 wounds, roll a D6 before removing it from the battlefield and before any embarked models disembark; on a 6 it explodes, and each unit within 6" suffers D3 mortal wounds.
TRANSPORT	This model can transport 10 <Legion> Infantry models. It cannot, however, transport Terminators, Cult of Destruction or Jump Pack models.
FACTION KEYWORDS	Chaos, <Mark of Chaos>, Heretic Astartes, <Legion>
KEYWORDS	Vehicle, Transport, Chaos Rhino

9 POWER

HELDRAKE

NAME	M	WS	BS	S	T	W	A	Ld	Sv
Heldrake	*	*	4+	7	7	12	*	8	3+

A Heldrake is a single model equipped with a hades autocannon and Heldrake claws.

DAMAGE

Some of this model's characteristics change as it suffers damage, as shown below:

REMAINING W	M	WS	A
7-12+	30"	3+	4
4-6	20"	4+	3
1-3	10"	5+	2

WEAPON	RANGE	TYPE	S	AP	D	ABILITIES
Baleflamer	18"	Assault D6	6	-2	2	This weapon automatically hits its target.
Hades autocannon	36"	Heavy 4	8	-1	2	-
Heldrake claws	Melee	Melee	User	-1	D3	When attacking models that can **FLY**, add 1 to this weapon's hit roll.

WARGEAR OPTIONS	• This model may replace its hades autocannon with a baleflamer.

ABILITIES	**Daemonic:** This model has a 5+ invulnerable save.	**Crash and Burn:** If this model is reduced to 0 wounds, roll a D6 before removing the model from the battlefield; on a 6 it crashes in a fiery explosion and each unit within 6" suffers D3 mortal wounds.
	Infernal Regeneration: At the start of your turn, this model regains 1 lost wound.	

FACTION KEYWORDS	**CHAOS, <MARK OF CHAOS>, HERETIC ASTARTES, <LEGION>**

KEYWORDS	**VEHICLE, DAEMON, DAEMON ENGINE, FLY, HELDRAKE**

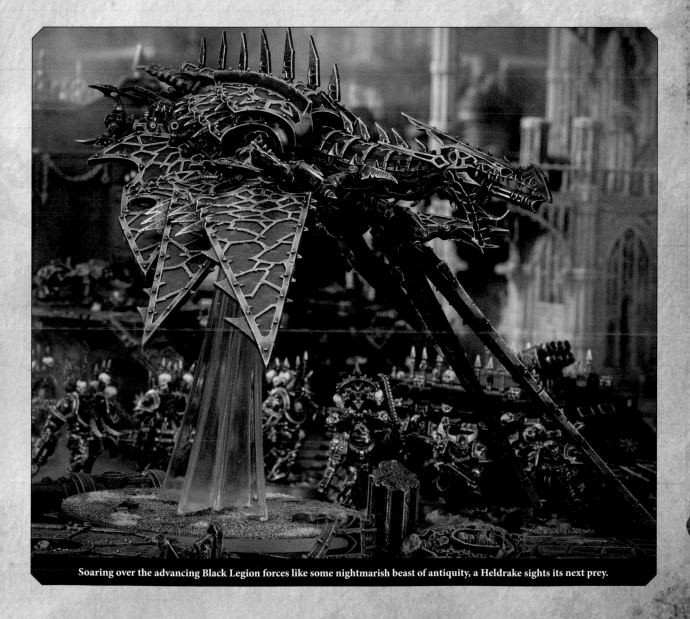

Soaring over the advancing Black Legion forces like some nightmarish beast of antiquity, a Heldrake sights its next prey.

KHORNE LORD OF SKULLS

30 POWER

NAME	M	WS	BS	S	T	W	A	Ld	Sv
Khorne Lord of Skulls	*	3+	3+	*	8	28	*	8	3+

A Khorne Lord of Skulls is a single model equipped with a gorestorm cannon, a hades gatling cannon, and a great cleaver of Khorne.

DAMAGE
Some of this model's characteristics change as it suffers damage, as shown below:

REMAINING W	M	S	A
14-28+	10"	10	4
7-13	7"	8	6
1-6	4"	5	8

WEAPON	RANGE	TYPE	S	AP	D	ABILITIES
Daemongore cannon	18"	Heavy D6	User	-2	3	This weapon automatically hits its target.
Gorestorm cannon	18"	Heavy D6	User	-2	2	This weapon automatically hits its target. When attacking units with 10 or more models, change this weapon's Type to Heavy 2D6.
Hades gatling cannon	48"	Heavy 12	8	-2	2	-
Ichor cannon	48"	Heavy D6	7	-4	D3	-
Skullhurler	60"	Heavy D6	9	-3	D3	When attacking units with 10 or more models, change this weapon's Type to Heavy 2D6.
Great cleaver of Khorne	When attacking with this weapon, choose one of the profiles below.					
- Smash	Melee	Melee	x2	-4	6	-
- Slash	Melee	Melee	User	-2	D3	Make 3 hit rolls for each attack made with this weapon.

WARGEAR OPTIONS	• This model may replace its gorestorm cannon with an ichor cannon or daemongore cannon. • This model may replace its Hades gatling cannon with a skullhurler.

ABILITIES	**Daemonic:** This model has a 5+ invulnerable save. **Infernal Regeneration:** At the start of your turn, this model regains 1 lost wound. **Explodes:** If this model is reduced to 0 wounds, roll a D6 before removing the model from the battlefield; on a 6 it explodes, and each unit within 2D6" suffers D6 mortal wounds.	**Titanic Daemon Engine:** A Khorne Lord of Skulls can shoot if there are enemy models within 1" of it, as long as all of the enemy models have the **INFANTRY** keyword. In this case it can shoot the enemy unit that is within 1" of it, or any other visible enemy unit that is within range and more than 1" away from any friendly models. In addition, a Khorne Lord of Skulls can move and fire Heavy weapons without suffering the penalty to its hit rolls. Finally, a Khorne Lord of Skulls only gains a bonus to its save in cover if at least half of the model is obscured from the firer.

FACTION KEYWORDS	**CHAOS, KHORNE, HERETIC ASTARTES, <LEGION>**
KEYWORDS	**TITANIC, VEHICLE, DAEMON, DAEMON ENGINE, LORD OF SKULLS**

NOCTILITH CROWN

NAME	M	WS	BS	S	T	W	A	Ld	Sv
Noctilith Crown	-	-	4+	-	8	14	-	-	3+

A Noctilith Crown is a single model equipped with lashing warp energies.

WEAPON	RANGE	TYPE	S	AP	D	ABILITIES
Lashing warp energies	6"	Pistol D6	7	-2	2	-

ABILITIES		
	Malevolent Locus: **PSYKERS** attempting to manifest powers within 24" of this model will suffer Perils of the Warp on any double result rolled for the Psychic test, rather than only double 1 or double 6. **CHAOS PSYKERS** are not affected by this ability. **Loathsome Aura:** **CHAOS** units have a 5+ invulnerable save while they are wholly within 6" of this model. In addition, you can re-roll Psychic tests for **CHAOS PSYKERS** while they are within 6" of this model. At the start of the second and third battle rounds, the range of both these aura abilities is increased by 3" (i.e. it is 9" in the second battle round, and 12" in the third and subsequent battle rounds).	**Immobile:** This model cannot move for any reason, nor can it fight in the Fight phase. Enemy models automatically hit this model in the Fight phase – do not make hit rolls. However, friendly units can still target enemy units that are within 1" of this model in the Shooting phase. **Unstable Energies:** If this model is reduced to 0 wounds, roll a D6 before removing it from the battlefield. On a 6, each unit within D6" of this model suffers D6 mortal wounds.

FACTION KEYWORDS	**CHAOS**
KEYWORDS	**BUILDING, VEHICLE, NOCTILITH CROWN**

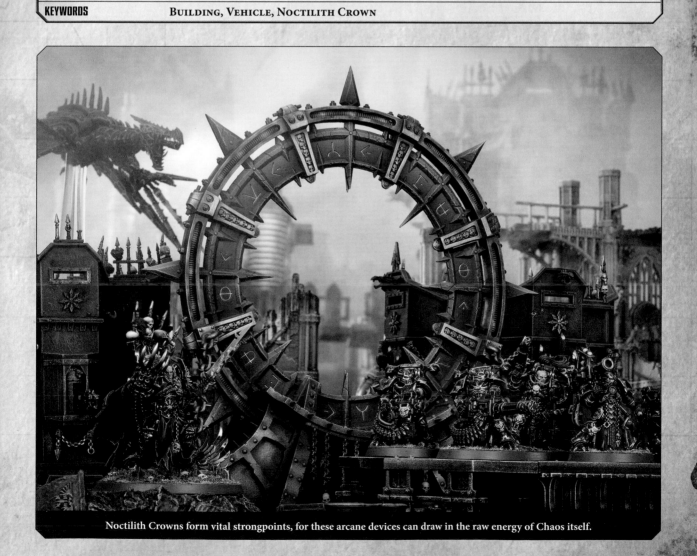

Noctilith Crowns form vital strongpoints, for these arcane devices can draw in the raw energy of Chaos itself.

THE FORBIDDEN ARMOURY

Having severed themselves from the industry of the Imperium, the Chaos Space Marines have been forced to become self-sufficient. The weaponry and armour they bear is often a mix of ancient marks, more recent designs plundered during raids, and the insane creations of the Warpsmiths, though all of it is heavily twisted by the energies of the warp to reflect the blackened soul of the bearer.

RANGED WEAPONS

WEAPON	RANGE	TYPE	S	AP	D	ABILITIES
Autocannon	48"	Heavy 2	7	-1	2	-
Autogun	24"	Rapid Fire 1	3	0	1	-
Autopistol	12"	Pistol 1	3	0	1	-
Baleflamer	18"	Assault D6	6	-2	2	This weapon automatically hits its target.
Battle cannon	72"	Heavy D6	8	-2	D3	-
Blastmaster	When attacking with this weapon, choose one of the profiles below.					
- Single frequency	48"	Heavy D3	8	-2	D3	Units do not receive the benefit of cover to their saving throws for attacks made with this weapon.
- Varied frequency	36"	Assault D6	4	-1	1	
Blight grenade	6"	Grenade D6	3	0	1	You can re-roll wound rolls of 1 for this weapon.
Blight launcher	24"	Assault 2	6	-2	D3	You can re-roll wound rolls of 1 for this weapon.
Bolt pistol	12"	Pistol 1	4	0	1	-
Boltgun	24"	Rapid Fire 1	4	0	1	-
Combi-bolter	24"	Rapid Fire 2	4	0	1	-
Combi-flamer	When attacking with this weapon, choose one or both of the profiles below. If you choose both, subtract 1 from all hit rolls made for this weapon.					
- Boltgun	24"	Rapid Fire 1	4	0	1	-
- Flamer	8"	Assault D6	4	0	1	This weapon automatically hits its target.
Combi-melta	When attacking with this weapon, choose one or both of the profiles below. If you choose both, subtract 1 from all hit rolls made for this weapon.					
- Boltgun	24"	Rapid Fire 1	4	0	1	-
- Meltagun	12"	Assault 1	8	-4	D6	If the target is within half range of this weapon, roll two dice when inflicting damage with it and discard the lowest result.
Combi-plasma	When attacking with this weapon, choose one or both of the profiles below. If you choose both, subtract 1 from all hit rolls made for this weapon.					
- Boltgun	24"	Rapid Fire 1	4	0	1	-
- Plasma gun	24"	Rapid Fire 1	7	-3	1	*See plasma gun*
Coruscating flames	18"	Assault 2	User	0	1	-
Cypher's bolt pistol	16"	Pistol 3	4	-1	1	-
Cypher's plasma pistol	12"	Pistol 2	8	-3	2	-
Daemongore cannon	18"	Heavy D6	User	-2	3	This weapon automatically hits its target.
Demolisher cannon	24"	Heavy D3	10	-3	D6	When attacking units with 5 or more models, change this weapon's Type to Heavy D6.
Doom siren	8"	Assault D6	5	-2	1	This weapon automatically hits its target. Units do not receive the benefit of cover to their saving throws for attacks made with this weapon.
Ectoplasma cannon	24"	Heavy D3	7	-3	D3	-
Excruciator cannon	36"	Assault D3	+2	-2	D3	-
Flamer	8"	Assault D6	4	0	1	This weapon automatically hits its target.
Fleshmetal guns	24"	Assault 6	6+D3	-D3	D3	*See Obliterators datasheet (pg 147)*
Frag grenade	6"	Grenade D6	3	0	1	-
Gorestorm cannon	18"	Heavy D6	User	-2	2	This weapon automatically hits its target. When attacking units with 10 or more models, change this weapon's Type to Heavy 2D6.
Hades autocannon	36"	Heavy 4	8	-1	2	-
Hades gatling cannon	48"	Heavy 12	8	-2	2	-
Havoc launcher	48"	Heavy D6	5	0	1	-
Heavy bolter	36"	Heavy 3	5	-1	1	-
Heavy flamer	8"	Heavy D6	5	-1	1	This weapon automatically hits its target.
Heavy stubber	36"	Heavy 3	4	0	1	-

RANGED WEAPONS

WEAPON	RANGE	TYPE	S	AP	D	ABILITIES
Helbrute plasma cannon	36"	Heavy D3	8	-3	2	For each hit roll of 1, the Helbrute suffers 1 mortal wound after all of this weapon's attacks have been resolved.
Helspear	12"	Assault 1	+1	-3	D3	-
Ichor cannon	48"	Heavy D6	7	-4	D3	-
Inferno bolt pistol	12"	Pistol 1	4	-2	1	-
Inferno boltgun	24"	Rapid Fire 1	4	-2	1	-
Khârn's plasma pistol	12"	Pistol 1	8	-3	2	Each time you roll a hit roll of 1 when firing this weapon, the bearer suffers 1 mortal wound.
Krak grenade	6"	Grenade 1	6	-1	D3	-
Lascannon	48"	Heavy 1	9	-3	D6	-
Lash of Torment	6"	Assault 2	User	-1	2	This weapon can be fired within 1" of an enemy unit, and can target enemy units within 1" of friendly units.
Lashing warp energies	6"	Pistol D6	7	-2	2	-
Magma cutter	6"	Pistol 1	8	-4	3	-
Meltagun	12"	Assault 1	8	-4	D6	If the target is within half range of this weapon, roll two dice when inflicting damage with it and discard the lowest result.
Missile launcher	When attacking with this weapon, choose one of the profiles below.					
- Frag missile	48"	Heavy D6	4	0	1	-
- Krak missile	48"	Heavy 1	8	-2	D6	-
Multi-melta	24"	Heavy 1	8	-4	D6	If the target is within half range of this weapon, roll two dice when inflicting damage with it and discard the lowest result.
Plague belcher	9"	Assault D6	4	0	1	You can re-roll wound rolls of 1 for this weapon. This weapon automatically hits its target.
Plague spewer	9"	Heavy D6	5	-1	1	You can re-roll wound rolls of 1 for this weapon. This weapon automatically hits its target.
Plasma gun	When attacking with this weapon, choose one of the profiles below.					
- Standard	24"	Rapid Fire 1	7	-3	1	-
- Supercharge	24"	Rapid Fire 1	8	-3	2	On a hit roll of 1, the bearer is slain after all of this weapon's attacks have been resolved.
Plasma pistol	When attacking with this weapon, choose one of the profiles below.					
- Standard	12"	Pistol 1	7	-3	1	-
- Supercharge	12"	Pistol 1	8	-3	2	On a hit roll of 1, the bearer is slain.
Predator autocannon	48"	Heavy 2D3	7	-1	3	-
Reaper autocannon	36"	Heavy 4	7	-1	1	-
Reaper chaincannon	24"	Heavy 8	5	-1	1	-
Shotgun	12"	Assault 2	3	0	1	If the target is within half range, add 1 to this weapon's Strength.
Skullhurler	60"	Heavy D6	9	-3	D3	When attacking units with 10 or more models, change this weapon's Type to Heavy 2D6.
Sonic blaster	24"	Assault 3	4	0	1	Units do not receive the benefit of cover to their saving throws for attacks made with this weapon.
Soulreaper cannon	24"	Heavy 4	5	-3	1	-
Talon of Horus (shooting)	24"	Rapid Fire 2	4	-1	D3	-
Twin heavy bolter	36"	Heavy 6	5	-1	1	-
Twin heavy flamer	8"	Heavy 2D6	5	-1	1	This weapon automatically hits its target.
Twin lascannon	48"	Heavy 2	9	-3	D6	-
Tyrant's Claw (shooting)	9"	Assault D6	5	-1	1	This weapon automatically hits its target.
Warp bolter	24"	Assault 2	4	-1	2	-
Warpflame pistol	6"	Pistol D6	3	-2	1	This weapon automatically hits its target.
Warpflamer	8"	Assault D6	4	-2	1	This weapon automatically hits its target.
Xyclos Needler	18"	Pistol 3	*	0	1	This weapon wounds on a 2+, unless it is targeting a **VEHICLE**, in which case it wounds on a 6+.

MELEE WEAPONS

WEAPON	RANGE	TYPE	S	AP	D	ABILITIES
Accursed crozius	Melee	Melee	+1	-1	2	-
Axe of dismemberment	Melee	Melee	x2	-3	D3	Each time you make a wound roll of 6+ for this weapon, the target unit suffers 1 mortal wound in addition to any other damage.
Bladed limbs and tail	Melee	Melee	+3	-2	D3	After the Lord Discordant makes his close combat attacks, you can attack with his Helstalker. Make a number of additional attacks as shown in the damage chart, using this weapon profile.
Brutal assault weapon	Melee	Melee	User	0	1	Each time the bearer fights, it can make 1 additional attack with this weapon.
Bubotic axe	Melee	Melee	+1	-2	1	You can re-roll wound rolls of 1 for this weapon.
Chainaxe	Melee	Melee	+1	-1	1	-
Chainfist	Melee	Melee	x2	-4	2	When attacking with this weapon, you must subtract 1 from the hit roll.
Chainsword	Melee	Melee	User	0	1	Each time the bearer fights, it can make 1 additional attack with this weapon.
Close combat weapon	Melee	Melee	User	0	1	-
Crushing fists	Melee	Melee	+1	-1	D3	-
Daemon jaws	Melee	Melee	User	-1	2	-
Daemonic axe	Melee	Melee	+1	-3	3	When attacking with this weapon, you must subtract 1 from the hit roll.
Daemonic mutations	Melee	Melee	User	-2	D3	-
Defiler claws	Melee	Melee	x2	-3	D6	-
Defiler scourge	Melee	Melee	+4	-2	3	Each time the bearer fights, it can make 3 additional attacks with this weapon.
Drach'nyen	Melee	Melee	+1	-3	3	Roll a D6 each time the bearer fights. On a 1 they suffer 1 mortal wound and cannot use this weapon further during this phase. On a 2+ they can make that many additional attacks with this weapon.
Eviscerating claws	Melee	Melee	+2	-3	3	-
Flail of corruption	Melee	Melee	+2	-2	2	You can re-roll wound rolls of 1 for this weapon. Make D3 hit rolls each time you attack with this weapon. Excess damage from this weapon is not lost; instead, keep allocating damage to another model in the target unit until either all the damage has been allocated or the target is destroyed.
Fleshmetal weapons	Melee	Melee	+D3	-D3	D3	*See Mutilators datasheet (pg 144)*
Force axe	Melee	Melee	+1	-2	D3	-
Force stave	Melee	Melee	+2	-1	D3	-
Force sword	Melee	Melee	User	-3	D3	-
Gorechild	Melee	Melee	+1	-4	D3	This weapon always hits on a roll of 2+, regardless of any modifiers.
Great cleaver of Khorne	When attacking with this weapon, choose one of the profiles below.					
- Smash	Melee	Melee	x2	-4	6	-
- Slash	Melee	Melee	User	-2	D3	Make 3 hit rolls for each attack made with this weapon.
Great plague cleaver	Melee	Melee	x2	-3	D6	You can re-roll wound rolls of 1 for this weapon. When attacking with this weapon, you must subtract 1 from the hit roll.
Helbrute fist	Melee	Melee	x2	-3	3	-
Helbrute hammer	Melee	Melee	x2	-4	D6	When attacking with this weapon, you must subtract 1 from the hit roll.
Heldrake claws	Melee	Melee	User	-1	D3	When attacking models that can **FLY**, add 1 to this weapon's hit roll.
Hellblade	Melee	Melee	User	-3	1	Each time you make a wound roll of 6+ for this weapon, that hit is resolved with a Damage of 2.
Hellforged sword	Melee	Melee	User	-2	3	-
Hideous mutations	Melee	Melee	User	-2	2	-
Horrifying mutations	Melee	Melee	User	-2	1	-
Impaler chainglaive	Melee	Melee	+2	-2	2	If the bearer made a charge move or performed a Heroic Intervention this turn, attacks with this weapon are made with a Strength characteristic of x2 instead of +2.
Lasher tendrils	Melee	Melee	User	-2	2	Each time the bearer fights, it can make 6 additional attacks with this weapon.
Lightning claw	Melee	Melee	User	-2	1	You can re-roll failed wound rolls for this weapon. If a model is armed with two lightning claws, each time it fights it can make 1 additional attack with them.
Mace of contagion	Melee	Melee	+2	-1	3	You can re-roll wound rolls of 1 for this weapon. When attacking with this weapon, you must subtract 1 from the hit roll.

MELEE WEAPONS

WEAPON	RANGE	TYPE	S	AP	D	ABILITIES
Malefic talons	Melee	Melee	User	-2	2	Each time a model with malefic talons fights, it can make 1 additional attack with this weapon. A model armed with two sets of malefic talons can make 3 additional attacks with them instead.
Master-crafted power sword	Melee	Melee	User	-3	2	-
Maulerfiend fists	Melee	Melee	x2	-3	3	-
Mechatendrils	Melee	Melee	User	0	1	Each time the bearer fights, it can make 2 additional attacks with this weapon.
Piercing claws	Melee	Melee	User	-1	1	Each time you make a wound roll of 6+ for this weapon, that hit is resolved with an AP of -4.
Plague knife	Melee	Melee	User	0	1	You can re-roll wound rolls of 1 for this weapon.
Plaguesword	Melee	Melee	User	0	1	You can re-roll failed wound rolls for this weapon.
Power axe	Melee	Melee	+1	-2	1	-
Power fist	Melee	Melee	x2	-3	D3	When attacking with this weapon, you must subtract 1 from the hit roll.
Power maul	Melee	Melee	+2	-1	1	-
Power scourge	Melee	Melee	+2	-2	2	Each time the bearer fights, it can make 3 additional attacks with this weapon.
Power sword	Melee	Melee	User	-3	1	-
Rod of Torment	Melee	Melee	User	-1	D3	When attacking a **Vehicle**, this weapon has a Damage of 1.
Soulflayer tendrils	Melee	Melee	User	-2	2	Each time the bearer fight, it can make 2 additional attacks with this weapon.
Talon of Horus (melee)	Melee	Melee	x2	-4	D3	-
Techno-virus injector	Melee	Melee	+4	-4	D3	After the Lord Discordant makes his close combat attacks, you can attack with his Helstalker. Make a single attack using this weapon profile in addition to the Helstalker's bladed limbs and tail. Each time a wound roll for an attack made with this weapon is successful when targeting a **Vehicle** unit, that unit suffers D3 mortal wounds in addition to any normal damage.
Thunder hammer	Melee	Melee	x2	-3	3	When attacking with this weapon, you must subtract 1 from the hit roll.
Tyrant's Claw (melee)	Melee	Melee	x2	-3	D3	When attacking with this weapon, you must subtract 1 from the hit roll.

CHAOS ICONS

ICON	UNIT	EFFECT
Icon of Wrath	**Khorne** units only	You can re-roll charge rolls for units with an Icon of Wrath.
Icon of Flame	**Tzeentch** units only	At the start of your Psychic phase, roll a D6 for each unit from your army with an Icon of Flame. On a roll of 6 inflict 1 mortal wound on the closest enemy unit within 12" of the model carrying the Icon of Flame.
Icon of Despair	**Nurgle** units only	Enemy units that are within 6" of any units from your army with an Icon of Despair must subtract 1 from their Leadership characteristic.
Icon of Excess	**Slaanesh** units only	If a unit has an Icon of Excess, its Death to the False Emperor ability takes effect on any hit rolls of 5+, rather than 6+.
Icon of Vengeance	Cannot be taken by **Khorne**, **Tzeentch**, **Nurgle** or **Slaanesh** units	Add 1 to the Leadership of all models in a unit that has an Icon of Vengeance.

A teeming force of Heretic Astartes surges forwards to crush the defenders of this Imperial world. Infantry, war machines and Daemon Engines work in brutal concert to obliterate their foes, filling the battlefield with the sounds of carnage and profane prayer.

THE LOST AND THE DAMNED

In this section you'll find rules for Battle-forged armies that include Chaos Space Marine Detachments – that is, any Detachment which only includes Chaos Space Marine units (as defined below). These rules include the abilities below and a series of Stratagems. This section also includes the Chaos Space Marines' unique Warlord Traits, Psychic Disciplines, Relics and Tactical Objectives. Together, these rules reflect the character and fighting style of the Chaos Space Marines in your games of Warhammer 40,000.

CHAOS SPACE MARINE UNITS

In the rules described in this section we often refer to 'Chaos Space Marine units'. This is shorthand for any unit that has one of the following Faction keywords: <Legion>, Black Legion, Word Bearers, Iron Warriors, Alpha Legion, Night Lords, World Eaters, Emperor's Children, Fallen or Red Corsairs. A Chaos Space Marine Detachment is therefore one which only includes units with one of these keywords.

Note that the Death Guard and Thousand Sons Legions deviate significantly in terms of organisation and therefore cannot make use of any of the rules or abilities listed in this section; instead they have bespoke rules and abilities detailed in their own codexes.

ABILITIES

Chaos Space Marine Detachments gain the following abilities:

DESPOILERS OF THE GALAXY

Consumed by hatred of the Imperium, the Chaos Space Marines advance not to conquer, but to set the galaxy ablaze.

If your army is Battle-forged, all Troops units in Chaos Space Marine Detachments gain this ability. Such a unit that is within range of an objective marker controls it even if there are more enemy models within range of it. If an enemy unit within range of the objective marker has a similar ability, then it is controlled by the player who has the most models within range as normal.

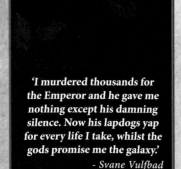

'I murdered thousands for the Emperor and he gave me nothing except his damning silence. Now his lapdogs yap for every life I take, whilst the gods promise me the galaxy.'

- Svane Vulfbad

Legion Traits

Each of the Traitor Legions has been uniquely twisted by the Ruinous Powers, and has perfected its own methods of slaughter and destruction.

If your army is Battle-forged, all Daemon Prince, **INFANTRY**, **BIKERS** and **HELBRUTE** units in Chaos Space Marine Detachments gain a Legion Trait, so long as every unit in that Detachment is from the same Legion. The Legion Trait gained depends upon the Legion they are from, as shown in the table opposite. For example, all such units in a **NIGHT LORDS** Detachment gain the Terror Tactics trait.

If your Chaos Space Marines are from a Renegade Chapter, or if they do not otherwise have an associated trait, use the Renegade Chapters trait opposite. For example, all of the units described above that are in a **RED CORSAIRS** Detachment would have the Dark Raiders trait.

Mere Mortals

CHAOS CULTIST units do not gain a Legion Trait.

Shadowy Allies

The inclusion of Fabius Bile or **FALLEN** units in a Detachment does not prevent other units in that Detachment from gaining a Legion Trait. However, Fabius Bile and the **FALLEN** units can never themselves benefit from a Legion Trait.

LEGION TRAITS

BLACK LEGION: BLACK CRUSADERS

Inexorable and unflinching, the Black Legion exemplify the threat posed by the Heretic Astartes, emerging from the Eye of Terror for the sole purpose of erasing the Imperium from the galaxy.

Add 1 to the Leadership characteristic of models in units with this trait. In addition, if a unit with this trait Advanced, it treats all its Rapid Fire weapons as Assault weapons until the end of the turn (e.g. a Rapid Fire 2 weapon is treated as an Assault 2 weapon).

IRON WARRIORS: SIEGE LORDS

Cold-hearted warriors whose only faith is in their wargear, the Iron Warriors have perfected siege warfare, and are able to gouge out even the most stubbornly entrenched enemies.

Enemy units attacked by units with this trait do not gain any bonus to their saving throws for being in cover. In addition, you can re-roll failed wound rolls for units with this trait when they target a **BUILDING**.

RENEGADE CHAPTERS: DARK RAIDERS

Freed from the constraints of the Imperium, Renegade Astartes indulge their enhanced capacity for violence.

Units with this trait can Advance and charge in the same turn.

WORLD EATERS: BUTCHER'S NAILS

Angron's sons hurl themselves towards their foe, intent on tearing them apart in a brutal whirlwind of violence.

When a unit with this trait makes a successful charge, you can make one additional attack with each of its models in the subsequent Fight phase.

NIGHT LORDS: TERROR TACTICS

The Night Lords revel in fear and mayhem, and will take apart an opposing army piecemeal, dividing and isolating the weakest enemies so that their confused cries can be savoured.

Models in enemy units must subtract 1 from their Leadership characteristic for each unit with this trait that is within 6" of theirs (to a maximum of -3).

EMPEROR'S CHILDREN: FLAWLESS PERFECTION

Inured to everyday sensations by lifetimes of indulgence, the Emperor's Children find stimulation only in excess, be it shocking acts of violence or gratuitous displays of martial prowess.

Units with this trait always fight first in the Fight phase even if they didn't charge. If the enemy has units that have charged, or that have a similar ability, then alternate choosing units to fight with, starting with the player whose turn is taking place.

ALPHA LEGION: HIDDEN IN PLAIN SIGHT

The warriors of the Alpha Legion are masters of duplicity, able to mislead and misdirect even the most vigilant of enemies before delivering the killing blow.

Your opponent must subtract 1 from hit rolls that target units with this trait if they are more than 12" away.

WORD BEARERS: PROFANE ZEAL

The Word Bearers march to war for the glory of the Chaos pantheon, stirred into a rapturous state of fanaticism by blasphemous catechisms and the dark promises of the Ruinous Powers.

You can re-roll failed Morale tests for units with this trait.

STRATAGEMS

If your army is Battle-forged and includes any Chaos Space Marine Detachments (excluding Auxiliary Support Detachments), you have access to the Stratagems shown here, meaning you can spend Command Points to activate them. These help to reflect the unique strategies used by the Heretic Astartes on the battlefield.

DAEMON SHELL

1CP

Chaos Space Marines Stratagem

Crafted on tainted forge worlds and infused with warp energy, Daemon shells release a mind-sickening scream as they are launched. If they cannot consume the soul of their target, they will seek out another's essence.

Use this Stratagem just before a **HERETIC ASTARTES CHARACTER** attacks with a bolt pistol, boltgun, combi-bolter or the boltgun profile of a combi-weapon. You can only make a single hit roll with the weapon (or boltgun profile) this phase, which you cannot re-roll. If the shot hits, the target suffers D3 mortal wounds; if the shot misses, your character suffers D3 mortal wounds.

GIFTS OF CHAOS

1CP/3CP

Chaos Space Marines Stratagem

Though fickle with their gifts, the Chaos Gods will reward those champions who continue to prove themselves worthy.

Use this Stratagem before the battle. Your army can have one extra Artefact of Chaos for 1 CP, or two extra Artefacts of Chaos for 3 CPs. All of the Artefacts of Chaos that you include must be different and be given to different Chaos Space Marine **CHARACTERS**. You can only use this Stratagem once per battle.

BESEECH THE CHAOS GODS

1CP

Chaos Space Marines Stratagem

The Chaos Gods will always reveal themselves to the willing.

Use this Stratagem at the start of any of your turns. Select a unit with the **<MARK OF CHAOS>** keyword that has not dedicated itself to one of the Chaos Gods. You can immediately dedicate that unit to one of the Chaos Gods as described on page 118.

BLASPHEMOUS MACHINES

1CP

Chaos Space Marines Stratagem

Heretic Astartes vehicles can be goaded to fury like wild beasts.

Use this Stratagem just before a **HERETIC ASTARTES VEHICLE** attacks in the Shooting phase. Until the end of the phase, that vehicle can ignore the penalties for moving and firing Heavy weapons, or for Advancing and firing Assault weapons.

CHAOS BOON

1CP

Chaos Space Marines Stratagem

The path of Chaos can lead a warrior to daemonhood, or it can see him transformed into a gibbering Chaos Spawn.

Use this Stratagem at the end of a Fight phase in which one of your **HERETIC ASTARTES CHARACTERS** (excluding **DAEMON CHARACTERS**) slays an enemy **CHARACTER**, **VEHICLE** or **MONSTER**. Roll 2D6 and look up the result below.

2D6	Boon
2	**Spawndom:** Your character is slain. However, before removing the model as a casualty, you can add a Chaos Spawn to your army. If you do, set up the Chaos Spawn within 6" of your character before removing them.
3	**Arcane Occulum:** Add 6" to the Range of all of the character's ranged weapons.
4	**Temporal Distortion:** Add 3" to the character's Move characteristic.
5	**Strength of the Berzerker:** Add 1 to the character's Strength characteristic.
6	**Warp Frenzy:** Add 1 to the character's Attacks characteristic.
7	**The Eye Opens:** Choose a boon of your choice (you cannot choose Spawndom or Daemonhood).
8	**Blademaster:** Subtract 1 from hit rolls that target the character in the Fight phase.
9	**Cosmic Fate:** Add 1 to all saving throws made for the character.
10	**Crystalline Body:** Add 1 to the character's Toughness characteristic.
11	**Fragment of Immortality:** Add 1 to the character's Wounds characteristic.
12	**Daemonhood:** Your character is slain. However, before removing the model as a casualty, you can add a Daemon Prince to your army. If you do, set up the Daemon Prince within 6" of your character before removing them.

Boons last for the rest of the battle. The same boon cannot be received by a model more than once – if this happens, choose a result the model has not yet received (excluding Spawndom and Daemonhood). Chaos Spawn or Daemon Princes created by a boon must have the same Mark of Chaos as the model had (if any), and they do not cost any reinforcement points in a matched play game.

VETERANS OF THE LONG WAR

1CP

Chaos Space Marines Stratagem

The hatred of the Traitor Legions has burned for millennia.

Use this Stratagem when a **HERETIC ASTARTES INFANTRY** or **BIKER** unit is selected to attack in a Shooting or Fight phase (excluding units from Renegade Chapters). You can add 1 to all wound rolls made for the unit until the end of the phase.

GRANDFATHER'S BLESSINGS

2CP

Chaos Space Marines Stratagem

Grandfather Nurgle is eager to bestow daemonic fecundity upon his faithful servants, sealing their gaping wounds with pulsating growths and replacing their spilt blood with curdling ichor.

Use this Stratagem at the end of your Movement phase. Select a **HERETIC ASTARTES NURGLE INFANTRY** or **BIKER** unit. One model in the unit heals D3 wounds. If there are no wounded models in the unit, a single model in the unit that was slain earlier in the battle is returned to the unit with a single wound remaining.

DAEMONFORGE

1CP

Chaos Space Marines Stratagem

The Daemon Engines of the Chaos Space Marines are driven by a fathomless hatred born of the warp.

Use this Stratagem in your Shooting or Fight phase when a Chaos Space Marine **DAEMON VEHICLE** is chosen to attack. You can re-roll all failed hit and wound rolls for that model until the end of the phase.

CHAOS FAMILIAR

1CP

Chaos Space Marines Stratagem

Though diminutive in stature, many lesser warp entities whisper dark secrets that can shift the tide of battle.

Use this Stratagem at the start of your Psychic phase. Select a friendly **HERETIC ASTARTES PSYKER**. That model can replace any of its psychic powers with a power of your choice from the Dark Hereticus discipline.

THE GREAT SORCERER

1CP

Chaos Space Marines Stratagem

Those not driven mad by the worship of Tzeentch are given the power to harness the energies of the warp like no other, so long as this gift is used against the Great Mutator's enemies.

Use this Stratagem at the end of your Psychic phase. Select a **HERETIC ASTARTES TZEENTCH PSYKER**. The psyker can immediately attempt to manifest one additional psychic power this turn.

TIDE OF TRAITORS

2CP

Chaos Space Marines Stratagem

The galaxy is filled with pathetic wretches who give themselves willingly to Chaos for the chance to win power and glory.

Use this Stratagem at the end of your Movement phase. If you do, pick a unit of Chaos Cultists and remove it from the battlefield. You can then set it up again wholly within 6" of the edge of the battlefield and more than 9" from any enemy models, at its full starting strength. You can only use this Stratagem once per battle.

LINEBREAKER BOMBARDMENT

1CP

Chaos Space Marines Stratagem

The Chaos Space Marines learnt long ago that excessive force pays for itself in the terror that it causes.

Use this Stratagem in your Shooting phase if a **<LEGION>** Chaos Vindicator is within 6" of 2 other friendly **<LEGION>** Chaos Vindicators. If you do so, the Vindicators cannot fire their demolisher cannons this phase – instead, select a visible point on the battlefield within 24" of all three vehicles. Roll a D6 for each unit within 3" of that point. Add 1 to the result if the unit being rolled for has 10 or more models, but subtract 1 if the unit being rolled for is a **CHARACTER**. On a 4+ that unit suffers 3D3 mortal wounds.

KILLSHOT

1CP

Chaos Space Marines Stratagem

The bloodthirsty Predator battle tanks of the Heretic Astartes hunt in packs to bring down especially large foes.

Use this Stratagem in your Shooting phase if a **<LEGION>** Chaos Predator is within 6" of 2 other friendly **<LEGION>** Chaos Predators. Add 1 to the wound rolls and damage for all of the Predators' attacks that target **MONSTERS** or **VEHICLES** this phase.

ENDLESS CACOPHONY

2CP

Chaos Space Marines Stratagem

In the clangour of battle the worshippers of Slaanesh hear sweet music, and they compete to be loudest in this deafening chorus.

Use this Stratagem at the end of your Shooting phase. Select a **HERETIC ASTARTES SLAANESH INFANTRY** or **BIKER** unit – that unit can immediately shoot again.

FURY OF KHORNE

3CP

Chaos Space Marines Stratagem

The bloodlust of Khorne's followers is never sated, and is only heightened by the arterial sprays of their enemies.

Use this Stratagem at the end of the Fight phase. Select a **HERETIC ASTARTES KHORNE INFANTRY** or **BIKER** unit – that unit can immediately fight again.

FLAKK MISSILE
Chaos Space Marines Stratagem

Flakk missiles are designed to eliminate light aircraft by unleashing a payload of shrapnel that shreds armour and ruptures vital systems.

Use this Stratagem just before a friendly **HERETIC ASTARTES INFANTRY** model attacks a unit that can **FLY** with a missile launcher. You only make a single hit roll with the weapon this phase; however, add 1 to the hit roll and, if it hits, the target suffers D3 mortal wounds.

1CP

FIRE FRENZY
Chaos Space Marines Stratagem

The unbridled wrath of a Helbrute is a useful tool in the hands of a commander who can direct it.

Use this Stratagem in your Shooting phase, just before a Helbrute shoots. If that Helbrute did not move in its Movement phase, it can fire all of its weapons twice but all of its attacks must target the nearest visible enemy unit.

1CP

FORWARD OPERATIVES
Alpha Legion Stratagem

The deceitful strategies of the Alpha Legion are as illusive as a shadow and as tangled as a nest of vipers.

Use this Stratagem when you can set up an **ALPHA LEGION INFANTRY** unit during deployment. You can set up the unit in concealment instead of placing it on the battlefield. At the beginning of the first battle round but before the first turn begins, the unit emerges from its hiding place – set it up anywhere on the battlefield that is more than 9" away from any enemy models.

1CP

DARK PACT
Word Bearers Stratagem

The Word Bearers are expert at drawing the twisted minions of the Dark Gods into realspace using profane rituals and gruesome sacrifices.

Use this Stratagem when a **WORD BEARERS CHARACTER** attempts to summon a unit of **DAEMONS** to the battlefield using a Daemonic Ritual. You can re-roll any of the dice used in the summoning roll, and your character will not suffer any mortal wounds for rolling doubles or triples.

1CP

IRON WITHIN, IRON WITHOUT
Iron Warriors Stratagem

Hardened by the most gruelling theatres of war in the galaxy, the Iron Warriors will continue to fight long after others of their ilk have fallen.

Use this Stratagem when an **IRON WARRIORS** unit loses a wound. Roll a D6 for that wound, and for each wound lost by the unit for the rest of the phase; on a 6, that wound is not lost.

1CP

SCORN OF SORCERY
World Eaters Stratagem

Like the god they worship, the warriors of the World Eaters despise psykers and their trickery, and through sheer force of Khorne-fuelled hatred can sever the sorcerous powers of others.

Use this Stratagem when an enemy **PSYKER** manifests a psychic power within 24" of a friendly **WORLD EATERS** unit. Roll a D6; on a 4+, the effects of that psychic power are negated.

1CP

EXCESS OF VIOLENCE
Emperor's Children Stratagem

The visceral sensation of every fresh kill causes the warriors of the Emperor's Children to enter an ecstatic frenzy of butchery and dismemberment.

Use this Stratagem just before an **EMPEROR'S CHILDREN INFANTRY** unit attacks in the Fight phase. Each time a model in your unit slays an enemy model, it can immediately make another hit roll using the same weapon at the same target (these bonus attacks cannot themselves generate any further attacks).

1CP

IN MIDNIGHT CLAD
Night Lords Stratagem

Having fought countless campaigns of terror in complete darkness, the Night Lords know how to make an ally of the shadows.

Use this Stratagem when a **NIGHT LORDS INFANTRY** unit is targeted by a shooting attack. For the rest of the phase, your opponent must subtract 1 from all hit rolls that target that unit.

1CP

LET THE GALAXY BURN
Black Legion Stratagem

Drawing upon millennia of festering bitterness and hate, the Black Legion attack with a ferocity that is terrible to behold .

Use this Stratagem when a **BLACK LEGION INFANTRY** or **BIKER** unit is selected to attack in a Shooting or Fight phase. You can re-roll all hit rolls of 1 for that unit for the rest of the phase. If the unit is a Chaos Space Marine squad, you can re-roll all failed hit rolls for it instead.

1CP

PRAYERS TO THE DARK GODS

The Dark Apostles of Chaos have a singular connection with their deities. It is not for warrior glory nor for self-aggrandisement they fight, but for the furtherance of their patron god's cause – as such they can call upon the favour of the Ruinous Powers to lend them strength at a critical moment.

Before the battle, generate the prayers for **PRIESTS** that can chant prayers from Prayers to the Dark Gods using the table below. You can either roll a D6 to generate their prayers randomly (re-roll duplicates), or you can select the prayers you wish them to have.

MARK OF CHAOS PRAYERS

A <**MARK OF CHAOS**> **PRIEST** that can chant prayers from the Prayers to the Dark Gods also knows the appropriate <**MARK OF CHAOS**> prayer on the right.

D6 PRAYER

1 BENEDICTION OF DARKNESS

As their words grow louder, inky blackness pours from the priest's eyes, forming a swirling mist around their allies.

If this prayer is heard, pick one friendly <**LEGION**> unit within 6" of this priest. Subtract 1 from hit rolls made for attacks with ranged weapons that target that unit.

2 LITANY OF DESPAIR

The priest calls upon the Dark Gods to offer his foes all manner of whispered temptations, sapping their will to fight.

If this prayer is heard, your opponent rolls two D6, discarding the lowest result, each time they take a Morale test for a unit within 6" of this priest.

3 OMEN OF POTENCY

The priest begins to glow with the unbridled power of the warp.

If this prayer is heard, add 3 to this priest's Attacks characteristic. In addition, if this prayer is heard, this priest's melee weapons have an Armour Penetration characteristic of -4.

4 WARP-SIGHT PLEA

The priest entreats his dark masters to guide his followers' aim, granting their shots unerring accuracy.

If this prayer is heard, pick one friendly <**LEGION**> unit within 6" of this priest. Add 1 to hit rolls for attacks made with ranged weapons by models in that unit.

5 SOULTEARER PORTENT

The priest's flock strike at their victim's very souls, the better to release them from their mortal bonds as an offering to the Dark Gods.

If this prayer is heard, pick one friendly <**LEGION**> unit within 6" of this priest. Add 1 to wound rolls for attacks made with melee weapons by models in that unit.

6 ILLUSORY SUPPLICATION

Chanting words that would drive most mortals mad, the priest alters the very fabric of reality, creating shadowy doppelgängers of nearby allies.

If this prayer is heard, friendly <**LEGION**> models have a 5+ invulnerable save while they are within 6" of this priest.

WRATHFUL ENTREATY

Drawing blood from his palm, the priest requests Khorne impart a measure of his godly strength to him.

KHORNE PRIEST only. If this prayer is heard, add 2 to this priest's Strength characteristic.

MUTATING INVOCATION

Speaking riddles, the priest bargains with the Master of Fate to make his flesh flow like liquid, absorbing enemy blows.

TZEENTCH PRIEST only. If this prayer is heard, this priest regains D3 lost wounds. Note that unlike other prayers, whose effects last only until the end of the battle round, wounds regained from this prayer are not lost again at the end of the battle round.

FECULENT BESEECHMENT

Belching a cloud of flies, the priest begs Grandfather Nurgle to bless his form with wondrous diseases.

NURGLE PRIEST only. If this prayer is heard, add 2 to this priest's Toughness characteristic.

BLISSFUL DEVOTION

The priest asks beloved Slaanesh to grant him the unnatural swiftness of the Dark Prince's daemonic children.

SLAANESH PRIEST only. If this prayer is heard, this priest can Advance and charge in their turn in this battle round.

DARK HERETICUS DISCIPLINE

Chaos Space Marine psykers open their minds fully to the horrors of the warp, drawing immense power from this nightmare dimension to rip apart their enemies and infuse their allies with strength. Only those already inured to the maddening taint of Chaos can wield such raw power without losing all remnants of sanity.

Before the battle, generate the psychic powers for **PSYKERS** that can use the Dark Hereticus discipline using the table below. You can either roll a D6 to generate their powers randomly (re-roll duplicates), or you can select the powers you wish them to have.

MARK OF CHAOS PSYCHIC POWERS

A <**MARK OF CHAOS**> **PSYKER** that can use powers from the Dark Hereticus discipline can replace one of its Dark Hereticus powers with the appropriate <**MARK OF CHAOS**> psychic power on the right.

D6 RESULT

1 INFERNAL GAZE

Unholy power streams from the psyker's eyes, charring and melting everything caught in its path.

Infernal Gaze has a warp charge value of 5. If manifested, select a visible enemy unit within 18" of the psyker and roll 3 dice. The target suffers 1 mortal wound for each roll of 4+.

2 DEATH HEX

The Sorcerer places a dire hex upon his enemies. Wards and energised shields flicker and fail, leaving the foe exposed.

Death Hex has a warp charge value of 8. If manifested, select a visible enemy unit within 12" of the psyker. Until the start of your next Psychic phase, that unit cannot take invulnerable saves.

3 GIFT OF CHAOS

As the power of the warp surges through the psyker's victim, bones snap and flesh rips as a new form takes shape.

Gift of Chaos has a warp charge of 6. If manifested, select an enemy unit that is within 6" of the psyker and visible to him and roll a D6. If the result is greater than the target's Toughness, it suffers D3+3 mortal wounds. If a **CHARACTER** is slain by this power, you can add a Chaos Spawn to your army and set it up within 1" of the character before it is removed.

4 PRESCIENCE

By focusing his warp-sight the psyker can guide the aim of his allies, bringing a swift and merciless death to their foes.

Prescience has a warp charge value of 7. If manifested, select a **HERETIC ASTARTES** unit within 18" of the psyker. You can add 1 to all hit rolls made for that unit until the start of your next Psychic phase.

5 DIABOLIC STRENGTH

The unholy energies of Chaos course through the recipient, swelling his frame with the strength to tear a tank in two.

Diabolic Strength has a warp charge value of 6. If manifested, select a **HERETIC ASTARTES** model within 12" of the psyker. Until the start of your next Psychic phase, add 2 to that model's Strength characteristic and 1 to its Attacks characteristic.

6 WARPTIME

The power of the immaterium bursts from the psyker, warping time and heightening the speed of his allies.

Warptime has a warp charge value of 6. If manifested, pick a **HERETIC ASTARTES** unit within 3" of the psyker. That unit can immediately move as if it were its Movement phase. You cannot use *Warptime* on a unit more than once per Psychic phase.

MARK OF TZEENTCH: WEAVER OF FATES

The psyker traces the skeins of the future to see the fates of battle. Forewarned of imminent danger, warriors dodge bullets and sword blows with seemingly supernatural reflexes.

Weaver of Fates has a warp charge value of 6. If manifested, select a visible **TZEENTCH HERETIC ASTARTES** unit within 18" of the psyker. Until the start of your next Psychic phase, the invulnerable save of that unit is improved by 1 (to a maximum of 3+). Models that do not have an invulnerable save instead gain a 5+ invulnerable save.

MARK OF NURGLE: MIASMA OF PESTILENCE

As the psyker chants in a phlegm-choked drone, a dark cloud of filth and flies shrouds his allies from view.

Miasma of Pestilence has a warp charge value of 6. If manifested, select a visible **NURGLE HERETIC ASTARTES** unit within 18" of the psyker. Until the start of your next Psychic phase, your opponent must subtract 1 from all hit rolls that target that unit.

MARK OF SLAANESH: DELIGHTFUL AGONIES

Those whose minds are touched by the psyker's caress are wracked by waves of exquisite pain, over which physical trauma has no hold.

Delightful Agonies has a warp charge value of 6. If manifested, select a visible **SLAANESH HERETIC ASTARTES** unit within 18" of the psyker. Until the start of your next Psychic phase, roll a D6 each time a model in that unit loses a wound; on a 5+ it does not lose that wound.

MALEFIC DISCIPLINE

Masters of Possession have studied the profane lore of conjuration, learning how to draw forth daemonic beings, taint their surroundings with the mutating energies of Chaos, and blast asunder the souls of their foes.

Before the battle, generate the psychic powers for **Psykers** that can use powers from the Malefic discipline using the table below. You can either roll a D6 to generate their powers randomly (re-roll any duplicate results), or you can select the psychic powers you wish the psyker to have.

1 INCURSION

The psyker opens a portal to the Realm of Chaos, allowing the warp's daemonic denizens to spill forth into reality.

Incursion has a warp charge value of 7. If manifested, the psyker can immediately attempt to summon a unit of **Daemons** to the battlefield using the Daemonic Ritual ability (pg 119) as if it were the Movement phase. When doing so, roll up to 4 dice instead of up to 3. The psyker will not suffer any mortal wounds as a result of doubles or triples being rolled for this Daemonic Ritual.

2 SACRIFICE

The psyker uses a sacrificial soul to remould and repair an unholy Daemon-form. The tainted spirits of Warpsmiths are particularly invigorating offerings to those Daemon Engines that are in their charge.

Sacrifice has a warp charge value of 4. If manifested, choose any model within 2" of the psyker; that model suffers 1 mortal wound. Then, choose a friendly <Legion> **Daemon** model within 18" of the psyker. That model regains D3 lost wounds. If that <Legion> **Daemon** model is a **Daemon Engine** and the model you chose to inflict the mortal wound on was a friendly <Legion> **Warpsmith**, the model regains 3 lost wounds instead.

3 MUTATED INVIGORATION

A wave of insanity and mutation flows from the psyker's fingers, enveloping their Daemonkin allies with bountiful gifts.

Mutated Invigoration has a warp charge value of 7. If manifested, select a friendly **Chaos Spawn**, <Legion> **Possessed** or <Legion> **Cult of Destruction** unit within 18" of the psyker. Until the start of your next Psychic phase, that unit will gain a bonus depending on what unit it is, as follows:

- You can re-roll the dice when rolling for that Chaos Spawn's Mutated Beyond Reason ability.
- You can re-roll the dice when rolling for the Attacks characteristic of that unit of Possessed due to its Writhing Tentacles ability.
- You can re-roll one of the dice when rolling for the Strength, AP and Damage characteristics of that Cult of Destruction unit's weapons due to its Fleshmetal Guns or Fleshmetal Weapons ability.

4 POSSESSION

The psyker blasts away their enemy's soul so that the spiritless shell left behind can be possessed by a Daemon, who quickly transforms it into a more pleasing form. Vehicles so possessed are typically unable to contain the Daemon within, and explode in a scream of empyric energy.

Possession has a warp charge value of 5. If manifested, then until the start of your next Psychic phase, the Armour Penetration characteristic of the psyker's melee weapons is improved by 2 (e.g. an AP of -1 becomes -3). Furthermore, until the start of your next Psychic phase, each time the psyker destroys an enemy **Infantry Character** in the Fight phase, you can add a Chaos Spawn model to your army. If the destroyed model was **Adeptus Astartes** or **Heretic Astartes**, you can instead add a Greater Possessed model to your army. If a new model is added to your army, set it up within 6" of the psyker and more than 1" from any enemy models. In addition, each time the psyker destroys an enemy **Vehicle** model in the Fight phase that could explode, it automatically explodes; no dice roll is made and any mortal wounds suffered by the psyker in the resulting explosion are ignored.

5 CURSED EARTH

The psyker becomes a conduit through which the energies of the warp flow, tainting the very ground and sustaining the Daemonkin that walk upon it.

Cursed Earth has a warp charge value of 7. If manifested, then until the start of your next Psychic phase, the invulnerable save of friendly <Legion> **Daemon** units is improved by 1 (to a maximum of 3+) while they are within 6" of this psyker.

6 INFERNAL POWER

The fell power of the immaterium flows from the psyker, imbuing the Daemons that reside within his followers' bodies with even greater ferocity.

Infernal Power has a warp charge value of 6. If manifested, then until the start of your next Psychic phase re-roll hit and wound rolls of 1 for attacks made by friendly <Legion> **Daemon** units while they are within 6" of this psyker.

ARTEFACTS OF CHAOS

Amongst the myriad warbands of the Chaos Space Marines there exist tools of murder whose very names inspire terror. Some of these artefacts date back to before the Horus Heresy, before their bearers were corrupted by the whispers of the Dark Gods. Others were forged using the essences of Daemons, and exist only to sow destruction throughout the galaxy.

If your army is led by a Chaos Space Marine Warlord, you may give one of the following Artefacts of Chaos to a Chaos Space Marine **CHARACTER** in your army. Named characters such as Lucius the Eternal already have one or more artefacts, and cannot be given any of the following artefacts.

Note that some weapons replace one of the character's existing weapons. Where this is the case, you must, if you are playing a matched play game or are otherwise using points values, still pay the cost of the weapon that is being replaced. Write down any Artefacts of Chaos your characters may have on your army roster.

TALISMAN OF BURNING BLOOD

This talisman constantly drips with thick, bubbling gore. The air around it is so heavy with the charnel stench of the slaughterhouse that it imbues the bearer's limbs with a supernatural swiftness to match their eagerness to butcher the foe.

KHORNE model only. The bearer of the Talisman of Burning Blood can Advance and charge in the same turn. Furthermore, the bearer can re-roll failed charge rolls.

EYE OF TZEENTCH

The Eye of Tzeentch is a relic that has been exposed to wild psychic energies for ten millennia. Sorcerers who stare into the artefact's unblinking depths can glean the secrets of the warp, and use such knowledge to focus their own eldritch powers.

TZEENTCH PSYKER only. The bearer of the Eye of Tzeentch adds 1 to their Psychic test when attempting to manifest the *Smite* power.

INTOXICATING ELIXIR

This dispenser is filled with a self-replenishing liquid that is pumped into the bearer's bloodstream by the pint. Some say the liquid, which grants those that partake it with unholy physical power, is a nectar distilled from Slaanesh's own pleasure gardens.

SLAANESH model only. Add 1 to the bearer's Strength and Attacks characteristics.

PUSCLEAVER

This blade bears the infamous Gurgling Doom contagion. One struck by the blade typically has only a few agonising seconds left to live before they finally realise the glory of Nurgle's generosity and keel over gurgling phlegm.

NURGLE model with power sword only. Puscleaver replaces the bearer's power sword and has the following profile:

WEAPON	RANGE	TYPE	S	AP	D
Puscleaver	Melee	Melee	User	-2	D3

Abilities: This weapon wounds on a 2+, unless the target is a **VEHICLE**, in which case roll to wound as normal.

AXE OF BLIND FURY

Bound within this fabled axe is the essence of a Greater Daemon. It rages against its eternity of servitude, resulting in grievous violence against the enemy and, sometimes, its owner or his allies.

KHORNE model with power axe only. The Axe of Blind Fury replaces the bearer's power axe and has the following profile:

WEAPON	RANGE	TYPE	S	AP	D
Axe of Blind Fury	Melee	Melee	+3	-3	D3

Abilities: You cannot re-roll or modify hit rolls of 1 for attacks made with the Axe of Blind Fury. Instead, these attacks automatically hit a friendly unit within 1". Randomly determine which unit is hit if there is more than one. If there are no friendly units within 1", the hit is ignored.

THE BLACK MACE

This malefic mace is said to have been cursed by each of the Daemon Primarchs. One who is struck by it instantly collapses into a mouldering pile of bones, while the curse spreads in a deadly shock wave.

Model with power maul only. The Black Mace replaces the bearer's power maul and has the following profile:

WEAPON	RANGE	TYPE	S	AP	D
Black Mace	Melee	Melee	+3	-2	2

Abilities: Roll a D6 each time a model is slain by the Black Mace; on a 6, that model's unit suffers an additional mortal wound at the end of the phase.

THE MURDER SWORD

So deadly are the wounds from this blade that some believe it is actually the Anathame – the weapon suspected to have laid low Warmaster Horus within the swamps of Davin's moon. The sword is undoubtedly of eldritch provenance, for with a sacrificial ritual it can become the bane of a certain foe above all others.

Model with power sword only. The Murder Sword replaces the bearer's power sword and has the following profile:

WEAPON	RANGE	TYPE	S	AP	D
Murder Sword	Melee	Melee	+1	-4	1

Abilities: At the start of the first battle round but before the first turn has begun, you must nominate one enemy **CHARACTER** to be the target of the bearer of the Murder Sword (this can be a character that is not yet set up on the battlefield). Remember to tell your opponent which character you have nominated. Each attack made with the Murder Sword that hits the selected character automatically inflicts 1 mortal wound upon that character instead of the normal damage.

THE EYE OF NIGHT

One of the artefacts used by Abaddon to take command of the dreaded Blackstone Fortresses, the Eye of Night is a multifaceted obsidian crystal of unknown origin. The slightest caress of the ebon beam it can unleash causes machines to suffer massive power failure or catastrophic internal damage. Not even the thickest armour can resist its malignant touch.

Black Legion model only. The bearer can unleash the power of the Eye of Night once per battle, in their Shooting phase, instead of firing any other weapons. When they do so, select a visible **Vehicle** unit and roll a D6; on a 2+, that unit suffers D3 mortal wounds.

THE CURSED CROZIUS

This was once the rod of office for a founding member of Lorgar's Chaplains, one of the first of his kind to be sent into the Legiones Astartes in order to watch for signs of sedition. In truth, it has always been the weapon of an arch-traitor. First used in anger to bludgeon a Praetor of the White Scars to death, it still bears the indelible stains of that first treacherous kill to this day. The wielder of the Cursed Crozius is instilled with all the knowledge they need to slay the loyalist thralls of the Corpse God.

Word Bearers model with a power maul only. The Cursed Crozius replaces the bearer's power maul and has the following profile:

WEAPON	RANGE	TYPE	S	AP	D
Cursed Crozius	Melee	Melee	+2	-2	3

Abilities: Re-roll all failed wound rolls for this weapon when targeting an **Imperium** unit.

FLESHMETAL EXOSKELETON

The fleshmetal exoskeleton so prized by the Eye of Terror's Warpsmiths bonds with the wearer's wargear and anatomy alike, so that they embody the maxim 'Iron Within, Iron Without' in a quite literal sense. A blade that manages to penetrate his armour will blunt itself on the hardened flesh beneath, and those enemies that somehow deal the warrior significant damage will see their adversary's cabled muscles reknit in a frenzy of silvered fibres until they are rebuilt as strong as ever.

Iron Warriors model only. The bearer of the Fleshmetal Exoskeleton has a Save characteristic of 2+. In addition, this model heals 1 wound at the start of each of your turns.

BRASS COLLAR OF BHORGHASTER

This collar of heavy brass is the bane of sorcerers, for bound within it is a Greater Daemon that despises magic. A psyker with the temerity to unleash eldritch power near this relic finds his mind screaming with pain. Moments later, the empyric energies he has conjured into being are turned back upon him in a raging inferno of white-hot flame. Those who succumb are immediately sucked into Khorne's realm, there to die a thousand times over.

World Eaters models only. The bearer of the Brass Collar of Bhorghaster can attempt to deny one psychic power in each enemy Psychic phase. If this model makes a successful Deny the Witch test, the psyker that was attempting to manifest the power immediately suffers Perils of the Warp.

BLADE OF THE HYDRA

Long ago, this oversized chainsword was of purely ceremonial use. Since the Daemon Prince Gharual of the Nine Sundered Souls was bound inside it, however, the blade has been a fiendish tool of destruction. Those with a will strong enough to control its multiple thirsting mindsets can cause the sawtoothed blade to shimmer into not one, but several swords that gnaw and gnash with an immortal hunger. These extra blades are insubstantial when the wielder wills it, and razor-sharp when the flesh of his enemies is near.

Alpha Legion model with chainsword only. The Blade of the Hydra replaces the bearer's chainsword and has the following profile:

WEAPON	RANGE	TYPE	S	AP	D
Blade of the Hydra	Melee	Melee	+1	-2	2

Abilities: Each time the bearer fights, it can make D3 additional attacks with this weapon.

CLAWS OF THE BLACK HUNT

These vicious hooked talons have spilt the blood of thousands of victims since their creation in the soul forges. Worn by the master of the Black Hunt, a vicious ritual that precedes the greatest of Night Lords invasions, they are so encrusted with gore they are almost black. This congealed fluid is so thick it cannot even be seared away by the vicious energy field that runs about each claw. This is seen by some as a clear sign of a gory blessing from destructive gods. Even when the wielder swipes the air near a foe, not quite making contact, the victim's armour and flesh still mysteriously part as if slashed open by a fierce and invisible beast.

Night Lords model with two lightning claws only. The Claws of the Black Hunt replaces both of the bearer's lightning claws and have the following profile:

WEAPON	RANGE	TYPE	S	AP	D
Claws of the Black Hunt	Melee	Melee	+1	-3	D3

Abilities: Increase the wielder's Attacks characteristic by 1. In addition, you can re-roll failed wound rolls for this weapon.

BLISSGIVER

This long-tongued whip can render those who feel its sting insensible with indescribable pleasure. Even those who put aside gratification for a greater duty find their oaths and promises forgotten, washed away in a tide of sensation that drowns the mind completely. So it is to feel the kiss of Slaanesh. Though their lives are cruelly torn away almost immediately afterwards, for a few short moments, they truly know ecstasy and agony entwined.

Emperor's Children model with bolt pistol only. Blissgiver replaces the bearer's bolt pistol and has the following profile:

WEAPON	RANGE	TYPE	S	AP	D
Blissgiver	6"	Assault D6	User	-1	1

Abilities: This weapon can be fired within 1" of an enemy unit, and can target enemy units within 1" of friendly units. If an enemy **Character** model is wounded by Blissgiver but not slain, roll a D6 at the end of the phase; on a 6, they suffer D3 mortal wounds.

WARLORD TRAITS

Those grim commanders who lead the armies of the Chaos Space Marines are fearsome warriors and ingenious strategists, whose barbarous campaigns across the Imperium are marked by corpse-strewn planets and nightmarish legends.

If a Chaos Space Marine **CHARACTER** is your Warlord, he can generate a Warlord Trait from the following table instead of the one in the *Warhammer 40,000* rulebook. You can either roll on the table below to randomly generate a Warlord Trait, or you can select the one that best suits his temperament and preferred style of waging war.

D6   WARLORD TRAIT

1   ETERNAL VENDETTA

This warlord has sworn never to rest in his dark crusade against his loyalist foes.

You can re-roll failed wound rolls for attacks made by your Warlord in the Fight phase against targets with the **ADEPTUS ASTARTES** keyword.

2   FLAMES OF SPITE

This warlord's bitterness burns so fiercely that his weapons flicker with the fires of Chaos.

If the wound roll for a melee weapon attack made by your Warlord is 6+, it inflicts 1 mortal wound on the target in addition to any other damage.

3   UNHOLY FORTITUDE

The power of the warp flows through this warlord's vein's, imbuing him with unnatural resilience.

Add 1 to the Wounds characteristic of your Warlord. In addition, roll a D6 each time your Warlord loses a wound. On a roll of 6, your warlord shrugs off the damage and does not lose the wound.

4   HATRED INCARNATE

The intense animosity that festers in this warlord's soul lends his strikes a terrible, hate-fuelled strength.

You can re-roll wound rolls of 1 for attacks made by your Warlord.

5   LORD OF TERROR

The aura of despair and hopelessness that surrounds this warlord hangs in the air and brings to mind all of his victims' worst nightmares.

The opposing player must roll an extra dice when taking Morale tests for units within 6" of your Warlord, and use the highest result.

6   EXALTED CHAMPION

Favoured amongst the Dark Gods, this warlord is bequeathed the fury of the warp itself.

Add 1 to your Warlord's Attacks characteristic.

> **'"Attack" is the only order worth remembering.'**
> - Khârn the Betrayer

LEGION WARLORD TRAITS

If you wish, you can pick a Legion Warlord Trait from the list below instead of the Chaos Space Marine Warlord Traits below, but only if your Warlord is from that Legion.

ALPHA LEGION: I AM ALPHARIUS

The Alpha Legion are experts in the art of deception, and none more so than this warlord.

In addition to this Warlord Trait, your Warlord has one randomly selected Chaos Space Marine Warlord Trait (see left). If your Warlord is slain, you can immediately select another **ALPHA LEGION CHARACTER** in your army to take their place and generate a Warlord Trait for them (including this one). If the mission you are playing grants victory points for slaying the enemy Warlord, your opponent will only achieve that objective if all of the **ALPHA LEGION CHARACTERS** in your army have been slain.

BLACK LEGION: FIRST AMONGST TRAITORS

Black Legion warlords have sworn never to rest in their eternal vendetta against their hated loyalist foes.

The Death to the False Emperor ability triggers an extra attack on rolls of 5+ instead of 6+ for models in friendly **BLACK LEGION** units that are within 6" of your Warlord.

EMPEROR'S CHILDREN: STIMULATED BY PAIN

The warlords of the Emperor's Children thrive on pain; the more grievous their injuries, the deadlier they become.

Add 1 to your Warlord's Attacks characteristic for each wound he has suffered (to a maximum of +3). If your Warlord heals any wounds, he loses the associated bonus attacks.

IRON WARRIORS: COLD AND BITTER

The Warlords of the Iron Warriors have little room for emotion left in their soul – they are driven only by bitterness and ruthless efficiency.

Friendly **IRON WARRIORS** units within 6" of your Warlord automatically pass Morale tests.

NIGHT LORDS: NIGHT HAUNTER'S CURSE

Some Night Lords warlords share the curse of foresight that plagued their Primarch.

Once per battle round, you can re-roll a single hit roll, wound roll, damage roll, Advance roll, charge roll or saving throw made for your Warlord.

WORLD EATERS: SLAUGHTERBORN

This warlord bears the favour of Khorne, his murderous prowess growing with each worthy skull claimed in his master's name.

Add 1 to your Warlord's Attacks and Strength characteristics each time he slays an enemy **CHARACTER**, **MONSTER** or **TITANIC** model.

WORD BEARERS: THE VOICE OF LORGAR

This warlord speaks with the authority of his Primarch; when he commands, others follow without question or hesitation.

Increases the range of any aura abilities on your Warlord's datasheet (e.g. Lord of Chaos, Demagogue) by 3".

'Each of the Legions has now nominated aspirants seeking to throw themselves upon our mercy in the vain hope that we may deem them worthy to join our ranks. Those loyal to the shrunken corpse on Terra still cling to their own processes by which perhaps one in a hundred neophytes may survive to become a battle-brother. The methods I have developed over the last millennia are more stringent, for we must be pure in our hatred and hard of heart, body and soul. Fewer than one in every thousand survive, and I strive each day to lengthen these odds still further.'

- Fabius Bile

NAMED CHARACTERS AND WARLORD TRAITS

If one of the following named characters is your Warlord, they must be given the associated Warlord Trait shown below. Cypher can never have a Warlord Trait.

NAMED CHARACTER	WARLORD TRAIT
Abaddon the Despoiler	First Amongst Traitors
Fabius Bile	Lord of Terror
Haarken Worldclaimer	Lord of Terror
Huron Blackheart	Eternal Vendetta
Khârn the Betrayer	Slaughterborn
Lucius the Eternal	Stimulated by Pain

POINTS VALUES

If you are playing a matched play game, or a game that uses a points limit, you can use the following lists to determine the total points cost of your army. Simply add together the points costs of all your models and the wargear they are armed with to determine your army's total points value.

HQ

UNIT	MODELS PER UNIT	POINTS PER MODEL (Excluding wargear)
Chaos Lord	1	74
Chaos Lord in Terminator Armour	1	95
Chaos Lord with Jump Pack	1	93
Daemon Prince	1	146
Daemon Prince with Wings	1	170
Dark Apostle	1	100
Exalted Champion	1	70
Lord Discordant on Helstalker	1	150
Master of Executions	1	70
Master of Possession	1	90
Sorcerer	1	90
Sorcerer in Terminator Armour	1	102
Sorcerer with Jump Pack	1	112
Warpsmith	1	35

TROOPS

UNIT	MODELS PER UNIT	POINTS PER MODEL (Excluding wargear)
Chaos Cultists	10-30	5
Chaos Space Marines	5-20	13

ELITES

UNIT	MODELS PER UNIT	POINTS PER MODEL (Excluding wargear)
Chosen	5-10	14
Dark Disciples	2	5
Fallen	5-10	14
Greater Possessed	1-2	70
Helbrute	1	60
Khorne Berzerkers	5-20	16
Mutilators	3	35
Noise Marines	5-20	15
Plague Marines	5-20	16
Possessed	5-20	20
Rubric Marines	5-20	16
Terminators	5-10	26

FAST ATTACK

UNIT	MODELS PER UNIT	POINTS PER MODEL (Excluding wargear)
Bikers	3-9	21
Chaos Spawn	1-5	25
Raptors	5-15	15
Warp Talons	5-10	12

FORTIFICATION

UNIT	MODELS PER UNIT	POINTS PER MODEL (Excluding wargear)
Noctilith Crown	1	100

HEAVY SUPPORT

UNIT	MODELS PER UNIT	POINTS PER MODEL (Excluding wargear)
Chaos Land Raider	1	200
Chaos Predator	1	90
Chaos Vindicator	1	125
Defiler	1	120
Forgefiend	1	100
Havocs	5	14
Maulerfiend	1	120
Obliterators	3	65
Venomcrawler	1	130

DEDICATED TRANSPORT

UNIT	MODELS PER UNIT	POINTS PER MODEL (Excluding wargear)
Chaos Rhino	1	70

FLYER

UNIT	MODELS PER UNIT	POINTS PER MODEL (Excluding wargear)
Heldrake	1	120

LORD OF WAR

UNIT	MODELS PER UNIT	POINTS PER MODEL (Excluding wargear)
Khorne Lord of Skulls	1	380

DAEMONS

UNIT	MODELS PER UNIT	POINTS PER MODEL (Including weapons)
Bloodletters	10-30	7
Daemonettes	10-30	6
Horrors - Blue Horrors - Pairs of Brimstone Horrors - Pink Horrors	10-30	5 3 7
Plaguebearers	10-30	7

NAMED CHARACTERS

UNIT	MODELS PER UNIT	POINTS PER MODEL (Including wargear)
Abaddon the Despoiler	1	240
Cypher	1	80
Fabius Bile	1	90
Haarken Worldclaimer	1	115
Huron Blackheart	1	105
Khârn the Betrayer	1	120
Lucius the Eternal	1	85

RANGED WEAPONS

WEAPON	POINTS PER WEAPON
Autocannon	10
Autogun	0
Autopistol	0
Baleflamer	30
Battle cannon	0
Blastmaster	20
Blight launcher	10
Bolt pistol	0
Boltgun	0
Combi-bolter	2
Combi-flamer	8
Combi-melta	15
Combi-plasma	11
Daemongore cannon	71
Demolisher cannon	0
Doom siren	8
Ectoplasma cannon	20
Excruciator cannon	0
Flamer	6
Fleshmetal guns	0
Gorestorm cannon	74
Hades autocannon	20
Hades gatling cannon	184
Havoc launcher	6
Heavy bolter	10
Heavy flamer	14
Heavy stubber	2
Helbrute plasma cannon	16
Ichor cannon	58
Inferno bolt pistol	0
Inferno boltgun	2
Lascannon	25
Lashing warp energies	0
Magma cutter	16
Meltagun	14
Missile launcher	20
Multi-melta	22
Plague belcher	7
Plague spewer	15
Plasma gun	11
Plasma pistol	5
Predator autocannon	40
Reaper autocannon	10
Reaper chaincannon	20
Shotgun	0
Skullhurler	98
Sonic blaster	4
Soulreaper cannon	10
Twin heavy bolter	17
Twin heavy flamer	28
Twin lascannon	40
Warp bolter	3
Warpflame pistol	3
Warpflamer	10

OTHER WARGEAR

WARGEAR	POINTS PER ITEM
Blight grenades	0
Daemonic Icon	15
Frag grenades	0
Instrument of Chaos	10
Krak grenades	0

ICONS

ICON	POINTS PER ICON
Icon of Despair	10
Icon of Excess	10
Icon of Flame	5
Icon of Vengeance	5
Icon of Wrath	10

MELEE WEAPONS

WEAPON	POINTS PER WEAPON
Accursed crozius	0
Axe of dismemberment	0
Bladed limbs and tail	0
Brutal assault weapon	0
Bubotic axe	5
Chainaxe	1
Chainfist	11
Chainsword	0
Crushing fists	0
Daemon jaws	8
Daemonic axe	10
Daemonic mutations	0
Defiler claws	0
Defiler scourge	12
Eviscerating claws	0
Flail of corruption	10
Fleshmetal weapons	0
Force axe	10
Force stave	8
Force sword	8
Great cleaver of Khorne	0
Great plague cleaver	15
Helbrute fist (single/pair)	30/40
Helbrute hammer	30
Heldrake claws	17
Hellforged sword	10
Hideous mutations	0
Horrifying mutations	0
Impaler chainglaive	0
Lasher tendrils	12
Lightning claws (single/pair)	8/12
Mace of contagion	7
Malefic talons (one set/two sets)	0/10
Maulerfiend fists	0
Mechatendrils	0
Plague knife	0
Plaguesword	1
Power axe	5
Power fist	9
Power maul	4
Power scourge	35
Power sword	4
Soulflayer tendrils	0
Techno-virus injector	0
Thunder hammer (**CHARACTERS**)	21
Thunder hammer (other models)	16

TACTICAL OBJECTIVES

Chaos Space Marines are as fearsome and versatile in warfare as their corpse-worshipping brothers, but where the Adeptus Astartes uphold the Imperium, the Heretic Astartes would see it burn.

If your army is led by a Chaos Space Marine Warlord, these Tactical Objectives replace the Capture and Control Tactical Objectives (numbers 11-16) in the *Warhammer 40,000* rulebook. If a mission uses Tactical Objectives, players use the normal rules for using Tactical Objectives with the following exception: when a Chaos Space Marines player generates a Capture and Control objective (numbers 11-16), they instead generate the corresponding Chaos Space Marines Tactical Objective, as shown below. Other Tactical Objectives (numbers 21-66) are generated normally.

D66	TACTICAL OBJECTIVE
11	For the Dark Gods!
12	Rise to Glory
13	The Will of Chaos
14	The Warp is Your Ally
15	Claim and Despoil
16	The Long War

---

11 | FOR THE DARK GODS! | Chaos Space Marines

Though they may differ in how they choose to achieve it, all of the Chaos Gods are united in their goal of spreading fear and wanton slaughter throughout the galaxy.

Score 1 victory point if an enemy unit was destroyed or failed a Morale test during this turn.

---

14 | THE WARP IS YOUR ALLY | Chaos Space Marines

The warp has ever been both a sanctuary and a source of terrible strength and for the mortal servants of Chaos.

Score 1 victory point if you manifested a psychic power during your turn or if you summoned a unit of **DAEMONS** to the battlefield with a Daemonic Ritual. Score D3 victory points instead if you manifested a psychic power and you summoned a unit of **DAEMONS** to the battlefield during your turn.

---

12 | RISE TO GLORY | Chaos Space Marines

If the deeds of their champions are worthy, the gaze of the Dark Gods will be drawn to the battlefield and the actions of their mortal vassals greatly rewarded.

Score 1 victory point if at least one enemy **CHARACTER**, **VEHICLE** or **MONSTER** was destroyed during this turn and the last wound it suffered was inflicted by a friendly **HERETIC ASTARTES CHARACTER**.

---

15 | CLAIM AND DESPOIL | Chaos Space Marines

When the Chaos Space Marines launch their raids into the galaxy, they often do so with the goal of despoiling that which their enemies hold sacred out of cruel spite.

Score D3 victory points if you control an objective marker that was controlled by your opponent at the start of the turn.

---

13 | THE WILL OF CHAOS | Chaos Space Marines

Though the bidding of the Chaos Gods can at times seem whimsical, rich reward awaits those with the wit to take advantage of their ephemeral desires.

Roll a D6 when this Tactical Objective is generated, and the start of each of your turns thereafter. Score 1 victory point if you control the objective marker whose number corresponds to the D6 result you rolled at the start of this turn.

---

16 | THE LONG WAR | Chaos Space Marines

Chaos Space Marines have been slaughtering the False Emperor's warriors enemies for millennia. This battle is but one of many.

Score 1 victory point if an enemy unit was destroyed during this turn. Score D3 instead if any enemy **IMPERIUM** units were destroyed this turn. If 3 or more enemy **IMPERIUM** units were destroyed during this turn, score 3 victory points, and if 6 or more enemy **IMPERIUM** units were destroyed during this turn, score D3+3 victory points instead.